BEERS
FROM AROUND THE
WORLD

This edition published by Parragon Books Ltd in 2018

Parragon Books Ltd
Chartist House
15–17 Trim Street
Bath BA1 1HA, UK
www.parragon.com

Written by Mark Kelly
Feature text by Stuart Derrick
Designed by Plum5 Limited
Project managed by Hannah Kelly

ISBN 978-1-4748-9743-3

Printed in China

Mark Kelly is a beer sommelier and writer living in south-west London. He can usually be found walking the streets of the UK capital on behalf of London's premier Cask Ale Microbrewer, Sambrook's Brewery or trying to burn off the previous night's drinking session by running them.

Stuart Derrick is a journalist, writer and editor with more than 20 years' experience writing for books, magazines, newspapers and organizations that need sparkling copy. As well as contributing to books on whisky and beer, he has written on subjects as diverse as travel, parenthood, finance, marketing and TV. He has also written a family facts book and is working on a series of books for children.

BEERS
FROM AROUND THE
WORLD

WITH OVER 400 OF THE WORLD'S GREATEST CRAFT BEERS, ALES, LAGERS & STOUTS

Bath • New York • Cologne • Melbourne • Delhi
Hong Kong • Shenzhen • Singapore

Contents

Introduction

8 **The Global Drink**
10 **Four Good Things**
12 **Beer – 9,000 Years in the Making**
14 **The Brewing Process**
16 **What are you Drinking?**

Beers by Region

19 The Americas

22 **United States of America**
55 **Canada** | 73 **Argentina**
73 **Brazil** | 74 **Mexico**
74 **Bahamas** | 75 **Trinidad and Tobago**
75 **Barbados**

77 Europe

80 **England** | 97 **Scotland**
102 **Ireland** | 109 **Wales**
113 **Germany** | 131 **Belgium**
149 **Austria** | 150 **Czech Republic**
153 **Italy** | 158 **France**
163 **Switzerland** | 164 **Luxembourg**
165 **Netherlands** | 167 **Spain**
169 **Denmark** | 174 **Sweden**
177 **Norway** | 180 **Iceland**
181 **Finland** | 185 **Poland**
186 **Russia** | 186 **Croatia**
187 **Serbia**

189 Australasia

192 **Australia**
197 **New Zealand**

203 Rest of the World

206 **Japan** | 207 **Singapore**
208 **China** | 210 **India**
212 **South Korea** | 214 **Vietnam**
214 **Indonesia** | 215 **Madagascar**
215 **Ghana** | 217 **South Africa**

Glossary & Index

218 **Glossary**
220 **Index**

The World's Favourite Drink...

Wherever you go in the world the locals have their own beers; finding out what they like to drink can be one of the joys of travelling.

This book will help you to discover some of the best beers from around the globe.

THE GLOBAL DRINK

Beer is the world's most widely consumed alcoholic drink. Wherever you go around the globe you will find people brewing, selling and, of course, drinking beer.

Frank Zappa said: 'You can't be a real country unless you have a beer and an airline. It helps if you have some kind of a football team, or some nuclear weapons, but at the very least you need a beer.'

Mr Zappa was – presumably – joking, but with the exception of a few countries in the Middle East, most countries do have a beer they call their own.

Why is beer so popular?

Every drinker can list their own answers to that question, but there are probably three main reasons:

Beer helps us to relax at the end of a hard day. It makes us feel good as we socialize with our friends.

It's refreshing and tastes good. Is there any better drink on a warm summer's day than an ice-cold Pilsner? And who would not gladden at the prospect of a drinking a comforting glass of stout in front of a pub fire on a winter's evening?

Finally, there is so much variety to choose from. 'I'll have a beer!' may be the common response to 'What are you drinking?' but which one to choose? Will it be a pale ale, porter, stout, fruit beer, cream ale, steam beer, best bitter, or barley wine? The choice is bewilderingly vast.

One of the great things about being a beer drinker is that there is always something new to try. Wherever you go in the world, the question 'What's yours?' remains a delightful invitation to ponder what's on offer locally. This book is here to help you make that all-important decision.

With more than 400 of the world's best beers described inside, it will no doubt reacquaint you with a few old favourites as well as provide suggestions for some new beers to drink. The past few years have been incredibly exciting from a beer drinker's

perspective. The rise of craft brewing has brought a new generation of inventive brewers to the fore who are combining the best of traditional know-how with innovative tastes and ingredients.

Even a small bar may now contain an array of beers from around the world, something that would not have been the case a few years ago. Beer drinkers' thirst for new experiences is driving the process.

This book will help you discover beers throughout the world. It takes a geographical approach, covering all the continents and the main beer-producing countries and looking at some of the most popular and distinctive beers available. For each beer it gives an overview of what to look out for and some tips on how best to enjoy it.

But that's not all. We'll also be looking at the history of beer and beer producers, the culture that surrounds beer in different countries, foods that go well with beer, and many fascinating beer facts to share with your friends the next time you're in a bar.

So pour yourself a glass, put your feet up and enjoy.

FOUR GOOD THINGS

Beer is a simple product made primarily of just four ingredients: malted barley, hops, water and yeast. It is the interplay of these elements, combined with the skill of the brewer, that can create a multitude of different flavours, aromas and types of beer.

Malt

Barley is the cereal grain that is commonly used in brewing. To create malt, barley is soaked in water until it begins to sprout, converting its starch reserves into sugars. This process is then halted by drying the grain in a kiln, providing a source of sugar and soluble starch for fermentation. The temperature of the kiln produces many different types of malt – such as pale, caramel or crystal, dark, and roasted malts – which are used to create specific beers. Malt contributes to the flavour, colour and mouthfeel of a beer.

While barley is the traditional grain for brewing, brewers may also use wheat, oats, rye or other grains.

Large commercial breweries sometimes use rice or corn to reduce their costs.

Hops

Prior to the 15th century, most ale was flavoured with a mixture of herbs, spices and berries, such as bog myrtle, yarrow, heather, juniper or caraway. There is evidence that Benedictine monks were using hops in brewing by the early 9th century, although their use did not become widespread in Europe until some centuries later.

Hops are the flowers from the hop vine and there are more than 50 recognized varieties. In brewing,

hops add a bitterness that balances the sweetness that remains in beer after the fermentation process ends. Some varieties are primarily used for their aroma. Hops also act as a preservative in the beer: unhopped beer goes off very quickly. Different hop varieties can be added at different stages of the brewing process, which influences the aroma, flavour and style of the beer. Popular varieties include Fuggles, Goldings, Cascade and Saaz.

Water

Beer is more than 95 per cent water, so it is little surprise that water quality has historically been an important determinant of where brewers locate. The flavour of a beer is strongly influenced by its water. Areas such as Burton upon Trent in the UK and Pilsen in the Czech Republic became great brewing capitals because the composition of their water was suited to particular types of beer – English bitter and Pilsner lager in these examples. Nowadays, chemical analysis and tinkering allows brewers to replicate the type of water needed for a particular beer, and many famous beers are now brewed in completely different areas to where they originated.

Yeast

These single-cell organisms are the catalysts that make the whole magical process of beer-making work. In consuming the sugar released from the malt, they produce alcohol and carbon dioxide during fermentation. Yeast occurs naturally in the environment, but specific yeasts are cultured for individual beers.

Although malt and hops are the main flavour components in beer, the strain of yeast also imparts its own flavour, prized by brewers. When the Truman beer brand of London was revived in 2013, it used yeast that had been cryogenically stored in 1958.

Ale production uses top-fermenting yeast, which rises to the top of the fermentation vessel and works at warm temperatures. Lager yeast is bottom fermenting and works more slowly, at lower temperatures, to produce lager's distinctive clean taste.

Belgian Lambic beers use wild yeasts in a process of spontaneous fermentation. Champagne yeast can be used in beer production, particularly for secondary fermentation of high-strength brews.

BEER – 9,000 YEARS IN THE MAKING

Today, millions of people worldwide knock back almost 42 billion gallons/190 billion litres of beer a year, but beer has been with us for a very long time. In fact, it is one of the oldest processed foodstuffs.

Archaeologists have found evidence of beer being produced and drunk as far back as the Neolithic period. Early Mesopotamian civilizations recorded their enjoyment of beer, and around 5,000 years ago, the ancient Egyptians lauded beer in their hieroglyphs, giving it wonderful names such as 'Joybringer' and 'Heavenly'.

It is thought that the first beers were produced by accident, perhaps by bread falling into a vat of soaking grain. This germinated and fed airborne yeasts to produce alcohol. This early beer bore little resemblance to the crystal-clear brews we sup today. It was more like an alcoholic soup and could be very strong at around 10 per cent ABV (Alcohol by Volume). Ancient engravings show it being drunk through tubes to filter out the solids. A smooth drink it was not.

Throughout history, beer was often considered as safer to drink than water, because the brewing process involves boiling the water. Even children drank a weak 'small beer'.

In the Middle Ages, brewing was largely a home-based activity undertaken by women or 'ale wives'. They would indicate that there was a brew ready by putting an ale wand outside their house. As beer was drunk with every meal, there was a ready market locally.

Monks were also important early brewers, producing beer for their community and the people who lived locally, selling it to support their orders. As this brewing was on a larger scale, monks helped develop more rigorous processes for brewing, advancing knowledge and improving quality along the way. Today, Trappist communities in Belgium, Austria and the Netherlands produce distinctive beers such as Chimay, Orval and Westmalle.

Early beer was flavoured with a mixture of herbs, known as a gruit, but over several centuries hops began to be cultivated for use in beer. For a time, hopped 'beer' and unhopped 'ale' existed side by side, but by the 15th century hops were the flavouring agent of choice throughout much of Europe.

The Industrial Revolution helped transform brewing from a cottage industry to big business. As millions of people moved to cities, often to work in hot, sweaty factories, demand for beer boomed. Large-scale urban breweries developed to serve this market, helped by advances in manufacturing and transportation.

Throughout the 18th and 19th centuries, industrial advances helped improve the quality of beer further. Coked coal allowed cleaner, more controllable malt kilns to produce lighter malt that could be used in paler ales. Industrial glass production replaced ceramic drinking cups with transparent vessels, allowing drinkers to see the quality of their beer, and encouraging brewers to improve it.

In 1840, Anton Dreher isolated the lager yeast – Saccharomyces pastorianus – and brewed the first Vienna lager. In 1842, Josef Groll brewed the first Pilsner lager, a clear golden beer in Pilsen, Czech Republic. It was a style that soon swept around the world, not least to the United States, where European brewers brought their skills to serve this huge new market.

Throughout the 20th century, beer production became more commercial as improvements in transportation and storage allowed brewers to sell beer far from its place of origin. This helped create massive global brands such as Heineken, Carlsberg and Budweiser.

In recent years, these have been complemented by something of a return to the smaller-scale roots of many brewers with the birth and growth of microbreweries and the ongoing craft brewing revolution.

This is just the latest turn in the story of beer, a tale that continues to evolve.

THE BREWING PROCESS

Whether it's a massive global beer brand like Carlsberg, or a craft ale 'curated' in somebody's garage, the process for brewing beer has not changed in its essentials for hundreds of years.

Malting

The brewing process starts with barley, although other grains, including wheat, rye or rice, can be used. The barley is soaked and allowed to begin germinating for several days, with the grains being turned occasionally.

When a small leaf, or acrospire, is almost the length of the grain, the process is halted by heating and drying. This 'kilning' process is usually undertaken by hot air being blown through the malt. The length of time and the temperature of malting help determine the type of malt produced. Lighter malts, for paler beers, are malted for a shorter time, while dark malts receive longer in the kiln, at a higher temperature.

The mash

Next, the malt is cracked by being run through a malt mill. This eases the release of the sugars, which are converted from starch in the malt as it is mixed with hot water. This process, called 'mashing', takes place in a vessel known as the mash tun (see pictures above). The liquid is then drained off and recirculated through the grains to ensure that all the sugars have been captured. This is known as lautering and sparging.

Boiling

This liquid goes into a brew kettle for 'the boil'. Hops are added throughout the boiling stage to give

bitterness, aroma and flavour. The liquid is now known as wort and goes through a filtering process to remove any solids.

The wort is then cooled quickly using pipes filled with cold water. This is to get the wort to a temperature at which yeast can be added before atmospheric yeast can contaminate the liquid. The beer is now ready to ferment and is transferred to a fermenting tank.

Fermentation

Time is the next key ingredient. Each type of beer requires a specific period of fermentation during which the yeast can get to work. The yeast feeds on the sugary mixture, producing alcohol and carbon dioxide. Each brewer has its own strain of yeast, which helps to create the particular flavour of the beer.

There are two main types of yeast in brewing. Top-fermenting yeast is used to create ales. This yeast typically operates at temperatures of between 10°C and 25°C (50–77°F). The yeast rises to the top of the fermentation tank and is skimmed off. Bottom-fermenting yeast is used to produce lager. It operates at lower temperatures of between 7°C and 15°C (46–49°F), so the fermentation process takes longer.

Filtering and conditioning

When the yeast has almost completely devoured the sugars in the fermenting beer, it is ready to be conditioned. The beer may be filtered to enhance its clarity and stabilize its flavour. Not all beer is filtered: wheat beers are often cloudy and some new craft beers present 'haziness' as a mark of authenticity.

Ales may be cask- or bottle-conditioned, which means that an additional, secondary fermentation takes place. A little extra yeast and sugar or wort may be added to aid this stage. This creates a natural carbonation in the beer. Cask-conditioned ales are served without additional carbonation.

For lagers to mature, the lagering process involves storing the beer at near freezing temperatures for anything from one to six months. Towards the end of the process the beer is filtered to create the crystal clarity drinkers prize. The beer is then bottled or kegged and is ready to serve.

WHAT ARE YOU DRINKING?

Just as it is said that Inuits have hundreds of words for different types of snow, there are many different names for the beverages known collectively as beer.

Beer experts often struggle to assign a beer to a particular style as there is no universally agreed method of categorizing them. What the experts do agree on is that there are an awful lot of different styles. These are just some of the beer styles you may come across.

Lager

The most common beer in the world is clear, golden lager. To 'lager' means to store in German, and relates to the long period of maturation at low temperatures that lagers traditionally undergo. Although lager seems a fairly homogenous product, there are many different varieties, notably in Germany, where you might enjoy a light 'helles', a dark 'dunkel' or a strong 'bock' lager.

Porter

This dark beer originated in 18th-century London, where it was a favourite drink of manual labourers, such as market porters. Made with dark malt, the beer declined in popularity as new, lighter ales became available, although it has experienced a resurgence in recent years.

Stout

Made famous by Dublin brewer Arthur Guinness in the late 18th century, dry stout is the best-known version of this beer, originally named stout (meaning strong) porter. Other variants include the stronger imperial stout, oatmeal stout and sweet 'milk' stouts.

Bitter

The classic British 'session' ale is clear amber-coloured and hoppy. It is naturally conditioned with a secondary fermentation in the cask. An ordinary bitter might be around 3.5 per cent ABV, with best bitter weighing in at about 4 per cent. Stronger bitters are also available.

Mild

This lightly hopped ale was a favourite with manual and agricultural workers owing to its relatively low alcohol content. This meant they could drink pints of it to refresh themselves without getting too drunk. It is harder to find these days, although some craft brewers have revived the style.

Barley wine

Particularly strong beers were given the name barley wine, perhaps to align their quality and potency with wine. Strengths of between 8 and 12 per cent ABV are common. Some beer writers see barley wines as a subset of old ales, or winter warmers, which are typically stronger than standard brews.

IPA

By the 18th century, English maltsters were able to regulate kilning to produce lighter malt to create new, paler ales. India pale ale is a highly hopped, strong pale ale originally brewed to withstand export from England to India by ship. The term IPA became widely used by brewers mimicking the style, and it is now brewed around the world.

Wheat beers

Wheat beers have a refreshing taste and may be spiced with flavours such as cloves, coriander or dried orange peel. Traditional in both Belgium and Germany, in the late 20th century the style was dying out until brands like Hoegaarden discovered a younger audience and revived the market. The beers are often cloudy, hence the terms witbier, weisse, or white beer, but they can also be clear or even dark dunkelweizen.

Fruit beers

Fruit has been added to beer for hundreds of years, producing interesting and refreshing drinks. Among the most well-known are Belgian Lambic beers, which commonly use cherries and raspberries – or occasionally peaches or other fruit.

Golden ales

These beers offer the depth of flavour of an ale with the clarity and refreshment of a lager. They are fruity, fragrant and clean-tasting, but some – especially the Belgian-style blonde ales – can be deceptively strong.

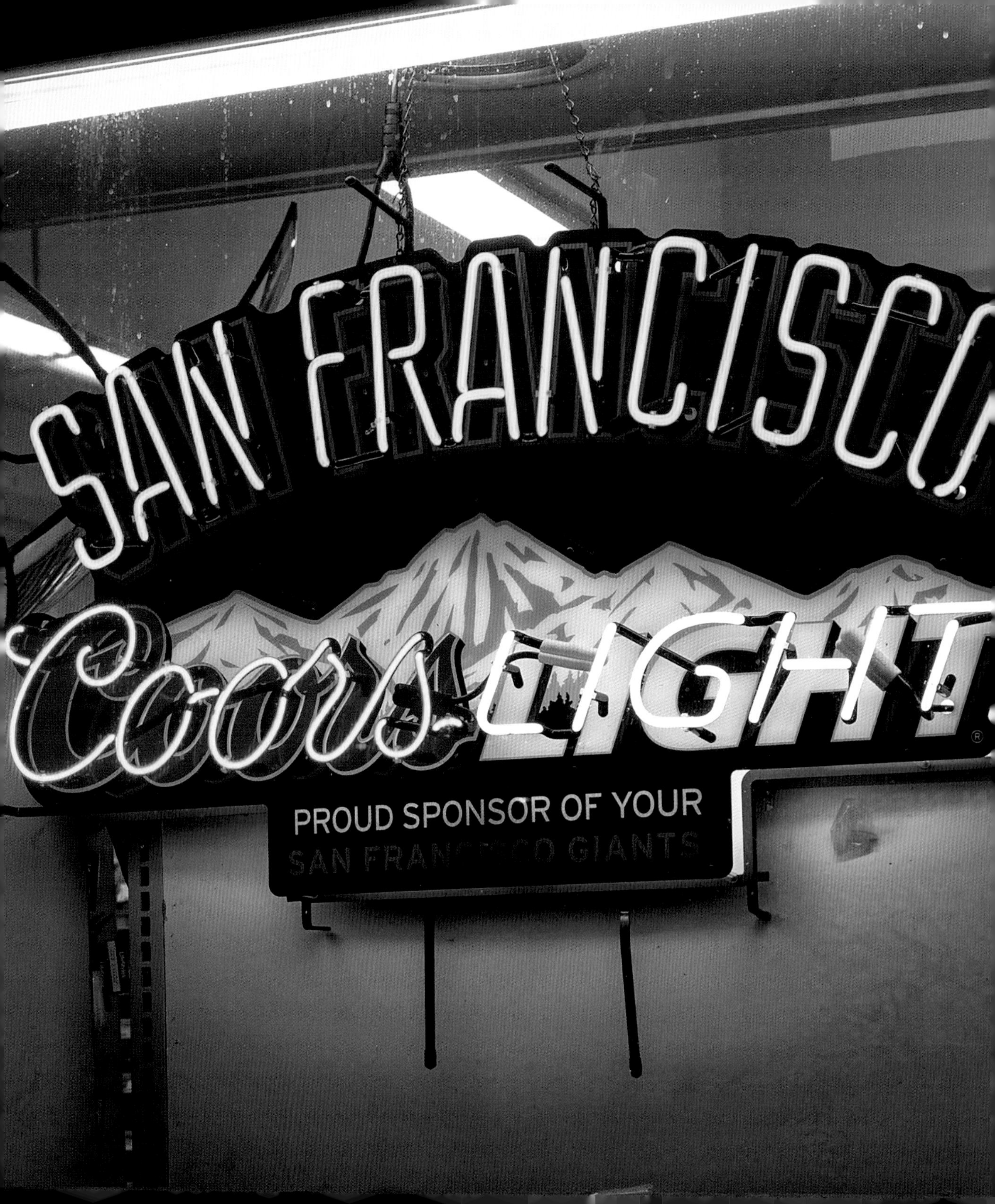
SAN FRANCISC
Coors LIGHT
PROUD SPONSOR OF YOUR

CHAPTER 1

The Americas

From the North to the South of these great continents, the European roots of American culture can be seen in the drinks that are enjoyed.

Throughout North and South America, beer reigns supreme, and with both continents being so large and diverse, the range of beers encompasses everything from pale ales and lagers to stouts and barley wine.

The United States is the second-biggest producer of beer in the world after China, with more than 2,000 breweries. Beers such as Budweiser, Coors and Miller are famous throughout the United States and sell in huge quantities.

Today the United States is experiencing a new revolution in brewing with craft and microbreweries producing exciting and innovative beers. Companies like Lagunitas, Magic Hat, Stone Brewing and a host of others are now highly regarded by beer drinkers. Even before the craft-brewing explosion, however, the United States produced distinctive styles of beer that stood out from the sea of weak lager, including Pennsylvania porter, American IPA and steam beer.

Names like August Krug of the Schlitz company, and Eberhard Anheuser and Adolphus Busch, of Anheuser-Busch show the importance of German know-how in American brewing. It's no surprise that when lager

yeast arrived in the United States in the mid-19th century brewers began to produce the Pilsners and bocks of their homeland, adapting their recipes to use the different types of barley and hops available. They also included corn and rice in the grain mix – and this resulted in the creation of American lager. This found a thriving market in such German strongholds as Ohio, Indiana, Missouri and Nebraska – more than 5.5 million German immigrants arrived in the United States between 1820 and 1910.

This influence is also felt in Central and South America, where pale lager-style beers predominate. Breweries such as Bohemia in Brazil, Quilmes in Argentina and Modelo in Mexico were established by immigrants from Germany and Austria, while Bauernfest is an annual German-themed beer festival held in Brazil.

Cool, refreshing, golden lagers are understandably popular in the hotter countries of South America. Dark beers such as Brazil's Eisenbahn Dunkel and Peru's Cusqueña Malta demonstrate a taste for other styles. Meanwhile, stout has always been popular in

the Caribbean, where strong brews like Dragon Stout and Royal Extra Stout are a mainstay in Jamaica and Trinidad.

South America has not been immune to the growth in craft brewing. Inspired by the United States, microbreweries, or *cervecerías*, are opening up throughout Central and South America, including Antares in Argentina and DaDo Bier in Brazil.

To encourage this new breed of brewers, the first annual South Beer Cup was held in Buenos Aires, Argentina, in 2011. The competition provides a place to showcase what's new in South American brewing, share best practice and to allow some good-natured competition.

For the first competition, 280 beers were entered in 20 categories, from 72 breweries, representing Argentina, Brazil, Chile and Uruguay. More than 40 medals were awarded.

The event continues to grow, as does the status of craft brewing, although it remains some way behind the United States. Such is the vibrancy of the US scene that it is often cited as an influence on a new breed

The United States is the second-biggest producer of beer in the world after China

of European brewers, inspired by the experimentalism and dynamism of the United States.

Just as the British took American blues and rock 'n' roll, and tweaked them to make them their own, so American brewers are doing something similar with beer.

And it is increasingly big business. Jim Koch, the creator of Samuel Adams, one of the original United States craft beers, was recently listed in the Bloomberg Billionaires Index. In less than 30 years, Samuel Adams grew from being a homebrew to become one of the largest United States-owned breweries.

🇺🇸 BISSELL BREWING SWISH IPA

Originally operating out of a small double bay unit in Portland, Maine, the Bissell brothers quickly hit their stride as brewers and relocated to larger premises to accommodate their taproom faithful and expand volume. This double IPA is one of the finest beers in their stable with a fiery mix of Citra, Mosaic and Simcoe hops and a hefty 8% alcohol. You can find it most of the year in their ominous black cans but they only brew it during winter from October to April.

TASTING NOTES: Mango, orange, tangerine and a medley of other boozy tropical fruits. Surprisingly easy to drink!
- **Country:** USA
- **Brewer:** Bissell Brothers Brewing Co.
- **Style:** Double IPA
- **Appearance:** Hazy yellow
- **Alcohol:** 8%
- **Serving temp:** 4–7°C

🇺🇸 COUNCIL BEATITUDE BOYSENBERRY BARREL AGED IMPERIAL TART SAISON

Brewing is so often a case of 'suck it and see'. When Council Brewing first put this tart saison beer together it was only brewed to 4%. However, after tasting, it was decided that it needed ageing in some boozy barrels of bourbon. Cue an increased malt bill bumping the alcohol up to 9.7% to withstand a long ageing process. Boysenberries complete the effect for an incredibly bold and complex flavour profile.

TASTING NOTES: Jammy fruits, red berries and raspberry sourness with a light and easy bourbon kick at the end.
- **Country:** USA
- **Brewer:** Council Brewing Co.
- **Style:** Flemish sour red
- **Appearance:** Deep red
- **Alcohol:** 9.7%
- **Serving temp:** 6–9°C

🇺🇸 FREMONT BREWING CO. BOURBON BARREL AGED DARK STAR

Freemont Brewing Co. in Seattle is a family-owned brewery which was set up during the depths of the recession in 2009. Dark Star is a gorgeous barrel-aged imperial stout, made using real Kentucky bourbon barrels and a heady combination of six roasted malts with a healthy dose of smoothing oats. It is a touch stronger than the average imperial stout in both alcohol and flavour and makes a great match with some plain vanilla ice cream.

TASTING NOTES: Silky cocoa and milk chocolate on the nose with an explosion of roasted coffee and molasses.
- **Country:** USA
- **Brewer:** Fremont Brewing Co.
- **Style:** Imperial stout
- **Appearance:** Black
- **Alcohol:** 14.5%
- **Serving temp:** 10–13°C

🇺🇸 CORE OATMEAL STOUT

Core Brewery is known for its distilling as well as brewing skills. Oatmeal is added to this stout alongside the usual dark roasted barley malt to give a smoother mouthfeel. This is emphasized even more by the use of nitrogen in the dispensing of this beer giving way to smaller bubbles, less 'fizz' and a creamier head. This makes for one of the smoothest beers in the United States and a tribute to the classic stout style.

TASTING NOTES: Toasted caramel, nutty cream sweetness and a dark chocolate bitterness.
- **Country:** USA
- **Brewer:** Core Brewing & Distilling Co.
- **Style:** Stout
- **Appearance:** Dark brown
- **Alcohol:** 5.9%
- **Serving temp:** 10–13°C

🇺🇸 THE BRUERY MISCHIEF

American craft brewers are renowned for their habit of taking styles of beer from around the world and tinkering with them. The Bruery has taken a Belgian blonde strong ale and added extra-fruity American hops during the boil stage of brewing, and also at the fermentation stage during the dry-hopping process. This adds another dimension to an already flavoursome and challenging style of beer. A delight at any dinner table – try it with crispy skinned duck or chicken.

TASTING NOTES: Dry with big flavours of ripe peach and melon, sitting against a peppery backdrop.
- **Country:** USA
- **Brewer:** The Bruery
- **Style:** Belgian blonde ale
- **Appearance:** Golden
- **Alcohol:** 8.5%
- **Serving temp:** 4–8°C

🇺🇸 COORS LIGHT

People in the late 1970s wanted a low-calorie beer to avoid the danger of a beer belly. Coors Light was born during this time and by 1994 was one of a small number of pale lagers accounting for 35 per cent of all beer sold in the USA. Brewed in Golden, Colorado where Adolph Coors founded his brewery in 1873, much is made of its use of Rocky Mountain water. However, as with many North American mass-market beers, cheaper grains are used instead of some of the barley malt to keep costs low.

TASTING NOTES: Light corn sweetness and a thin texture that is best served ice cold.
- **Country:** USA
- **Brewer:** Molson Coors
- **Style:** Pale lager
- **Appearance:** Pale yellow
- **Alcohol:** 4.2%
- **Serving temp:** 1–2°C

Pabst brewery produced the first six-pack of beer in the 1940s, after studies found that six cans were the ideal weight for the average housewife to carry home from the store.

🇺🇸 SLY FOX 113

Based in Pennsylvania, Sly Fox is renowned for canning many of its products to keep them fresh as they are shipped around the world. It also serves beer on tap at its brewpub and eatery in Phoenixville. Its success has been swift – with production beginning in January 2012 it is still a newcomer to the American craft-brewing scene. This is its year-round IPA. Made with hops grown in the Yakima region of Washington state, the high alpha acid content guarantees big citrus, pine and bitterness.

TASTING NOTES:
Powerful bitterness and lots of mixed fruity tones.
- **Country:** USA
- **Brewer:** Sly Fox Brewing Co.
- **Style:** IPA
- **Appearance:** Dark amber
- **Alcohol:** 7%
- **Serving temp:** 4–7°C

🇺🇸 LIVE OAK HEFEWEIZEN

Live Oak Brewing was founded in 1997 as part of what had become a fast-moving wave of new microbrewers setting up in the south-east of the USA. After 19 years of brewing in East Austin the brewery moved downtown in 2015 to incorporate a taproom. The brewing style is extremely faithful to old traditions and this HefeWeizen is modelled after the classic wheat beers made in Bavaria and beyond. The key is in the yeast, which produces the trademark HefeWeizen flavours.

TASTING NOTES: Banana, clove and sweet meringue combine in classic traditional Bavarian style.
- **Country:** USA
- **Brewer:** Live Oak Brewery Co.
- **Style:** Hefeweizen
- **Appearance:** Hazy straw
- **Alcohol:** 5.3%
- **Serving temp:** 6–8°C

🇺🇸 OFF COLOR APEX PREDATOR

A huge proportion of good brewing is down to sound chemistry and simple equations. Sometimes though a little artistry is required, and in Off Color's Apex Predator, the final product sings to the tune of the yeast. Turning off the temperature control in the fermentation vessel allows the feisty strain of yeast to improvise and ferment with the naturally changing temperature of the brewery cellar. The beer is finished with a generous dose of Crystal for dry hopping, and the addition of flaked wheat ensures a superbly fluffy white 'mane' to this beast of a farmhouse ale. A clean bready finish ensures versatility at the dinner table as well.

TASTING NOTES: Refreshing grassy hop flavours with a slightly funky but doughy pizza base finish.
- **Country:** USA
- **Brewer:** Off Color Brewing
- **Style:** Saison
- **Appearance:** Cloudy gold
- **Alcohol:** 6.5%
- **Serving temp:** 4–7°C

🇺🇸 FOUNDERS ALL DAY IPA

Many American craft beers (especially IPAs) come with a high alcohol content that gets you drunk after one or two bottles. This beer is an exception, designed to have maximum flavour while keeping the ABV low enough to drink, well… all day! At only 4.7%, Founders has worked something of a miracle by creating a quaffable but delightful little flavour bomb that doesn't scare away the casual drinking crowd. A truly great beer.

TASTING NOTES: Lots of peach and grapefruit hop aromas in the nose and in the taste, well matched by sweet, doughy malts.
- **Country:** USA
- **Brewer:** Founders Brewing Co.
- **Style:** IPA
- **Appearance:** Golden yellow
- **Alcohol:** 4.7%
- **Serving temp:** 4–7°C

🇺🇸 ODELL CUTTHROAT PORTER

High up in the Rocky Mountains there lives a freshwater fish named the Cutthroat trout. A favourite among anglers, it gives its name to Odell's London-inspired porter, brewed in Fort Collins, Colorado. A relatively easy-going beer for its style, a lightweight body belies its big flavour. This is one of Odell's regular beers and it has won various awards on both sides of the Atlantic.

TASTING NOTES: Slightly salty, savoury malt flavours work well with hints of coffee and chocolate.
- **Country:** USA
- **Brewer:** Odell Brewing Co.
- **Style:** Porter
- **Appearance:** Clear black
- **Alcohol:** 4.8%
- **Serving temp:** 5–10°C

🇺🇸 LEFT HAND BREWING MILK STOUT

Milk stouts are traditionally said to have certain health benefits. Sadly this isn't exactly true! They just include milk sugar (lactose) – a type of sugar that can't be fermented and therefore stays in the beer. Left Hand Brewing produces a fantastic version at its Colorado brewery. Like adding cream to your coffee, it might make you pile on a pound or two, but once you've tried it you won't go back to semi-skimmed milk any time soon.

TASTING NOTES: Sweet, creamy with big hints of chocolate and coffee. Like a boozy chocolate milkshake.
- **Country:** USA
- **Brewer:** Left Hand Brewing Co.
- **Style:** Milk stout • **Appearance:** Black
- **Alcohol:** 6% • **Serving temp:** 7–12°C

🇺🇸 BUDWEISER

Known affectionately as Bud, Budweiser has claimed it is the 'King of Beers' since it became a world bestseller in the 1950s. This pale lager is brewed using up to 30 per cent rice along with the barley malt to make it more cost-effective; this results in an incredibly 'lite' taste that needs to be drunk ice cold. Massive sales have helped Anheuser-Busch InBev become the world's largest brewing company, with more than 25 per cent of the market share worldwide.

TASTING NOTES: Very light aroma of grain and a carbonated texture in the mouth, with very little bitterness.
- **Country:** USA
- **Brewer:** AB InBev
- **Style:** Pale lager
- **Appearance:** Pale yellow
- **Alcohol:** 4.8%
- **Serving temp:** 1–2°C

🇺🇸 ALASKAN AMBER

The Alaskan Brewing Company's flagship beer has been on every beer drinker's must-try list since it was voted Best Beer in the Nation in 1988. Alaskan Amber is based on a classic recipe for a beer the Alaskan gold miners used to drink around the turn of the 20th century. It's an Alt (old) style beer, a style that originated in Germany, using ale yeasts that ferment slowly and at colder temperatures than most ales.

TASTING NOTES: Heavy malt aroma, rich caramel taste with hints of soft peachy fruit. Try it with smoked salmon.
- **Country:** USA
- **Brewer:** Alaskan Brewing Co.
- **Style:** Altbier
- **Appearance:** Amber
- **Alcohol:** 5.3%
- **Serving temp:** 8–12°C

🇺🇸 BLUEJACKET RHEINARD DE VOS

An interesting take on the Flemish red beers of Europe. Bluejacket uses the infamous Brettanomyces yeast strain to ferment this tart and sour beer. The natural fermentation takes place in wine barrels from the Auvergne region of France, resulting in a beer that is fruity forward with a distinctly funky yeast vibe, tasting a little more like wine than you'd expect.

TASTING NOTES: Wild strawberries and black pepper. Works great with a rich dish like duck à l'orange.
- **Country:** USA
- **Brewer:** Bluejacket
- **Style:** Flemish red
- **Appearance:** Dark cherry red
- **Alcohol:** 6.7%
- **Serving temp:** 10–13°C

🇺🇸 RIVER NORTH BREWERY MR. SANDMAN

Founded in 2012 by the husband and wife team of Matt and Jessica Hess, River North Brewery specializes in yeast-centric Belgian-style beers. The esters produced by such yeast lend a different hue to this out-of-the-ordinary imperial stout. In June 2017 the couple finally found premises in their namesake neighbourhood in Denver, RiNo, and they now can all their brews so they are available further afield.

TASTING NOTES: Fruity apple aromas coupled with sweet milky chocolate and a smoky aftertaste.
- **Country:** USA
- **Brewer:** River North Brewery
- **Style:** Imperial stout
- **Appearance:** Black
- **Alcohol:** 12.9%
- **Serving temp:** 10–13°C

🇺🇸 DOGFISH HEAD 90 MINUTE IMPERIAL IPA

One of the most important parts of any brewing process is the boil. This is the stage where hops are added for aroma, bitterness and preservation, and usually lasts one hour. Dogfish Head produces 60, 90 and 120 minute IPAs with varying levels of bitterness. The 90 minute version is a 9% double IPA with extra malt to balance out the bitterness imparted by the extremely high level of hops.

TASTING NOTES: Sweet malt and pungent hops combine to create candied alcohol fruit-cake-like flavours. Barbecue pulled pork would match well.
- **Country:** USA
- **Brewer:** Dogfish Head Brewery
- **Style:** Imperial IPA
- **Appearance:** Golden/orange
- **Alcohol:** 9%
- **Serving temp:** 8–12°C

🇺🇸 BOULEVARD HIBISCUS GOSE

The quintessentially North German style of beer gets a makeover with the addition of fresh and floral hibiscus. During the early boil phase, Boulevard Brewery throws in a whole heap of salt and some coriander seeds for additional savoury spice. The addition of hibiscus flowers instead of the more usual aroma hops towards the end of the process results in a beautiful pink colouring to the beer.

TASTING NOTES: Tangy, slightly sour and refreshing with hints of lime and coriander.
- **Country:** Germany
- **Brewer:** Boulevard Brewing Co.
- **Style:** Gose
- **Appearance:** Pink
- **Alcohol:** 4.2%
- **Serving temp:** 4–7°C

🇺🇸 BRIDGE BREW WORKS DUN GLEN DUBBEL

Inspired by the legendary Dun Glen hotel which burned down in 1930, Bridge Brew Works created this classy Belgian-style beauty. The story goes that the longest game of poker ever was played at the hotel – lasting 14 years in total. With that in mind, the brewers intended this dubbel as a perfect sipping beer when you're winning at the tables.

TASTING NOTES: Sticky brioche bread, raisins and toasted hazelnuts.
- **Country:** USA
- **Brewer:** Bridge Brew Works
- **Style:** Dubbel
- **Appearance:** Dark brown
- **Alcohol:** 6.5%
- **Serving temp:** 8–10°C

DID YOU KNOW?

President George Washington certainly appreciated beer – he had his own brewhouse in the grounds of his house at Mount Vernon, Virginia, and insisted that the soldiers in his Continental Army be permitted a quart of beer in their daily rations.

🇺🇸 BLACKFOOT RIVER SINGLE MALT IPA

Despite the suggestive name, Blackfoot River doesn't actually brew this beer with any whisky. It does however stick to one type of high-quality Maris Otter barley malt – in the same way that malt whisky does – without adding any speciality grains. Single Malt IPA is the brewery bestseller and is highly drinkable with anything spicy such as Indian or Thai curries. This beer also pairs well with cheese, especially anything veined with blue like a Stilton.

TASTING NOTES: Tangerine hops aromas with tinned peaches and cream.
- **Country:** USA
- **Brewer:** Blackfoot River Brewing Company
- **Style:** IPA
- **Appearance:** Golden
- **Alcohol:** 6.9% • **Serving temp:** 4–7°C

🇺🇸 BROOKLYN NARANJITO

Sometimes beers are created purely to go with delicious food that the brewers love. And so it was with Naranjito! The plethora of Mexican cuisine in and around New York City was the inspiration here, so this is a beer with lots of natural zest due to the use of whole sweet orange peel in the kettle alongside the hops. Perfect for those hearty burritos and spicy tacos you find in Williamsburg markets.

TASTING NOTES: Orange blossom, lime zest and juicy mandarins.
- **Country:** USA
- **Brewer:** Brooklyn Brewery
- **Style:** Pale ale
- **Appearance:** Pale gold
- **Alcohol:** 4.5%
- **Serving temp:** 4–7°C

🇺🇸 YARDS GENERAL WASHINGTON TAVERN PORTER

After homebrewing their way through their degrees, gaining experience at an English-style brewing company and spending every spare penny they had on beer, Tom Kehoe and Jon Bovit pooled their savings, maxed out their credit cards and in 1994 founded the Yards Brewing Company. This porter was created as part of their 'Ales of the Revolution' series and is based on an original recipe from one of America's Founding Fathers, George Washington. A delicious lesson in American history.

TASTING NOTES: Butter, chocolate, and with a slight hint of molasses. This would be great with slow-cooked brisket.
- **Country:** USA
- **Brewer:** Yards Brewing Co.
- **Style:** Porter
- **Appearance:** Clear brown
- **Alcohol:** 7% • **Serving temp:** 8–12°C

🇺🇸 VICTORY GOLDEN MONKEY

When they first met on the way to school in 1973, fifth-graders Bill Covaleski and Ron Barchet could scarcely imagine they'd end up starting one of America's best-loved breweries together. Their Golden Monkey is based on a classic Belgian abbey beer recipe but with that all-important American twist – extra hops. Spicy, bubbly and very refreshing – you'd never guess it was 9.5% from its quaffable character.

TASTING NOTES: Ripened fruit, lots of bubblegum from the yeast and a full-bodied, bubbly character. Great with creamy cheese such as Brie.
- **Country:** USA
- **Brewer:** Victory Brewing Co.
- **Style:** Abbey tripel
- **Appearance:** Yellow-orange
- **Alcohol:** 9.5%
- **Serving temp:** 4–7°C

MARBLE IMPERIAL RED

Founded in 2008 in the centre of Albuquerque, New Mexico, Marble Brewery is something of a local legend. Now occupying three locations around the state, its taprooms are a great place to find some of its more limited-edition beers like this Imperial Red ale, full of red fruits, tangy citrus and a hint of roasted cocoa beans.

TASTING NOTES: A great match with barbecue ribs and blue cheeses.
- **Country:** USA
- **Brewer:** Marble Brewery
- **Style:** Red ale
- **Appearance:** Hazy red
- **Alcohol:** 8%
- **Serving temp:** 10–13°C

MENDOCINO BLACK HAWK STOUT

Technically this is an Irish-style dry stout, and the most important ingredient is the dark roasted grain, which gives the matt black colour you'd expect in a pint of Guinness, the classic Irish dry stout. A fantastic example of traditional Irish-style beer from a modern American brewer.

TASTING NOTES: Dry roasted bitterness that balances the sweet dark malts. Great served with an Irish stew.
- **Country:** USA
- **Brewer:** Mendocino Brewing Co.
- **Style:** Dry stout
- **Appearance:** Black
- **Alcohol:** 5.2%
- **Serving temp:** 10–14°C

DID YOU KNOW?

President Jimmy Carter signed the bill to legalize homebrewing in 1978, but Americans have been brewing ever since English settlers reached the New World and they didn't stop – even during Prohibition!

🇺🇸 MAGIC HAT #9

Magic Hat's famous 'Not Quite Pale Ale' is almost impossible to describe, because there's never been anything quite like it. Put your scepticism aside until you try it though. The reason behind the #9 name is clouded in secrecy as part of the brewing sorcerers' image the Magic Hat brewery cultivates. It is a brewer with bags of personality and a wide range of impressive beers that always have that little special something.

TASTING NOTES: Perfume, light malt and a hint of citrus fruits in the nose are paired with sweet peach flavours on the tongue.
• **Country:** USA
• **Brewer:** Magic Hat Brewing Co.
• **Style:** Pale ale
• **Appearance:** Medium orange
• **Alcohol:** 5.1%
• **Serving temp:** 4–7°C

🇺🇸 MENDOCINO EYE OF THE HAWK

Part of the Mendocino 'Select Collection', Eye of the Hawk may not be available all year round, but what's certain is that it is always included in the yearly brew schedule. Coppery red in colour, the taste is a fusion of Cluster, Cascade and the classic lagering hop Saaz for a crisp grassy finish to go alongside its intense dark caramel flavours.

TASTING NOTES: Meadow grassiness, cinder toffee and honeycomb.
• **Country:** USA
• **Brewer:** Mendocino Brewing Company
• **Style:** American strong ale
• **Appearance:** Copper red
• **Alcohol:** 8%
• **Serving temp:** 10–13°C

🇺🇸 NARRAGANSETT AUTOCRAT COFFEE MILK STOUT

Narragansett Brewery has been brewing beer since the 1890s in Rhode Island. It was only natural therefore that it teamed up with Autocrat Coffee which has been bringing Rhode Islanders their morning coffee for the same length of time! A smooth stout, this one took silver at the World Beer Championships in 2014 with good reason.

TASTING NOTES: Coffee, toffee and chocolate milkshake makes it a great match for any chocolate dessert.
• **Country:** USA
• **Brewer:** Narragansett
• **Style:** Milk stout
• **Appearance:** Dark brown
• **Alcohol:** 5.3%
• **Serving temp:** 8–10°C

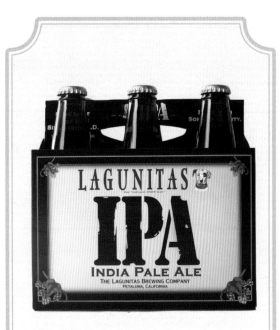

🇺🇸 LAGUNITAS IPA

Lagunitas IPA was first brewed in 1995 as a sessionable IPA that you could knock back for hours without wearying of being attacked by hops. More of a malt-forward, almost English-style IPA, Lagunitas proved so popular after its first batch that the brewery decided to make it an all-year-round brew, and now you can find it throughout America at the top of any craft beer list.

TASTING NOTES: Big toffee flavours, sweet, with a hoppy aroma that never overpowers you. Perfect with chargrilled meat.
- **Country:** USA
- **Brewer:** Lagunitas Brewing Co.
- **Style:** IPA
- **Appearance:** Amber
- **Alcohol:** 6.2%
- **Serving temp:** 4–7°C

🇺🇸 MOLSON COORS BLUE MOON

Originally named Bellyslide Belgian White when first created in 1995 by Blue Moon's brewmaster Keith Villa, this is a fresh take on the Belgian witbier styles revived in the 1960s by Pierre Celis. Using a combination of malted wheat, barley and oats for extra body, Villa also adds the classic elements of Belgian witbier including orange peel and coriander. A finishing touch of a slice of orange adds an extra bit of drama at the taps.

TASTING NOTES: Zesty orange, mildly soapy with a unique almost celery-like finish. Classic with steamed mussels and fries.
- **Country:** USA
- **Brewer:** Molson Coors
- **Style:** Witbier
- **Appearance:** Hazy yellow
- **Alcohol:** 5.4%
- **Serving temp:** 4–7°C

🇺🇸 OSKAR BLUES BOURBON JAVA TEN FIDY

Some of the best-rated beers in the world are imperial stouts and this style certainly seems to be a recurrent theme among the beer geeks of America. Bourbon Java Ten FIDY is given an extra dimension by barrel-ageing and a good healthy injection of coffee from a 'craft' Colorado roastery, Hotbox. The result is an extra dose of bitterness, a tobacco-like finish and the usual barrel-aged finish of booze and warmth.

TASTING NOTES: Molasses, coffee and a smooth hit of dark chocolate.
- **Country:** USA
- **Brewer:** Oscar Blues Brewery
- **Style:** Imperial stout
- **Appearance:** Black
- **Alcohol:** 10.5%
- **Serving temp:** 10–13°C

🇺🇸 BRASSERIE SAINT JAMES DAILY WAGES

The farmhouse-style saisons of Northern France and Belgium were traditionally brewed as a replacement for drinking water. They were vital in the payment of seasonal workers in the summertime but needed to be brewed in winter and fermented at cool temperatures. Brasserie Saint James in Reno has been as true to the original style as possible using a French yeast strain, subtle use of spices and a sensible but healthy hop character to ensure a long life.

TASTING NOTES: Hints of lemon, fresh white bread and lightly herbal sweetness.
- **Country:** USA
- **Brewer:** Brasserie Saint James
- **Style:** Saison
- **Appearance:** Pale gold
- **Alcohol:** 4.7%
- **Serving temp:** 4–7°C

🇺🇸 PARISH GHOST IN THE MACHINE

Not content with the volume or intensity of hoppy beers on the market, Parish Brewery decided to create a monster with its Ghost in the Machine beer. Hitting the shelves usually only once per year, beer geeks from around the country line up to grab a six-pack. The beer was created to combat the desensitization of hoppy beer and uses over five kilograms (ten pounds) of hops per barrel during brewing. Prepare your taste buds!

TASTING NOTES: Citric lemon rind and pithy orange with a juicy hop finish.
- **Country:** USA
- **Brewer:** Parish Brewing Co.
- **Style:** Double IPA
- **Appearance:** Hazy gold
- **Alcohol:** 8%
- **Serving temp:** 4–7°C

🇺🇸 DUCK-RABBIT BALTIC PORTER

Beer specialists don't come with weirder names (or logos) than this! The Duck-Rabbit brewery in North Carolina specializes in dark beers, from amber ale to milk stout – there are no hoppy pale ales here. Duck-Rabbit's Porter and Baltic Porter are very much 21st-century American beers, only distantly related to the porters of 18th-century London.

TASTING NOTES: Earthy, nutty aromas with hints of spice and smoke. Medium-bodied and easy to drink.
- **Country:** USA
- **Brewer:** Duck-Rabbit Brewery
- **Style:** Porter
- **Appearance:** Dark brown
- **Alcohol:** 9%
- **Serving temp:** 8–13°C

🇺🇸 YUENGLING DARK BREWED PORTER

Originally called the Eagle Brewery when it was first established in 1829 in Pottsville, Pennsylvania, the Yuengling brewery is the oldest in the United States. After brewery fires, Prohibition and a whole host of hardships, the brewery surpassed two-million barrels in 2009, making it not just the oldest, but also one of the most successful breweries in the US. This is its traditional British-style porter and one of the flagship products.

TASTING NOTES: Notes of sweetened coffee, liquorice and a hint of chocolate.
- **Country:** USA
- **Brewer:** D.G. Yuengling & Son
- **Style:** Porter • **Appearance:** Brown
- **Alcohol:** 5% • **Serving temp:** 8–13°C

🇺🇸 PABST BLUE RIBBON

Pabst beer apparently won America's Best at the World's Columbian Exposition in Chicago in 1893. Since then, it has been known as Pabst Blue Ribbon, although the beer never actually won a blue ribbon. In fact, it's unclear whether it won any awards at all that year, with many official accounts claiming that only bronze medals were awarded. What is clear though is that this has established itself as one of America's go-to beers. Usually at the top of the list in any bar and attractively priced, PBR has had a surge in sales since it became popular among hipsters, artists and musicians.

TASTING NOTES: Plenty of toffee-like malt with a very mellow and refreshing aftertaste. To be drunk alongside live music!
• **Country:** USA
• **Brewer:** Pabst Brewing Co.
• **Style:** Pale lager
• **Appearance:** Pale yellow
• **Alcohol:** 5% • **Serving temp:** 2–5°C

🇺🇸 ARROGANT BASTARD ALE

Arrogant Brewery is well known for its belligerent marketing style and this beer is one of its more famous brews, partly due to the slightly confrontational name but also of course for the taste! This is one of the first American strong ales – released way back in 1997. The recipe hasn't changed much – deep, satisfying and full of spice and caramel.

TASTING NOTES: Try it alongside a bowl of spicy chilli or a hefty burrito.
Country: USA
Brewer: Arrogant Brewing
Style: Strong ale
Appearance: Amber brown
Alcohol: 7.2%
Serving temp: 10–13°C

🇺🇸 PULPIT ROCK SAFTIG

Brewing from an old dairy facility next door to a laundromat in Decorah, Iowa, Pulpit Rock might be what you'd call a nanobrewery rather than a microbrewery. Comprising four friends fuelled by a passion for brewing beer, the Pulpit rock team have a tap list that is constantly changing. This northeastern-style IPA is served hazy and is true to its name which in Norwegian simply means 'juicy'.

TASTING NOTES: Juicy citrus, bright and refreshing with a good bit of spice in the finish to round it out.
• **Country:** USA
• **Brewer:** Pulpit Rock Brewing Co.
• **Style:** IPA
• **Appearance:** Hazy gold
• **Alcohol:** 6.1%
• **Serving temp:** 4–7°C

🇺🇸 AGAINST THE GRAIN LONDON BALLING

Brewed with Maris Otter pale barley, there's a distinctive British character to this barrel-aged barley wine. Not only does it use the highest-quality malt to be found in the British Isles, it also makes full use of Kentish hops including English Nugget and First Goldings. The only hint that this beer is from Kentucky is the bourbon barrels in which it's aged. Rich, silky and smooth, it's also incredibly punchy!

TASTING NOTES: Mahogany woody notes with toffee apple and bourbon caramel finish.
- **Country:** USA
- **Brewer:** Against the Grain
- **Style:** Barley wine
- **Appearance:** Dark gold
- **Alcohol:** 12.5%
- **Serving temp:** 10–13°C

🇺🇸 SKA MODUS HOPERANDI

There's nothing quite like a good beer-related pun. Ska Brewing's Modus Hoperandi is mainly found in cans – which some people might regard as inferior. In reality, though, cans keep a tighter seal so the beer stays fresher as well as cool faster! Which is a good thing, as you'll want to drink this 6.8% American-style IPA as fresh and as cool as possible. One of the best American IPAs around.

TASTING NOTES: A pine-infused mix of grapefruit, citrus and sweet hearty malts. Perfect alongside a Thai curry. Even better with spicy kebabs.
- **Country:** USA
- **Brewer:** SKA Brewing
- **Style:** IPA
- **Appearance:** Deep orange
- **Alcohol:** 6.8%
- **Serving temp:** 4–7°C

🇺🇸 MAUI COCONUT HIWA PORTER

A visit to Hawaii wouldn't be complete without a trip to an authentic island beach bar, and Maui Brewing has exactly what every tourist needs with its amazing locally-inspired cuisine and a host of imaginative brews. This creative take on the porter is made with a blend of six different roasted malts, those classic American flavours of Cascade and Columbus hops and a whole heap of hand-toasted coconut. The subtleness of the coconut flavour keeps it from being overpowering and makes what could be another standard-issue porter into something very special indeed. Sold in Maui's kookily-designed cans to keep the beer extra fresh.

TASTING NOTES: Dusty coconut and chocolate aroma, coffee and sweetness on the palate with more of that coconut subtly coming through at the end.
- **Country:** USA
- **Brewer:** Maui Brewing Co.
- **Style:** Porter
- **Appearance:** Black
- **Alcohol:** 6%
- **Serving temp:** 7–12°C

🇺🇸 PELICAN UMBRELLA NEW-WORLD IPA

Adorned with a sketch of Phil the Pelican, the brewery mascot, Pelican's Umbrella New-World IPA features a slightly more exotic ingredient – Ella hops, which are grown in Australia and have a bright acidic fruit flavour. The Pelican's oceanfront pub and brewery in Pacific City, Oregon, is famous for fine cuisine from its executive chef, Ged Aydelott, and the fine beer of brewmaster Darron Welch – a must-visit attraction for any beer lover.

Tasting notes: Gooseberry, pineapple and sour grapes with a digestive biscuit finish.
Country: USA
Brewer: Pelican Brewing Company
Style: IPA
Appearance: Light gold
Alcohol: 7.4%
Serving temp: 4–7°C

🇺🇸 FLYING DOG RAGING BITCH

Flying Dog is one of America's best-loved microbrewers. Adorned with the distinctive artwork of legendary British-born illustrator Ralph Steadman, its Raging Bitch Belgian IPA is perhaps not the ideal gift for your wife on Valentine's Day. It is, however, well worth a go on other occasions. The standout factor is the yeast – a Belgian strain known as Diablo that imparts a bubblegum and banana flavour combination often found in German wheat beers. Here it floats on a backdrop of hoppy American IPA to astounding effect, producing a unique beer.

TASTING NOTES: Banana, bubblegum and toffee. Like Banoffee pie in a bottle.
• **Country:** USA
• **Brewer:** Flying Dog Brew Co.
• **Style:** Belgian IPA
• **Appearance:** Dark amber
• **Alcohol:** 8.3%
• **Serving temp:** 8–12°C

🇺🇸 NEBRASKA BREWING MÉLANGE A TROIS

After over a decade of consistently scooping award after award, Mélange a Trois is well worth seeking out if you find yourself in Nebraska with a thirst for quality Belgian-style blonde ale. A fairly standard brewing process brings a great blonde colour and honey sweetness but the beer is really elevated when it gets an additional six-month maturation in French oak wine barrels previously used for Chardonnay.

TASTING NOTES: Oaky tannins, tangy grape and zesty orange combine with those sweet honey malts.
• **Country:** USA
• **Brewer:** Nebraska Brewing Co.
• **Style:** Belgian blonde
• **Appearance:** Golden
• **Alcohol:** 11.3%
• **Serving temp:** 4–7°C

🇺🇸 TRILLIUM METTLE

A beer created to mark the anniversary of the opening of the Trillium brewery, Mettle combines three classically American hops in Citra, Columbus and Amarillo for intense peach and nectarine fruit. The addition of rye to the malt bill means the liquid is given an extra dimension of spice too with an acidic, almost white wine-like nature in the nose.

TASTING NOTES: A dry finish and bold hops make this a great match for an aromatic curry.
• **Country:** USA
• **Brewer:** Trillium Brewing Company
• **Style:** Imperial IPA
• **Appearance:** Yellow gold
• **Alcohol:** 8.4%
• **Serving temp:** 4–7°C

🇺🇸 GOOSE ISLAND IPA

It seems like the Goose Island brewery from Chicago has been delighting us with its IPA for ever. This was one of the first hoppy IPAs to become widely available. Goose Island is now owned by global brewing group AB InBev. Happily the recipe has not changed one bit since the buyout and hopefully it never will.
A perfect balance of sweet, sour and bitter.

TASTING NOTES: Salted caramel popcorn, lovely floral hops with a hint of spice and a giant whiff of citrus in the nose.
- **Country:** USA
- **Brewer:** Goose Island Beer Co.
- **Style:** IPA
- **Appearance:** Hazy amber
- **Alcohol:** 5.9%
- **Serving temp:** 4–7°C

🇺🇸 SMUTTYNOSE REALLY OLD BROWN DOG

Featuring a picture of Olive, the brewery dog and official 'spirit guide' of Smuttynose Brewery, Old Brown Dog is a full-bodied brown ale with some real punch. Drinking like the iconic 'old ales' of Great Britain, it has deep notes of intense fruit, luscious sweet malts and a sweet aftertaste. One to enjoy late at night with some stinky cheese.

TASTING NOTES: Redcurrant jam, blueberries and Caramac sweetness.
- **Country:** USA
- **Brewer:** Smuttynose Brewing Company
- **Style:** Old ale
- **Appearance:** Brown
- **Alcohol:** 11.1%
- **Serving temp:** 10–13°C

🇺🇸 OTHER HALF ALL CITRA EVERYTHING

With its fluorescent colouring and simple minimalist design, a can of this double dry hopped Citra showpiece is as eye-catching as it is delicious. As you might suspect, only Citra hops are used to create this punchy IPA, adding the hops in steadily throughout the boil and again after fermentation. The result is a wonderful demonstration of what makes Citra the most sought-after hop in the world.

TASTING NOTES: A jumble of grapefruit, gooseberry, lychees and passion fruit in the aroma and light peachy notes in the finish.
- **Country:** USA
- **Brewer:** Other Half Brewing Co.
- **Style:** Imperial IPA
- **Appearance:** Cloudy gold
- **Alcohol:** 8.5%
- **Serving temp:** 4–7°C

🇺🇸 JACKIE O'S PUB & BREWERY SPIRIT BEAST 2016

It's not often you get two beers for the price of one. But Jackie O's has gone even further and given us six! Spirit Beast is a blend of five separate bourbon-aged imperial stouts together with a strong Belgian quad. The blending effect is different each time this incredible beer is brewed depending on what barrel-aged beers are available for blending so the flavours will vary somewhat. One thing they all have in common is that they are amazingly complex and as such need to be drunk slightly warmer than fridge temperature.

TASTING NOTES: Nutty sweetness, vanilla nibs, coconut and bitter chocolate with a slightly smoky undertone and a boozy finish.
- **Country:** USA • **Brewer:** Jackie O's Pub & Brewery
- **Style:** Imperial stout
- **Appearance:** Black • **Alcohol:** 12.5%
- **Serving temp:** 10–13°C

🇺🇸 TWO ROADS OL' FACTORY PILS

Two Roads Brewery is all about community. Using grand old heritage properties and transforming them from derelict post-industrial white elephants into thriving businesses has long been its goal. In this 'Factory Pilsner' a traditional German recipe is used and is given a modern American twist with the addition of a dry hopping process. Dry hopping adds almost zero extra bitterness and amps up the aromas to make a Pilsner fit for any hard-working American after a long day.

TASTING NOTES: Biscuit malt flavours with grassy, almost floral light hops give way to tangy green apple in the finish.
- **Country:** USA
- **Brewer:** Two Roads Brewing Co.
- **Style:** Pilsner
- **Appearance:** Clear yellow
- **Alcohol:** 5%
- **Serving temp:** 4–7°C

🇺🇸 KUHNHENN RASPBERRY EISBOCK

Since its first release in 2004, Kuhnhenn's Raspberry Eisbock has developed a manic following in the States. The brew starts out a little like a dark lager but, after a long boil, fresh raspberries are added with extra juice. The dark, chocolate malts combine with these tangy fruits to create a great balance that is intensified by the huge 15.5% alcohol. Finally, the end product is aged to provide some much-needed mellowing.

TASTING NOTES: Masses of red fruit with caramel and toffee sweetness.
- **Country:** USA
- **Brewer:** Kuhnhenn Brewing Co.
- **Style:** Fruit beer
- **Appearance:** Dark red
- **Alcohol:** 15.5%
- **Serving temp:** 10–13°C

🇺🇸 BEER VALLEY LEAFER MADNESS

Oregon's brewing scene is one of the most prolific in the world, with around 150 brewing companies. Such a hive of activity is bound to produce some outstanding beers and Leafer Madness by the Beer Valley Brewery is definitely one of them. A double or imperial pale ale – the generous quota of bittering hops help make this one of the few beers in the world that has 100 IBUs.

TASTING NOTES: Mouth-puckering bitterness, huge grapefruit citrus notes and probably best enjoyed without food.
- **Country:** USA
- **Brewer:** Beer Valley Brewing Co.
- **Style:** Imperial IPA
- **Appearance:** Hazy orange
- **Alcohol:** 9%
- **Serving temp:** 12–14°C

🇺🇸 FIRESTONE WALKER DOUBLE BARREL PALE ALE

Using traditional methods of ageing dating back to the first IPAs made in Burton upon Trent in the UK, Firestone Walker has based its flagship beer not on the modern, boldly hopped beers so popular in America, but on a style popular in Great Britain in the late 19th century. Rather than using stainless steel tanks, the beer is aged in oak barrels, which introduce slightly smokier, charred wood and vanilla flavours to produce a classic British-style pale ale.

TASTING NOTES: Toasted bread, caramel, wood and vanilla combine with a slight spice in the finish.
- **Country:** USA
- **Brewer:** Firestone Walker Brewing Co.
- **Style:** Premium pale ale
- **Appearance:** Dark amber
- **Alcohol:** 5%
- **Serving temp:** 8–12°C

🇺🇸 WEST SIXTH PAY IT FORWARD

'Paying it forward' simply means to do good deeds for no reason, which is exactly what West Sixth Brewing does with every bottle of this beer it sells, using proceeds from this delicious porter to support local charities in the community. So you can feel even better about enjoying the decadent, rich chocolate and coffee flavours that are amplified by the cacao nibs it's aged with.

TASTING NOTES: Nutty with hints of raisin and mochaccino.
- **Country:** USA
- **Brewer:** West Sixth Brewing
- **Style:** Porter
- **Appearance:** Hazy brown
- **Alcohol:** 7%
- **Serving temp:** 10–13°C

STRAIGHT TO ALE
LAIKA IMPERIAL STOUT

Straight to Ale brewing company was founded by a group of homebrewers who got together in 2009 with the goal of bringing better beer to Huntsville, Alabama. Dan Perry and Co. found their way into the heart of their community and now hold two locations in Huntsville, both producing cans and kegs of some of the finest beer in the state. Laika is a limited-release imperial stout that packs a real punch.

TASTING NOTES: Malt rich with notes of chocolate, hazelnuts and cream.
- **Country:** USA
- **Brewer:** Straight to Ale
- **Style:** Imperial stout
- **Appearance:** Black
- **Alcohol:** 11.7%
- **Serving temp:** 10–13°C

ALPINE BEER WINDOWS UP

America is famous for its hops – mostly grown in the Yakima Valley region in Washington State. The most in demand of these plants is Citra, a variety which produces a plethora of fruit flavours from the tropical to the citrus. This excellently balanced IPA from Alpine is one of the best examples of Citra. A relatively low IBU means the beer doesn't overwhelm the palate with bitterness and allows the fruity flavours of American hops to shine through.

TASTING NOTES: Melon, grapefruit, gooseberries, passion fruit and lime. All the fruits and a nice hit of caramel at the end.
- **Country:** USA
- **Brewer:** Alpine Beer Co.
- **Style:** IPA
- **Appearance:** Orange-gold
- **Alcohol:** 7%
- **Serving temp:** 4–7°C

TREE HOUSE JULIUS

Tree House brewery is not just big on hops but also big on style. Its distinctive and colourful cans catch the eye almost as much as its bold and brash flavours capture the palate. This is its flagship American IPA, loaded with 1.6 kilograms (3.5 pounds) of West Coast hops per barrel but with enough roundness from the malt to create a balanced drinking experience.

TASTING NOTES: Sweet orange and mango give the strong impression of tropical fruit and tart citrus.
- **Country:** USA
- **Brewer:** Tree House Brewing Company
- **Style:** IPA
- **Appearance:** Hazy orange
- **Alcohol:** 6.8%
- **Serving temp:** 4–7°C

In August 1997 a homebrewing club from Colorado scaled new heights in beer brewing when it brewed a batch of barley wine at 4,400m/14,333ft on the summit of Mt Elbert (the highest peak in Colorado).

TERRAPIN WAKE-N-BAKE COFFEE OATMEAL IMPERIAL STOUT

Often in America beer gets made in such a complicated way that the style becomes a mouthful in itself. Coffee Oatmeal Imperial Stout is exactly as it sounds – brewed with coffee from Jittery Joe's roaster in Athens, Georgia, Terrapin Beer Co. also added a healthy dose of oatmeal to achieve that trademark comforting and silky mouthfeel that we look for in an imperial stout.

TASTING NOTES: Coffee dominates the nose and translates to the taste as well. Liquorice, vanilla and burst caramel.

- **Country:** USA
- **Brewer:** Terrapin Beer Co.
- **Style:** Imperial stout
- **Appearance:** Black
- **Alcohol:** 9.4%
- **Serving temp:** 10–13°C

ANCHOR OLD FOGHORN BARLEY WINE

San Francisco's Anchor brewery was founded in the late 19th century and became famous for its California common beer or, as it is also known, steam beer. Old Foghorn is Anchor's take on classic British barley wine. Rich in sugars from two types of malt, the brewers balance out all that sweetness with bitterness and aroma from a mountain of Cascade hops – which lend their distinctive citrus aroma to many American beers.

TASTING NOTES: Strong caramel aroma and a long, dry, bitter finish. Try it with aged blue cheese or slow-cooked beef stew.

- **Country:** USA
- **Brewer:** Anchor Brewing Co.
- **Style:** Barley wine
- **Appearance:** Burnt copper
- **Alcohol:** 8.8%
- **Serving temp:** 8–13°C

🇺🇸 ANDERSON VALLEY
BOONT AMBER ALE

The story of Anderson Valley brewery is a quintessentially American one. Starting in 1987 with a ten-barrel brewhouse beneath the bustling Buckhorn Saloon in Boonville, California, production quickly expanded and as of 2011 was 40,000 barrels per year. The Boont Amber Ale is typical of its style. A blend of malts that includes the darker crystal and the slightly paler two-row combine to give a brilliant copper appearance. Brewed with a blend of four hop varieties, the finished product is well balanced and subtly complex, with an easy-going, light bitter finish.

TASTING NOTES: Toffee, butterscotch and caramel flavours. One to drink alongside almost any meal.
- **Country:** USA
- **Brewer:** Anderson Valley Brewing Co.
- **Style:** Amber
- **Appearance:** Amber ale
- **Alcohol:** 5.8%
- **Serving temp:** 8–12°C

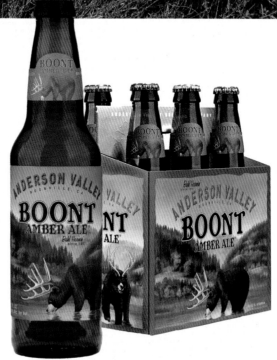

WORKING UP A STEAM

California is associated with one of America's unique beer styles – steam beer. In fact, some people regard steam beer as America's only native beer style.

When James Marshall found gold at Sutter's Mill, California, in 1848, it led to a rush of 300,000 gold seekers descending on the state by the following year. These '49ers' came in search of fortune; they also needed to be fed and watered.

Prospecting is thirsty work, so brewers also arrived in the Golden State on the lookout for a new market. At the time, lager was beginning to take over American brewing, so it is thought that some brewers arrived

with lager yeast. However, at this point they encountered a problem.

Lager requires a period of fermenting at very low temperatures. In the hot Californian climate, this was not possible. There was no refrigeration and the nearest source of ice that could have been used to create a cooler fermenting environment was too far away to collect.

Brewers had to improvise, so they brewed with the lager yeast at ale temperatures, resulting in a hybrid beer style that combined elements of both lager and ale. Open fermenting tanks were used to cool the beer down. Because the fermenting tanks were sometimes on the roofs of buildings, the cooling beer would give off a steam in the mornings, which may be one source of the name 'steam beer'.

Another possibility is that it derives from a traditional German beer called Dampfbier, which literally means steam beer. Many American brewers were of German descent; they may have known that Dampfbier was also fermented at high temperatures and adapted the recipe.

After primary fermentation, the beer was transferred to kegs with live beer added, so that it continued to ferment. Before it could be poured the barrel had to be vented to remove excess carbonation. The resulting explosive release, not unlike a steam train's brakes, may be a further explanation for the name.

Like German steam beer, the American version was viewed as a rough-and-ready drink for working men; it was sometimes known as 'California common'.

Many different brewers produced the beer, which used local ingredients to keep costs down. It was generally an amber beer, often compared to Munich beer. Caramel malt, roast malt and caramelized sugar were used in combination to produce the distinctive colour.

As brewing technology improved, demand for this low-end drink subsided. Following Prohibition, one of the few brewers remaining was San Francisco's Anchor brewery, which had been established in 1896. However, after a period of decline, the business was about to fold in 1965. Alerted to the death throes of his favourite beer, Fritz Maytag (a Stanford graduate and heir to the washing machine business) bought a controlling share in the brewery and attempted to kickstart the business.

By altering the recipe of the beer and focusing on better quality control, Maytag helped revive Anchor. Bar owners had complained that the beer spoiled easily, so he developed a bottled version of Anchor Steam Beer, which was launched in 1971 to almost instant acclaim.

Throughout his ownership of the company Maytag deliberately kept its size relatively small to ensure that the beer quality remained great. He can fairly be described as one of the godfathers of American craft brewing as he sought to help other microbreweries follow his example and develop products that were an alternative to mass-produced beer.

Because Anchor trademarked the term 'steam beer' in 1981, other brewers are not able to use it. They are stuck with the slightly more prosaic descriptor of 'California common beer'.

According to the Beer Judge Certification Program, a beer-tasting examiner, the term California common beer is 'narrowly defined around the prototypical Anchor Steam example'. The style 'showcases the signature Northern Brewer hops (with woody, rustic or minty qualities) in moderate to high strength', and is fermented with a lager yeast that was selected to thrive at the cool end of normal ale fermentation temperatures. Traditionally it was fermented in open fermenters, a process that Anchor still uses.

Other brewers have sought to revive the style, which is no longer regarded as a cheap bottle of suds, but as a premium beer. Examples include Dorothy's New World Lager and Linden Street Common Lager. The latter is brewed in Oakland and is described as a tribute to styles and brewing methods that originated in the Bay Area during the pre-Prohibition era.

🇺🇸 SAMUEL ADAMS BOSTON LAGER

Samuel Adams Boston Lager is brewed using an old family recipe dating back to the 1870s, and was one of the leading lights in the American craft brewing revolution in the 1980s. Now a hugely recognizable brand that hasn't compromised on flavour and brewing know-how to cut costs, Samuel Adams is an American institution and a six-pack would be a welcome sight in any beer-drinker's fridge. Best consumed while watching your favourite sports team.

TASTING NOTES: Toasty malt, toffee and caramel sweetness is balanced with refined hops.
- **Country:** USA
- **Brewer:** Samuel Adams Brewing
- **Style:** Amber lager
- **Appearance:** Amber
- **Alcohol:** 4.9%
- **Serving temp:** 4–7°C

🇺🇸 SIERRA NEVADA PALE ALE

Sierra Nevada Pale Ale has also found favour with drinkers all over the world. This timeless interpretation of American pale ale has become something of a benchmark beer. As is common in many American pale ales, Sierra Nevada is dry hopped with a generous helping of Cascade hops after the initial bittering hops have done their job, using the brewery's patented hop torpedo to impart all the fruity, citrus aromas of the plant without adding any further bitterness. The result is a nice balance of citrus fruits and bitter hops along with a helping of caramel flavours from the malts.

TASTING NOTES: Floral orange blossom on the nose, with a long, lingering bitter finish. Great with any spicy curry.
• **Country:** USA • **Brewer:** Sierra Nevada Brewing Co.• **Style:** Pale ale
• **Appearance:** Amber • **Alcohol:** 5.6%
• **Serving temp:** 4–7°C

🇺🇸 BIG SKY BREWING MOOSE DROOL BROWN ALE

The ingredients used in this beer bring together the best from both sides of the pond. It uses four types of malt and four hop varieties – including the famous Kent Goldings variety common in the UK's real ale scene. Moose Drool is easy-going and well-balanced, and the lower alpha acids in the UK hops allow more sweetness to come through.

TASTING NOTES: Chocolate, light orange and caramel aromas with a nutty malt finish. Try with hearty foods like smoked sausage.
• **Country:** USA
• **Brewer:** Big Sky Brewing Co.
• **Style:** Brown ale
• **Appearance:** Deep brown
• **Alcohol:** 5.1%
• **Serving temp:** 10–12°C

🇺🇸 GRAND TETON BITCH CREEK ESB

In the Targhee National Forest in Idaho runs a restless vein of water popular with fishermen and kayakers for its beauty and character. This famous landmark gives its name to one of the most decorated beers in the USA. Grand Teton's Bitch Creek has won 12 gold medals at brewing awards throughout the country and is – so locals will tell you – as feisty and complex as its namesake. A rich American brown ale made with a blend of five malts for a very robust flavour and a satisfying baseline of rich caramels topped off with a spicy, pine resin hop finish.

TASTING NOTES: Caramel, nuts, orange and a slightly spicy finish. Try it with barbecued meats or aged Gouda cheese.
• **Country:** USA
• **Brewer:** Grand Teton Brewing
• **Style:** Brown ale
• **Appearance:** Brown
• **Alcohol:** 6.5%
• **Serving temp:** 10–12°C

MICHELOB ORIGINAL LAGER

First brewed in 1896 by the American godfather of brewing (for better or worse) Adolphus Busch, Michelob is pitched as a beer for the more discerning drinker. Named after a Czech brewer from Saaz (a region famous for its hops), Michelob is similar to many other pale lagers on the US market.

TASTING NOTES: Some light malt notes, hints of corn and light hints of earthy hop flavour.
- **Country:** USA
- **Brewer:** AB InBev
- **Style:** Pale lager
- **Appearance:** Clear yellow
- **Alcohol:** 5%
- **Serving temp:** 1–2°C

ROGUE DEAD GUY ALE

Brewers are often proud of their yeast and the brewers at Rogue are no exception. Rouge's Pacman yeast is so named due to its extremely voracious nature – it eats a wide variety of sugars for a long time – making it perfect in the brewing of this German-style Helles (pale) lager. Using traditional Saaz and Perle hops from Europe together with four caramelized malts, Dead Guy Ale has all the bready character of a conventional Helles lager, but the brewers at Rogue have given it a slightly higher hop content for a fuller flavour.

TASTING NOTES: Grains, toasted bread and alcohol all contribute to the overall flavour of this beer, with a dry hoppy finish.
- **Country:** USA • **Brewer:** Rogue Ales
- **Style:** Helles lager • **Appearance:** Amber
- **Alcohol:** 6.6% • **Serving temp:** 4–7°C

DID YOU KNOW?

White House Honey Ale is the first beer known to have been brewed in the White House. In January 2011, then President Barack Obama purchased a home brewing kit and White House chefs brewed the beer.

🇺🇸 BELL'S AMBER ALE

The kilning of malt is a very subtle part of the brewing process: just a few degrees' variation in temperature can produce very different flavours. Bell's Amber Ale, brewed in Michigan, is made with Munich malt – a rich variety that is most notably used in Oktoberfest beers in Germany. The higher kiln temperature imparts an intense, sweet flavour that is balanced out by floral and citrus hops to make a classic American amber ale.

TASTING NOTES: Intense, toasted flavours; great with a wide variety of food. Pure liquid bread.
- **Country:** USA
- **Brewer:** Bell's Brewery
- **Style:** Amber ale
- **Appearance:** Amber
- **Alcohol:** 5.8%
- **Serving temp:** 8–12°C

🇺🇸 TOPPLING GOLIATH KING SUE

Part of the Toppling Goliath Brewing Co.'s 'Hop Patrol' series, King Sue uses what many consider to be the Cadillac of hops – Citra – in almost double the quantities of a normal IPA. Citra hops are in such high demand worldwide that it's simply not affordable in some parts of the world to use them. The profile of this double IPA is pinewood, sweet tangerine and grapefruit zest in vast quantities with a dramatic punchy bitterness at the end.

TASTING NOTES: Tangerine, grapefruit, mango, pine and all the best parts of Citra hops.
- **Country:** USA
- **Brewer:** Toppling Goliath Brewing Co.
- **Style:** Double IPA
- **Appearance:** Hazy orange
- **Alcohol:** 8.5%
- **Serving temp:** 4–7°C

🇺🇸 BROOKLYN LAGER

Since the late 1980s, the Brooklyn Brewery has been at the forefront of the resurgence in American craft brewing. This Vienna-style lager was for a while the only craft lager in a marketplace dominated by big business. Production is now largely based at company headquarters in trendy Williamsburg. Brewing is overseen by Garrett Oliver – an aficionado of beer and food pairing – who has been Brooklyn's brewmaster since 1994. Brooklyn Lager is today an iconic product, a symbol of New York and a go-to beer for beer drinkers around the world.

TASTING NOTES: Firm, malty base provides a robust backdrop for floral, fragrant hops. Goes with anything you can find in your fridge.
- **Country:** USA • **Brewer:** Brooklyn Brewery
- **Style:** Vienna lager
- **Appearance:** Dark amber
- **Alcohol:** 5.2% • **Serving temp:** 4–7°C

🇨🇦 LABATT BLUE

Without doubt the undisputed heavyweight brewer of Canada, Labatt Brewing Company sells more than any other in the Great White North – largely down to its flagship brand, Labatt Blue. Originally called Pilsener Lager when first introduced in 1951, the beer quickly gained the nickname 'Blue' from the colour of its label and the brewers' support of the Canadian Football League team, the Blue Bombers. Labatt Blue became Canada's bestselling beer by 1979. Although Budweiser now outsells it on home turf, this classic pale lager is still the most popular and bestselling Canadian beer in the world.

TASTING NOTES: Light malt and mild citrus aromas with the textbook crisp, clean, pale lager taste. Serve it ice cold with peanuts and your favourite sports team.
- **Country:** Canada
- **Brewer:** Labatt Brewing Company
- **Style:** Pale lager • **Appearance:** Pale yellow
- **Alcohol:** 5% • **Serving temp:** 1–2°C

🇨🇦 ALEXANDER KEITH'S INDIA PALE ALE

Alexander Keith's IPA is unlike any other India pale ale. It's not particularly strong at only 5% and has very low hop bitterness, so it doesn't resemble the modern American-style IPAs. It also lacks the fruitiness and full body associated with the traditional British style. But this IPA was around long before the current IPA revival. It has its own character and perhaps because of this has become Nova Scotia's most popular beer.

TASTING NOTES: Slight corn notes, very light hoppiness and a very smooth thin finish.
- **Country:** Canada
- **Brewer:** Oland Brewery
- **Style:** IPA • **Appearance:** Golden
- **Alcohol:** 5%
- **Serving temp:** 8–12°C

DID YOU KNOW?

French herbalist Louis Hébert and his wife were Canada's first brewers – emigrating to Quebec in 1617, they were granted farmland to grow barley and wheat from which they brewed beer for themselves and their neighbours.

⦿ ALLEY KAT OLDE DEUTERONOMY

Alley Kat, founded in 1994, is one of the longest-running microbrewers in Canada, but is still a relatively new outfit. Founders Neil and Lavonne Herbst are brewing some of the most exciting beers in North America. Some are best drunk immediately to retain their fresh hop character, while others are best kept for lengthy periods in cool dark cellars so the malt flavours will develop. Olde Deuteronomy barley wine definitely falls into the latter category.

TASTING NOTES: Heavy on toffee, dark fruit, brown sugar and a heady dose of alcohol in the nose. Aged versions may take on woody notes.
- **Country:** Canada
- **Brewer:** Alley Kat Brewing Co.
- **Style:** Barley wine
- **Appearance:** Copper
- **Alcohol:** 10.3%
- **Serving temp:** 13–15°C

⦿ COAL HARBOUR WOODLAND SOUR SAISON

As with many Belgian-style beers brewed in North America, the locally-produced hops give a completely different dimension from their European counterparts. Coal Harbour's Woodland Sour Saison is a twist on their modern witbier which is front-loaded with local hops. The twist? This is a kettle soured beer. Unlike standard sours which take a long time to develop their funky flavours in less than hygienic conditions, kettle souring introduces the bacteria between the mashing-in stage and boiling for a quick and simple shortcut to those dusty sour flavours. Orange peel, coriander and Sichuan peppercorns finish the job.

TASTING NOTES: Pine resin, floral orange bitters and lemon tart with light sourness in the finish.
- **Country:** Canada
- **Brewer:** Coal Harbour Brewing Co.
- **Style:** Saison
- **Appearance:** Cloudy gold
- **Alcohol:** 5.25%
- **Serving temp:** 8–10°C

DID YOU KNOW?

Beer has a major role in the Canadian economy, with one in a hundred jobs being supported by beer sales.

🍁 MILL STREET TANKHOUSE ALE

The Mill Street Brewery has been going strong since production started in 2002. Founders Steve Abrams, Jeff Cooper and Michael Duggan named it after the address 55 Mill Street in Toronto's historic distillery district. Its Tankhouse Ale is made using a recipe for a hoppy, well-balanced modern American-style pale ale that the head brewer developed 20 years ago – it was such a favourite he saw no need to change it.

TASTING NOTES: Loaded with spicy hop aromas from the American Cascade variety used for both bitterness and finishing.
- **Country:** Canada
- **Brewer:** Mill Street Brewery
- **Style:** Pale ale
- **Appearance:** Copper red
- **Alcohol:** 5.2%
- **Serving temp:** 4–7°C

🍁 AMSTERDAM BONESHAKER IPA

Some brewers aim for subtleties in their product that are only detectable to the seasoned beer lover. Amsterdam Brewery didn't care about subtleties when it made this continually hopped IPA. With an almost dangerous amount of Amarillo hops used, the question, 'How many hops can fit in one beer?' may never be 100 per cent settled but the Boneshaker IPA certainly comes close to providing the answer. Not for the faint of heart – hop lovers only.

TASTING NOTES: Pine-like resin aromas, forceful citrus fruits and a slight peppery spice from the hops.
- **Country:** Canada
- **Brewer:** Amsterdam Brewery
- **Style:** IPA
- **Appearance:** Hazy amber
- **Alcohol:** 7.1%
- **Serving temp:** 4–7°C

🍁 BRASSNECK NO BRAINER

The best lager takes at least six weeks to brew, and in the case of Brassneck's No Brainer corn lager it's actually more like ten weeks. As a result, it's quite rare they can even brew this beer because it takes up so much of their brewing capacity. Incredibly pale and not the kind of beer that beer geeks line up for, this is one brew that's about pure refreshment and thirst quenching.

TASTING NOTES: Super light, a touch of meadow spice and a delicious biscuity sweetness.
- **Country:** Canada
- **Brewer:** Brassneck Brewery
- **Style:** Lager
- **Appearance:** Hazy blonde
- **Alcohol:** 4.5%
- **Serving temp:** 4–7°C

🍁 SLEEMAN HONEY BROWN LAGER

After a few years of running their own pub, John Sleeman and his English wife were visited by his Aunt Florian one fateful day. Clutching a bottle of his family's historic Sleeman beer, she proceeded to tell him about his heritage and on that day an empire was reborn. The Sleeman brewery reopened in 1988 and its Honey Brown Lager is brewed in the style of the cottage breweries of old, with a touch of natural honey being added towards the end.

TASTING NOTES: Caramel, sweet honey and toasted malt in the aroma with a mellow, honey bitter taste.

- **Country:** Canada
- **Brewer:** Sleeman Breweries
- **Style:** Amber lager
- **Appearance:** Light amber
- **Alcohol:** 5.2%
- **Serving temp:** 4–7°C

🍁 POWELL STREET OLD JALOPY PALE ALE

The very definition of a microbrewery – technically a nanobrewery given its small production line – the husband and wife team of David Bowkett and Nicole Stefanopoulos began their Vancouver-based brewing adventure in 2012. A homage to the Burton upon Trent beer styles, this beautifully made English-style pale ale is as balanced and refined as you'd hope for, with equal amounts of American hops and roasted caramel malts giving the perfect balance of bitter and sweet.

TASTING NOTES: Lots of sweet malts and zesty citrus in the aroma and much the same story in the taste. Excellent with a chargrilled steak.

- **Country:** Canada
- **Brewer:** Powell Street Craft Brewery
- **Style:** Pale ale • **Appearance:** Orange
- **Alcohol:** 5.5% • **Serving temp:** 4–7°C

🇨🇦 MOLSON CANADIAN LAGER

One of the best selling pale lagers in Canada, this is a beer with a string of awards to its name. As well as a gold medal in the North American Lager category at the Canadian Brewing Awards in 1989, 1990, 1991, 1997, 2001 and 2002, it also won Gold Medal Distinction from the Monde Selection – a sort of Michelin star guide for food and drink products. Not bad for a simple, clean, easy-drinking lager.

TASTING NOTES: An easy-going blend of clean malts, a hint of lemon and a moreish sweetness that makes it hard to stop drinking.
- **Country:** Canada
- **Brewer:** Molson Coors
- **Style:** Pale lager
- **Appearance:** Pale yellow
- **Alcohol:** 5%
- **Serving temp:** 1–2°C

🇨🇦 PROPELLER LONDON STYLE PORTER

Yet another tribute to the brewers of the British Isles, this traditional London porter is based on the drink the cabbies and porters of London used to drink after their late-night shifts. Propeller Brewery's version is just about perfect and extremely true to the original recipe of pale, roasted and chocolate malts levelled out with a sensible amount of hops from either side of the Atlantic. Much softer and easier to drink than you'd expect.

TASTING NOTES: Bitter chocolate, light toffee and liquorice notes in the aroma with a sweet, malty taste in the mouth. Great with roasted meats or blue cheese.
- **Country:** Canada
- **Brewer:** Propeller Brewery
- **Style:** Porter
- **Appearance:** Clear brown
- **Alcohol:** 5%
- **Serving temp:** 8–13°C

🇨🇦 MUSKOKA KIRBY'S KÖLSCH

The kölsch style was brewed as an alternative to the bottom-fermented Pilsners and lagers of the early 1900s, with almost zero aroma hops to ensure maximum bready flavours. Muskoka brewery went a step further, as so many do in North America, by adding another sweet flavour in the form of fresh peach juice. A great match for seafood, sharp cheeses and anything that goes with white bread.

TASTING NOTES: Sweet fruity peach flavours with hints of orange blossom and lemon zest.
- **Country:** Canada
- **Brewer:** Muskoka Brewery
- **Style:** Fruit kölsch
- **Appearance:** Pale straw
- **Alcohol:** 4.6%
- **Serving temp:** 4–7°C

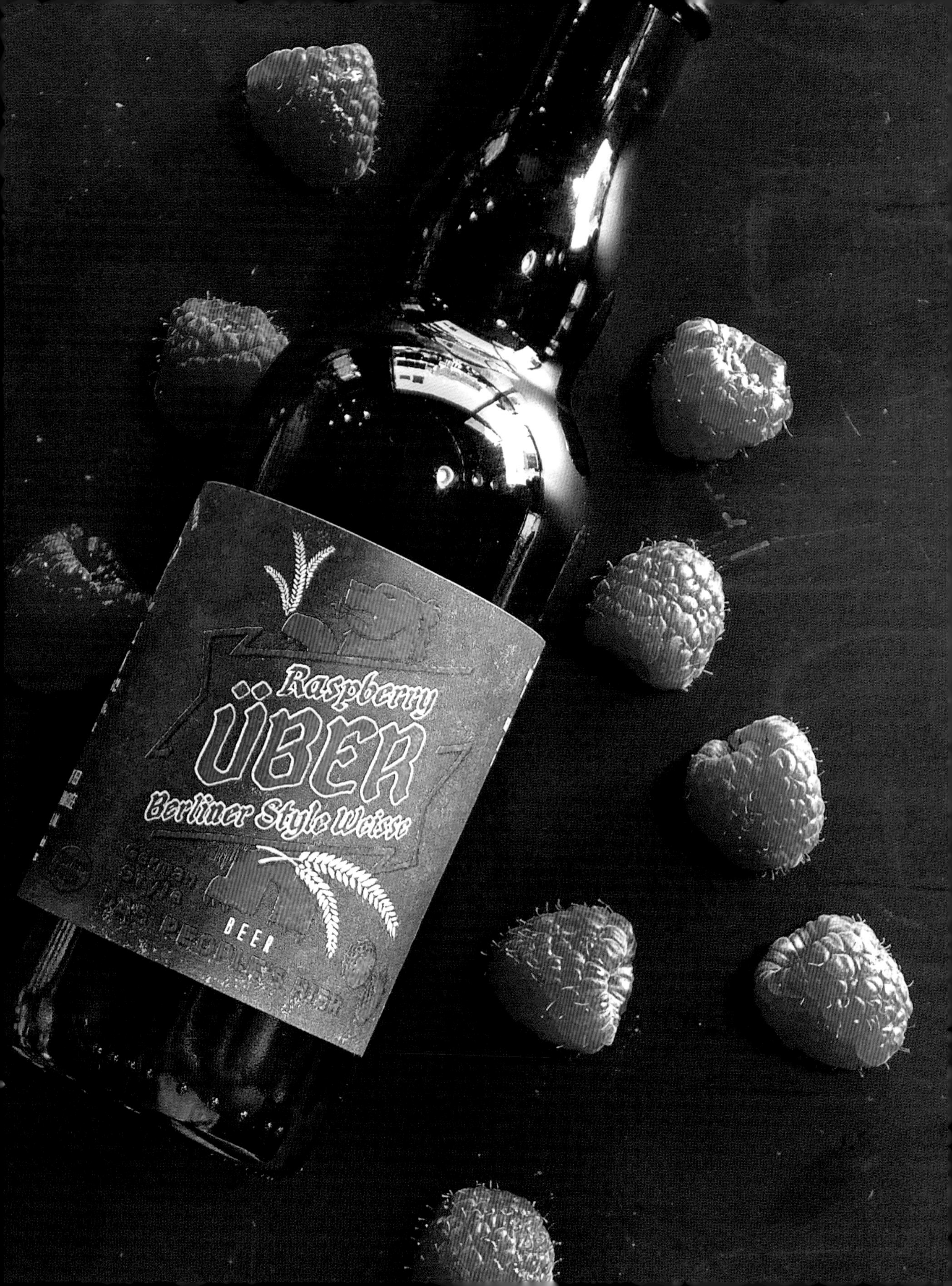
Raspberry
ÜBER
Berliner Style Weisse
BEER

🍁 NICKEL BROOK RASPBERRY UBER

The Berliner weisse style is given an extra spark of refreshment by a long ageing on fresh raspberries by Ontario-based Nickel Brook. As well as the sour raspberry flavours the fruit also imparts a gorgeous fruit juice-like red tint to the beer. The original Nickel Brook Brewery in Burlington is now exclusively brewing beers of this funky nature in order to let the yeast roam freely through the entire brewhouse.

TASTING NOTES: Fresh raspberry, tart apple and lighter notes of lime and barnyard.
- **Country:** Canada
- **Brewer:** Nickel Brook Brewing Co.
- **Style:** Berliner Weiss
- **Appearance:** Light red
- **Alcohol:** 3.8%
- **Serving temp:** 3–5°C

🍁 DIEU DU CIEL PÉCHÉ MORTEL

An incredibly rich and intense beer and not one for casual consumption. Péché Mortel is French for mortal sin – which is very appropriate in this instance. A hugely viscous and thick, black body comes with the calorie count you'd expect from a 9.5% imperial stout. These flavoursome, warming strong stouts were originally brewed by English brewers for export to the Russian Tsar. Dieu du Ciel's version includes coffee in the brewing process.

TASTING NOTES: Roasted coffee, sweet chocolate with hints of vanilla cream and spicy fruit. Great with vanilla ice cream on top for a beer float.
- **Country:** Canada
- **Brewer:** Dieu du Ciel
- **Style:** Imperial stout
- **Appearance:** Black
- **Alcohol:** 9.5%
- **Serving temp:** 8–13°C

🍁 GRANITE IPA

One of the few brewers outside of the UK to have a healthy mix of cask ales in its taproom, Granite Brewery has operated since 1985 in Halifax, Nova Scotia, and specializes in English-style beers straight from the cask. These beers need to be looked after by trained cellar men and woman in order to get the best out of them. Brothers Kevin and Ron Keefe created this recipe as a nod to the more full-bodied and malt-forward India pale ales that were first created in London in the 17th century, but with the addition of dry hops after fermentation in order to impart extra aroma.

TASTING NOTES: Spicy hop flavours with meadow grain aromas and a slightly caramelized orange note in the finish.
- **Country:** Canada
- **Brewer:** Granite Brewery • **Style:** IPA
- **Appearance:** Cloudy orange • **Alcohol:** 5%
- **Serving temp:** 10–13°C

🇨🇦 STONEHAMMER CONTINUITY BALTIC PORTER

Baltic porters were always brewed in the Baltic states of Latvia, Estonia and Lithuania in north-east Europe and derived much of their style from the porters and stouts of 17th century Great Britain. A touch stronger in order to stave off the cold, this fantastic example from StoneHammer is as faithful to the original style as can be. Thick, dark and super-rich with a pleasing warmth in the finish.

TASTING NOTES: Lots of coffee, molasses and ripe dark fruit and a hint of cherries.
- **Country:** Canada
- **Brewer:** StoneHammer Brewing
- **Style:** Porter
- **Appearance:** Dark amber
- **Alcohol:** 7.8%
- **Serving temp:** 8–10°C

🇨🇦 CENTRAL CITY RED RACER IPA

Central City's Red Racer IPA is its flagship product and is served up by the bucketload at its chic little brewpub in Surrey, east of Vancouver, British Columbia. The brewery is named after a fictional city created by DC comics as the home of its famous graphic novel character, The Flash.

TASTING NOTES: Floral, almost perfume like hops meld flowers and tropical fruit perfectly with a rich, biscuit toffee malt.
- **Country:** Canada
- **Brewer:** Central City Brewing Co.
- **Style:** IPA
- **Appearance:** Dark amber
- **Alcohol:** 6.5%
- **Serving temp:** 4–7°C

🇨🇦 GREAT LAKES HARRY PORTER

Great Lakes Brewing has a string of awards to its name for its Canuck Pale Ale, but it would be a shame to not include this seasonal favourite as well. Harry Porter (apparently JK Rowling is cool with the name) is a full-bodied dark roasty winter warmer that goes brilliantly with blue cheese or some good chocolate cake.

TASTING NOTES: Creamy, silky body with hints of mud pie and tray bake tiffin.
- **Country:** Canada
- **Brewer:** Great Lakes Brewery
- **Style:** Porter
- **Appearance:** Oak-brown
- **Alcohol:** 6.5%
- **Serving temp:** 10–13°C

🇨🇦 RIBSTONE CREEK OLD MAN WINTER

Ribstone Creek created this boozy and flavourful porter to coincide with the Christmas period and they still brew it to mark the holidays. A dark and warming beer to soothe the soul on a cold night, it makes a great match for the fruit puddings and chocolate treats that Christmas brings as well as being an excellent fireside sipper. Expect the beer to be slightly cloudy as it's left unfiltered with hints of the yeast remaining.

TASTING NOTES: Dried fruits, a touch of tobacco smoke and big smooth caramel flavours.

- **Country:** Canada
- **Brewer:** Ribstone Creek Brewery
- **Style:** Porter
- **Appearance:** Dark brown
- **Alcohol:** 6.6%
- **Serving temp:** 10–13°C

🇨🇦 WILD ROSE CHERRY PORTER

When you add whole cherries to the lusciously bitter and dark chocolate flavours and aromas of a classic London-style porter, then only good things can happen. Wild Rose's Cherry Porter does exactly that and is one of the best beers for a chilly winter evening. With a slightly smoky character as well as fruit, double cream and lashings of black cherry flavour, try pairing this award-winning beer with a big slice of Black Forest gateau.

TASTING NOTES: Rich chocolate, espresso coffee and a long-lasting impression of black cherry.
- **Country:** Canada
- **Brewer:** Wild Rose
- **Style:** Cherry porter
- **Appearance:** Dark burgundy
- **Alcohol:** 6.6%
- **Serving temp:** 12–14°C

🇨🇦 MT BEGBIE BRAVE LIVER SCOTCH ALE

Known in brewing circles as a 'wee heavy', the Scotch ale is always strong, dark and viscous with bold flavours and a warming touch to it. This version from Mt Begbie in Revelstoke has a tinge of oak imparted from a short ageing process with other hints of whisky and butterscotch. It makes an ideal match for any dark meat dishes but particularly venison and other game meats.

TASTING NOTES: Caramel, toasted malt and woodchip with a hint of double cream.
- **Country:** Canada
- **Brewer:** Mt Begbie Brewing Co.
- **Style:** Scotch ale
- **Appearance:** Mahogany
- **Alcohol:** 6.5%
- **Serving temp:** 10–13°C

🇨🇦 HOYNE BREWING DARK MATTER

The dark porter style is definitely more popular in the colder climes of Canada where the more warming flavours help stave off the chilly air. Dark Matter is a great example of this – sweet, biscuit malts lend a brown sugar note to this one with a subtle hint of cookies and hazelnut milk. Unlike some of the high-alcohol beers found all over the state, this one is easier to drink and goes well with most caramelized meat dishes or even some hard blue cheese.

TASTING NOTES: Nutty with light grassy hop flavours, cereal sweetcorn and walnut.
- **Country:** Canada
- **Brewer:** Hoyne Brewing Co.
- **Style:** Porter
- **Appearance:** Dark brown
- **Alcohol:** 5.3%
- **Serving temp:** 10–13°C

🍁 À LA FÛT LA BRITISH À L'ÉRABLE

A spring seasonal from the delightful Microbrasserie À la Fût, this beer is a marriage of that most Canadian of products, maple syrup, and walnuts. Much of the brewery's output is only available from its taproom and restaurant in St-Tite, Canada, but this one is available in pint-sized cans on a seasonal basis in many places. Dark, smooth and properly British with a French accent.

TASTING NOTES: Maple syrup, roasted nuts with some praline notes and a very soft texture. Easy to drink!
- **Country:** Canada
- **Brewer:** À la Fût
- **Style:** Brown ale
- **Appearance:** Ruby reddish-brown
- **Alcohol:** 4.1%
- **Serving temp:** 8–10°C

🍁 UNIBROUE LA FIN DU MONDE

'La Fin du Monde' refers to the thoughts of the intrepid European pioneers who believed Canada was literally The End of the World. They brought with them a specific strain of yeast that had been used for centuries. La Fin du Monde, first brewed in 1994, is Unibroue's recreation of one of those early beers and the first of its kind to be attempted in the Americas.

TASTING NOTES: Floral hops with aromas of honey, spice, coriander and a little orange peel coupled with a refreshing yeasty, dry finish.
- **Country:** Canada
- **Brewer:** Unibroue
- **Style:** Abbey tripel
- **Appearance:** Golden
- **Alcohol:** 9%
- **Serving temp:** 12–14°C

🍁 LEFT FIELD BANG-BANG

The baseball-loving co-founders of Left Field Brewery are Mark and Mandie Murphy. Their passion for brewing is matched only by their love of baseball and many of their beers get named after the sporting terminology which is their second language. Bang-Bang is their dry hopped sour – fermented with wild yeast and giving off hits of sour candy, pineapple sweets and the telltale resinous notes that Citra imparts.

TASTING NOTES: Fruity tropical punch with crisp and tart apple and a refreshing summery finish.
- **Country:** Canada
- **Brewer:** Left Field Brewery
- **Style:** Sour
- **Appearance:** Pale gold
- **Alcohol:** 5.3%
- **Serving temp:** 3–5°C

🍁 GRANVILLE ISLAND MAPLE SHACK CREAM ALE

Granville Island Brewing has been a mainstay in Canadian brewing since 1984, making it the oldest microbrewery in Canada and an inspirational success story. Its Maple Cream Ale isn't just a pretty name. It uses a hint of pure maple syrup in the brewing process in much the same way honey or sugar can be added during fermentation. The idea is to accentuate the naturally toffee-like flavours extracted from the caramel malt for an extra flavour dimension.

TASTING NOTES: Swirling caramel, sticky toffee and subtle hints of maple are balanced with the lightest of hop finishes.
- **Country:** Canada
- **Brewer:** Granville Island Brewing
- **Style:** Amber • **Appearance:** Bronze
- **Alcohol:** 5% • **Serving temp:** 4–7°C

🍁 MCAUSLAN ST-AMBROISE OATMEAL STOUT

The McAuslan brewery began in early 1989 and quickly established itself as a big hitter in the microbrewing world with its St-Ambroise pale ale. Soon after, Peter McAuslan expanded his range to include this nigh-on perfect oatmeal stout. Adding a percentage of oats to the brew makes for a smooth body, while the dark roasted malts give hints of espresso coffee alongside a generous slug of chocolate and liquorice.

TASTING NOTES: The coffee and chocolate flavours are all at once bitter and sweet and are carried along by a smooth and sumptuous black body.
- **Country:** Canada
- **Brewer:** McAuslan Brewing
- **Style:** Stout
- **Appearance:** Black
- **Alcohol:** 5%
- **Serving temp:** 8–13°C

🍁 BARLEY STATION BUSHWACKER BROWN ALE

Canada is a country known for its good beer, and the French settlers in the country have given it a reputation for excellent food as well. Barley Station is a brewpub that uses only the best ingredients both for its beer and for its dinner menu. Bushwacker blends a total of eight different coloured grains to create a British-style brown ale that demands to be drunk by the pint with a deep and rich-tasting stew.

TASTING NOTES: Hints of chocolate with coffee, nutty grains and a sweet and thin body.
- **Country:** Canada
- **Brewer:** Barley Station Brew Pub (Shuswap Lake Brewing Co.)
- **Style:** Porter
- **Appearance:** Dark brown
- **Alcohol:** 4.6%
- **Serving temp:** 10–13°C

🍁 BEAU'S LUG-TREAD LAGERED ALE

Named for the tyre treads of a small tractor that ploughs the fields of eastern Ontario, Lug-Tread Lagered Ale is somewhere between an ale and a lager. In Germany, the style is named kölsch. The long maturation period at a cool temperature means the beer develops a crisp, dry character while retaining all the fruitiness you'd expect from a smooth golden ale. A good demonstration of how beer can truly be bread in liquid form.

TASTING NOTES: Soft, doughy aromas of proving bread and light toast with a subtle hint of peach-like fruit before the crisp, bitter finish.
- **Country:** Canada
- **Brewer:** Beau's All Natural Brewing Co.
- **Style:** Kolsch
- **Appearance:** Golden
- **Alcohol:** 5.2%
- **Serving temp:** 3–6°C

🍁 SIDE LAUNCH MOUNTAIN LAGER

'From hard work comes good things' is the motto of the Side Launch brewery which took its name from the longstanding ties between the Collingwood region and the shipbuilding industry. The 'side launch' manoeuvre was always reserved for ships that were too big to be launched normally! This Mountain Lager is a refreshing take on a German-style Pilsner with plenty of grassy hops but a bready dough-like quality to balance it all out.

TASTING NOTES: Sweet grassy meadow herb-like hops with bready grains and a nice clean aftertaste.
- **Country:** Canada
- **Brewer:** Side Launch Brewing Co.
- **Style:** Lager
- **Appearance:** Bright gold
- **Alcohol:** 4.7%
- **Serving temp:** 4–7°C

🍁 HOWE SOUND PUMPKINEATER IMPERIAL PUMPKIN ALE

Halloween is taken extremely seriously in North America and many brewers take to celebrating it by brewing one of the most polarizing beer styles in existence – the Pumpkin Ale. Using the tough vegetable to give the beer a more viscous body, the wort is usually then used as a vessel for various spices – in this case star anise, nutmeg, cloves and cinnamon. Howe Sound only brews this in the autumn months so get it while you can.

TASTING NOTES: Nutmeg, cloves and mulled wine with warming flavours that match well with a carrot cake.
- **Country:** Canada
- **Brewer:** Howe Sound Brewing
- **Style:** Pumpkin Ale
- **Appearance:** Cloudy orange
- **Alcohol:** 8%
- **Serving temp:** 10–13°C

DID YOU KNOW?

Confusion over whether Canadian beer is stronger than American beer was caused because alcohol was measured differently in each country, with the United States using the alcohol-by-weight method, while Canadians use alcohol by volume.

 FLYING MONKEY'S BELLE OF THE BARREL

Flying Monkey's Brewery is well known for its mantra 'Brew Fearlessly'. Like many others the team began life as homebrewers on a small budget and you'll find their beers are all about making great liquid without relying on marketing to get them noticed. Belle of the Barrel is one of their seasonal masterpieces, a barley wine with real punch, a full body and oodles of strong boozy fruit flavours.

TASTING NOTES: Peppery spice, brandy-soaked peaches and honey in the finish.
- **Country:** Canada
- **Brewer:** Flying Monkey's Craft Brewery
- **Style:** Barley wine
- **Appearance:** Amber
- **Alcohol:** 11.5%
- **Serving temp:** 10–13°C

DRIFTWOOD FAT TUG IPA

The India pale ale style is one of the most popular in all of North America with very good reason. The Driftwood Fat Tug IPA is a typical example: it is intensely hopped to give vivid fruit flavours as well as a spicy bitterness at the end. Pairs superbly well with Mexican and other spicy fare.

TASTING NOTES: Grapefruit, melon and a healthy dose of spice sit atop a caramel malt baseline.
- **Country:** Canada
- **Brewer:** Driftwood Brewing Co.
- **Style:** IPA
- **Appearance:** Dark amber
- **Alcohol:** 7%
- **Serving temp:** 4–7°C

◈ BRASSERIE LES 2 FRÈRES PORTER BALTIQUE HICKSON

Inspired by their grandfather from a young age, Nicolas and Mathieu Gagnon-Oosterwaal launched the Brasserie Les 2 Frères in 2014 to a string of awards including a Platinum Medal at the 2015 World Beer Cup for their imperial IPA and a Gold for their classic IPA in 2017. Their Baltic Porter is a great showcase of the delicate Fuggles hop with only the softest fruit aromas complementing the blend of chocolate, Munich and Vienna malts nicely.

TASTING NOTES: Caramel, milk chocolate and a slightly nutty coffee note.
- **Country:** Canada
- **Brewer:** Brasserie Les 2 Frères
- **Style:** Porter • **Appearance:** Black
- **Alcohol:** 8.5%
- **Serving temp:** 10–13°C

◈ TOOTH AND NAIL TRUCE

Belgian-style beers are often noted for the addition of ingredients that are not traditional or conventional. This moody strong ale from Tooth and Nail Brewery utilizes this freedom to its absolute maximum, being brewed with dried figs, star anise and crucially, a strain of yeast used in Belgian monasteries in Europe. Prepare yourself for a truly over-the-top commotion of flavours in this Trappist style from some of Ottawa's most gastronomic beer geeks.

TASTING NOTES: Sticky dark fruits are complemented with spice kicks, orange peel and lively carbonation.
- **Country:** Canada
- **Brewer:** Tooth and Nail Brewing Co.
- **Style:** Belgian strong ale
- **Appearance:** Red-brown
- **Alcohol:** 8.75%
- **Serving temp:** 10–13°C

◈ FOUR WINDS OPERIS BRETT SAISON

Brettanomyces, or simply 'Brett' for short, is a type of wild yeast which grows naturally on the skins of fruit as they become ripe. Once the scourge of many a brewer, these days a skilfully-brewed brett beer can be a treasure. Four Winds ages this sour saison style in oak barrels previously used to hold red wine. The funky flavours apparent in this are all down to the yeast which imbues the liquid with a variety of odd flavours.

TASTING NOTES: Look for horse blanket, crisp apple and vinous fruit. Acidic finish.
- **Country:** Canada
- **Brewer:** Four Winds
- **Style:** Saison
- **Appearance:** Cloudy gold
- **Alcohol:** 7%
- **Serving temp:** 3–5°C

BRIMSTONE ENLIGHTENMENT BLONDE ALE

Recently picking up a respectable silver at the 2016 Canadian Beer awards, Enlightenment blonde ale doesn't play to the masses by following the script of big hop flavours. There's a gentler bitterness to this brew that makes it more akin to a Belgian-style blonde than a modern pale ale. When taken on its own terms, Enlightenment is a balanced, complex and almost sessionable take on the golden ale.

TASTING NOTES: Some grassy hops aromas, soft apple and a floral orange blossom.
- **Country:** Canada
- **Brewer:** Brimstone Brewing Co.
- **Style:** Blonde
- **Appearance:** Gold
- **Alcohol:** 5.5%
- **Serving temp:** 3–5°C

DID YOU KNOW?

The oldest brewery in Canada is Molson's in Montreal, established in 1786 and strategically located to take advantage of the Scottish and English fur traders' preference for the ales and porters of their home countries.

GREAT LAKES CANUCK PALE ALE

When a beer is described as an American or West Coast-style pale ale, it tends to mean that its central attraction is the hops rather than the malt (as in an English or East Coast-style). Canuck is Great Lakes' version of a West Coast pale ale, with a vivid hop personality and a relatively light malt content. Founded in 1987, the brewery is the oldest craft brewery in Toronto.

TASTING NOTES: Citrus, floral hops and a light maltiness in excellent balance. Great with a mild fish curry.
- **Country:** Canada
- **Brewer:** Great Lakes Brewery
- **Style:** Pale ale
- **Appearance:** Hazy amber
- **Alcohol:** 5.2%
- **Serving temp:** 4–7°C

OTROMUNDO STRONG RED ALE

The best brewers can often have humble beginnings. Founded in 2004, the OtroMundo Brewing Company is an Argentinian gem which began its operations in a dilapidated former brewery in the small town of San Carlos, Santa Fe. This iconic red ale takes plenty of influence from the classic red ales of the USA with a fruit hops profile and caramel malts.

TASTING NOTES: Sweet, yeasty toffee notes with a caramel sweet finish.
- **Country:** Argentina
- **Brewer:** OtroMundo Brewing Co.
- **Style:** Strong amber ale
- **Appearance:** Light amber
- **Alcohol:** 7.5%
- **Serving temp:** 8–10°C

QUILMES

Often known as Quilmes Cristal, this is without doubt the most famous Argentinian beer taking a massive 75 per cent of the market share in the country. Its colours match that of the Argentinian flag and it was created in 1888 by a German-born immigrant looking to bring a touch of European style to Argentinian lager.

TASTING NOTES: Malted grain, toasted grains and a sweet caramel aroma. Pairs well with spicy barbecue meat.
- **Country:** Argentina
- **Brewer:** Cervecería y malteria Quilmes
- **Style:** Pale lager
- **Appearance:** Yellow
- **Alcohol:** 4.9%
- **Serving temp:** 2–5°C

BAMBERG THUNDERSTRUCK

An unusual style of beer known as a Doppelkölsch, Bamberg has taken the kölsch style to the extreme. Top fermented as any kölsch worth its salt should be, Bamberg also gives this beer a healthy dose of hops post-fermentation – specifically the Hüll Melon variety which is closely related to Cascade. Lastly, this beer is given a huge malt bill boosting the alcohol to give it true punch.

TASTING NOTES: Bready, boozy flavours coupled with honeydew melon, strawberry and peach.
- **Country:** Brazil
- **Brewer:** Bamberg Bier
- **Style:** Kölsch
- **Appearance:** Golden
- **Alcohol:** 8.2%
- **Serving temp:** 7–10°C

DADO BIER ORIGINAL

Not many breweries in the world still profess to follow the Reinheitsgebot – an ancient German purity law which restricted the ingredients allowed in brewing beer. DaDo Bier was set up in 1995 and followed this law to the letter, in the process creating their flagship beer. This easy-going Pilsner is a homage to the beers of Germany.

TASTING NOTES: Grassy hops that don't overwhelm with light toasted grain notes and a creamy-white bubbly head.
- **Country:** Brazil
- **Brewer:** DaDo Bier
- **Style:** Pilsner
- **Appearance:** Bright yellow
- **Alcohol:** 4.5%
- **Serving temp:** 3–5°C

⊞•⊞ CORONA EXTRA

The number one bestselling beer in Mexico and increasingly popular worldwide, Corona is easily recognizable in bars all over the world thanks to the lime wedge that plugs the top of the bottle once opened. Some say this used to be a smart way of keeping flies out of your beer in hot weather – not to mention adding a citrus taste of lime to the beer. Nowadays (and in most cooler climes) this lime wedge is largely not needed but is a popular gimmick nonetheless.

TASTING NOTES: Very light and refreshing with small hints of citrus and light hay-like grains. A twist of lime is optional.
- **Country:** Mexico
- **Brewer:** Grupo Modelo
- **Style:** Pale lager
- **Appearance:** Yellow
- **Alcohol:** 4.6%
- **Serving temp:** 1–2°C

DID YOU KNOW?

Light beer in Mexico is often served as a cocktail called a *michelada* ('my beer, ice cold') – mixed with salt and lime juice and maybe also chilli powder, Worcestershire or soy sauce, or tomato juice.

▶ BAHAMIAN STRONG BACK STOUT

'Drink Strong Back every day 'cause it keeps the heart attacks away,' was the exclamation of one happy Bahamian shipyard worker. While that might not be strictly true, Strong Back is an export strength stout designed to appeal to men and women – despite the ultra-macho charging ram on the label. Brewed on the island of Grand Bahama.

TASTING NOTES: Aromas of raisins, caramel and cocoa with hints of chocolate and spice on the palate.
- **Country:** Bahamas
- **Brewer:** Bahamian Brewery & Beverage Co.
- **Style:** Export stout
- **Appearance:** Dark brown
- **Alcohol:** 7.6%
- **Serving temp:** 8-13°C

CARIB LAGER

If you're going to drink a lager on the isles of Trinidad and Tobago then it's safe to assume you'll be drinking Carib Lager. First brewed in 1950, it's been a mainstay of island life for decades and is the Carib brewery's flagship product. Pale and refreshing with the easy-going taste you'd expect from a tropical island beer.

TASTING NOTES: Slightly malty flavours with a soft carbonation and a thin texture. Very lightly bitter.
- **Country:** Trinidad and Tobago
- **Brewer:** Carib Brewery
- **Style:** Pale lager
- **Appearance:** Pale yellow
- **Alcohol:** 5.2%
- **Serving temp:** 1–2°C

DID YOU KNOW?

A beer expert is known as a Cerevisaphile, a word derived from the Latin name of the Roman Goddess of agriculture, Ceres, meaning strength.

10 SAINTS

This classy-looking beer is a lager with a difference. Many darker, stronger beers get the barrel-aged treatment, but there aren't many barrel-aged beers accessible to people who don't want to drink high-alcohol brews. 10 Saints lager fills this gap. Aged in Mount Gay Special Reserve rum casks for 90 days, it comes in at an easy-drinking 4.8%.

TASTING NOTES: Sweet vanilla, light spice and hints of rum overlay the clean flavours of pale lager.
- **Country:** Barbados
- **Brewer:** 10 Saints Brewery Co.
- **Style:** Premium lager
- **Appearance:** Gold
- **Alcohol:** 4.8%
- **Serving temp:** 2–5°C

CHAPTER 2

Europe

Europe is the home of most beer styles enjoyed around the world today, from refreshing pale lagers to warming strong ales.

In terms of the importance of brewing culture, the diversity of beers available and the influence of its brewing traditions on the rest of the world, Europe remains the most important brewing region.

Europeans certainly love beer: Europe accounts for well over half of the top 20 beer-consuming countries per capita in the world, including three of the first four places. The Czech Republic tops the table with an average of 250 pints (142 litres) of beer drunk per person every year.

Culturally, beer is an essential part of European society. It is consumed in a wide range of settings, as an accompaniment to food, to help relax and socialize, while watching sport or other events, and as a way of celebrating. Although consumption has been falling in recent years, the Continent still produces 25 per cent of all the beer in the world.

Quantity isn't everything, however, and Europe can rightly claim to have a greater range of beer styles than any other continent. It is home to some of the biggest beer brands in the world, such as Heineken, Guinness and Kronenbourg, but also to beers so local that they don't travel much beyond the shadow of the brewery. For the beer tourist, a road trip through Europe is strewn with possibilities.

England is the home of real ale – beer that is conditioned in the cask or bottle. It is a style that remains central to UK pub culture: most bars will have at least one and usually several ales on offer. Despite reaching a nadir in the 1970s when keg bitter and lager threatened to wipe it out, real ale is now in rude health. Brewers such as Adnams, Fuller's, Greene King and Timothy Taylor continue to create typically British-style beers.

Scottish and Irish brewers have beers that reflect their own brewing traditions, such as heather ales and stouts. Scotland has also emerged as the unlikely home of the brewers of the world's strongest beer. Craft brewer BrewDog set a record with its End of History beer, which had a strength of 55 per cent alcohol. However, this was superseded by a 67.5 per cent brew called Snake Venom, from the nearby Brewmeister.

Across the English Channel in Belgium, a long history of brewing has produced distinctively different

results. From Trappist and abbey beers to strong ales and Lambic beers fermented with wild yeast, Belgium has a huge number of beer styles. Belgians have resisted the seemingly invincible onward march of Pilsner lager, even though Stella Artois, its best-known beer, is just that. Alongside the ubiquitous lager, Belgium has maintained its rich brewing tradition.

Germany is sometimes thought of as the home of lager, and the image of foaming steins of golden beer is iconic. While that is what is served at the world's largest beer festival, Oktoberfest in Munich, German beer offers much more. Wheat beers are a speciality and are available in dark and light varieties. Other local brews include Cologne's Kölsch, the Altbiers of the Rhine, and regional specialities like Gose, which is centred on Leipzig.

Even traditional wine-drinking nations in Europe are waking up to beer. The heat of Spain makes beer one of the most popular drinks and the country is in the top ten beer producers in the world. Italy has a growing reputation as a destination for beer-themed tourism as a new generation of microbreweries has

Europe accounts for well over half of the top 20 beer-consuming countries per capita in the world

sprung up in the past 20 years. While large brewers like Peroni and Moretti cater for the mass market, Italy's craft brewers are creating beers to be savoured and which can be paired well with food.

These are just a few of the beers on offer. There is a new beer to be discovered around every corner in Europe and something for every taste.

✚ SAMBROOK'S WANDLE

In 2008, the London beer scene appeared to be virtually non-existent, and it took a leap of faith from Duncan Sambrook to bring it back to life. Wandle is the quintessential British best bitter, using Maris Otter barley and Kentish hops from as close as possible to the brewery premises in Battersea, south-west London. Clean and crisp, and easy to drink several pints dangerously quickly!

TASTING NOTES: Lemon, meadow herbs and lighter hints of spice.
- **Country:** England
- **Brewer:** Sambrook's Brewery
- **Style:** Best bitter
- **Appearance:** Golden sunset
- **Alcohol:** 3.8%
- **Serving temp:** 10–13°C

✚ ADNAMS BROADSIDE

A heartwarming example of Great British brewing. Adnams brewery in Southwold, Suffolk, was founded in 1872 and it really knows its craft. Broadside is a multi-award-winning English strong ale rich in fruity, Christmas-cake-like aromas and sweetness from the pale ale malts and First Gold hops. A fantastically authentic taste of the British Isles.

TASTING NOTES: Booze-soaked fruit cake and a healthy dose of floral hops to balance it out.
- **Country:** England
- **Brewer:** Adnams
- **Style:** Strong bitter
- **Appearance:** Dark ruby
- **Alcohol:** 6.3%
- **Serving temp:** 8–12°C

✚ BRICK BREWERY RED BRICK RYE

From a shed in a back garden to the Peckham Rye railway arch it now occupies, Brick Brewery takes inspiration from all over the world in the creation of its beers. Be it a Czech-style lager or a zingy double IPA, most of its beers can be found in its brewery tapyard in Peckham. Red Brick Rye is inspired by the distinctive colour of London clay and a classic American rye recipe.

TASTING NOTES: Loaded with C hop flavours, spice, citrus and caramel sweetness.
- **Country:** England
- **Brewer:** Brick Brewery
- **Style:** Rye
- **Appearance:** Brick red
- **Alcohol:** 5%
- **Serving temp:** 4–7°C

✠ EAST LONDON BREWING QUADRANT

Brewing is chemistry in no small part, so when industrial chemist Stuart Lascelles tired of his 20-year career in the exciting world of industrial latex research, he took naturally to the profession. Quadrant is one of the highlights of East London's range and a true stout in the old-fashioned sense of the word. Strong with rich dark flavours and a silky sweetness that makes it a perfect late-evening tipple.

TASTING NOTES: Coffee, dark raisins and plums with dark chocolate bitterness to finish.
- **Country:** England
- **Brewer:** East London Brewing Co.
- **Style:** Stout
- **Appearance:** Chocolate brown
- **Alcohol:** 5.8%
- **Serving temp:** 10–13°C

✠ BEAVERTOWN SMOG ROCKET

Started by the son of Led Zeppelin frontman Robert Plant and a foodie friend from his American adventures, Beavertown Brewery (named after the De Beauvoir area of Hackney) is fast becoming renowned not just for its excellent brewing creations – like this flavoursome and smooth smoked porter – but also for the creative food pairings served up in its American bar and grillhouse, Duke's Brew and Que in Hackney, London.

TASTING NOTES: Smoky, campfire-like aromas together with hints of coffee and a light body that's perfect served cellar-cool or slightly warmer.
- **Country:** England
- **Brewer:** Beavertown Brewery
- **Style:** Smoked porter
- **Appearance:** Dark brown
- **Alcohol:** 5.4%
- **Serving temp:** 4–12°C

✠ ANARCHY BREW CO ANARCHY LAGER

Initially starting out under the name 'Brew Star', Simon and Dawn Miles were forced to make the switch after becoming embroiled in a legal dispute over the name. Small brewers often fall foul of larger ones in this manner but it hasn't stopped them from creating some of the finest ales and lagers in the north-east of England. Anarchy Lager was the beer they turned to when they changed their name.

TASTING NOTES: Dry mouthfeel with fruit loaf, candied fruit and sweet brandy caramel.
- **Country:** England
- **Brewer:** Anarchy Brew Co
- **Style:** Imperial Pilsner
- **Appearance:** Hazy gold
- **Alcohol:** 7%
- **Serving temp:** 3–5°C

DID YOU KNOW?

The London Beer Flood occurred in October 1814, when a vat containing more than 135,000 gallons /600,000 litres of beer ruptured. The resulting tidal wave demolished houses and killed nine people, one from alcohol poisoning.

✠ TWICKENHAM FINE ALES NAKED LADIES

Twickenham Brewery was one of the very first microbrewers to set up near London in the early part of the noughties. This classic bitter is inspired by the water nymph statues of York House gardens in Twickenham and uses Pilgrim, Celeia and Chinook hops. Head Brewer Stuart Medcalf won a silver medal at the Champion Beer of Britain awards with this outstanding golden bitter.

TASTING NOTES: Citrus with tart apple and pineapple aromas and a light, easy drinking finish.
- **Country:** England
- **Brewer:** Twickenham Fine Ales
- **Style:** Golden ale
- **Appearance:** Deep gold
- **Alcohol:** 4.4%
- **Serving temp:** 10–13°C

✠ BRISTOL BEER FACTORY SOUTHVILLE HOP

Most strong IPA's come in a much smaller bottle! Bristol Beer Factory has gone fully American with the flavour profile but fully British with the serving size. Packed with tropical fruit flavours and aromas this amber-coloured IPA comes out with a strong malty base note to provide contrast to the hops and the bitterness. Works amazingly well with spicy foods like jerk chicken and barbecue pork ribs.

TASTING NOTES: Pineapple, grapefruit and passion fruit and biscuit malt chewiness.
- **Country:** England
- **Brewer:** Bristol Beer Factory
- **Style:** IPA
- **Appearance:** Amber
- **Alcohol:** 6.5%
- **Serving temp:** 7–10°C

✠ BURNING SKY PLATEAU

Formed by the ex-head brewer of Dark Star Brewery in Sussex, Burning Sky is a well-loved and now critically-acclaimed brewery based in picturesque Firle in the South Downs National Park. Mark Tranter is using the best of British and Belgian brewing knowledge with barrel ageing and spontaneously fermented beers in production. Plateau however is a session drinking pale ale filled to the brim with New Zealand and American hops.

TASTING NOTES: Soft mouthfeel with grassy hops to begin with before the tropical fruit flavours take hold.
- **Country:** England
- **Brewer:** Burning Sky
- **Style:** Pale ale
- **Appearance:** Pale gold
- **Alcohol:** 3.5%
- **Serving temp:** 10–13°C

🏴 DARK STAR REVELATION

Regarded by many in the business as one of the best brewers in the world, Dark Star's Rob Jones named his first brew for Dark Star brewery (then called Skinners) after a Grateful Dead song. The name stuck and became the name of the brewery soon after. Revelation is an American-style pale ale made with four North American hop varieties for that instantly recognizable fresh citrus aroma.

TASTING NOTES: A cheesecake biscuit-like base is followed by a wave of citrus fruits, pine and butterscotch.
- **Country:** England
- **Brewer:** Dark Star Brewing
- **Style:** American pale ale
- **Appearance:** Deep amber
- **Alcohol:** 5.7%
- **Serving temp:** 6–10°C

✠ SIREN LIQUID MISTRESS

Named best new brewery in England when it exploded on to the scene in 2014, Siren has built up a core range of exciting, US-influenced beers whilst constantly experimenting with one-offs, kooky flavours and barrel-ageing. Liquid Mistress is one of the best red ales you'll taste. West Coast hops from the United States give it brightness and spark while the dark malts contribute dark-brown sugars and hints of overdone biscuit. Available in cask, keg or bottle.

TASTING NOTES: Burnt dark fruit, biscuit caramel and with a zesty hop finish of pink grapefruit.
- **Country:** England
- **Brewer:** Siren Craft Brew
- **Style:** Red ale
- **Appearance:** Red
- **Alcohol:** 5.8%
- **Serving temp:** 8–10°C

✠ FULLER'S LONDON PRIDE

A beer that's synonymous with the city in which it is brewed, and highly regarded by its devotees. Fuller's London Pride is one of the most popular real ales in Great Britain and has won a multitude of awards from beer enthusiasts and CAMRA (Campaign for Real Ale) since it was first brewed in the 1950s.

TASTING NOTES: Spices, nuts and tea-like aromas from the dark malts, together with woody hops and peach.
- **Country:** England
- **Brewer:** Fuller's
- **Style:** Premium bitter
- **Appearance:** Golden
- **Alcohol:** 4.7%
- **Serving temp:** 8–12°C

DID YOU KNOW?

In olden days, a bride would provide ale to her wedding guests in exchange for a gift or donation; known as 'bride ale' this is where the word 'bridal' comes from.

✠ FLACK MANOR DOUBLE DROP

Flack Manor Brewery is based in the Hampshire market town of Romsey, and was founded by Nigel Welsh, who had already amassed nearly 35 years of experience as the former director of Ringwood Brewery in Salisbury. The 'Double Drop' is a method of brewing used in the early 20th century but extremely rare in the modern brewing world. Dropping the beer into a secondary, lower tank after an initial fermentation results in a cleaner wort and sometimes some butterscotch diacetyl.

TASTING NOTES: Roasty best bitter, blackberry jam flavours with caramel and French oak.
- **Country:** England
- **Brewer:** Flack Manor Brewery
- **Style:** Bitter
- **Appearance:** Red amber
- **Alcohol:** 3.7%
- **Serving temp:** 10–13°C

➕ PRESSURE DROP PALE FIRE

The dilapidated railway arches of London are being utilized by many an aspiring craft brewer. Pressure Drop brewery was inspired by the brewing boom of the early 2010s and views many of its recipes as fluid concepts – including this London favourite – Pale Fire. Each time it is brewed the hops, quantities thereof and boil times may differ so expect a unique flavour in every batch.

TASTING NOTES: Varies but mostly refreshing citrus, very light malt character and hints of spice.
- **Country:** England
- **Brewer:** Pressure Drop
- **Style:** Pale ale
- **Appearance:** Cloudy yellow
- **Alcohol:** 4.8%
- **Serving temp:** 4–7°C

➕ WEIRD BEARD BLACK PERLE

This light and easy-going coffee milk stout was inspired by an occasion when brewers Gregg Irwin and Bryan Spooner drank a single hop Perle IPA – a hop known for an earthy and spicy character which works well in darker beers. Combining this with lactose and coffee from Alchemy Coffee in Wimbledon, London, they have created a smooth and rich coffee milkshake of a beer.

TASTING NOTES: Coffee, creamy chocolate and cookie dough with a hint of burnt sugar.
- **Country:** England
- **Brewer:** Weird Beard Brewing
- **Style:** Stout
- **Appearance:** Off-black
- **Alcohol:** 4.5%
- **Serving temp:** 10–13°C

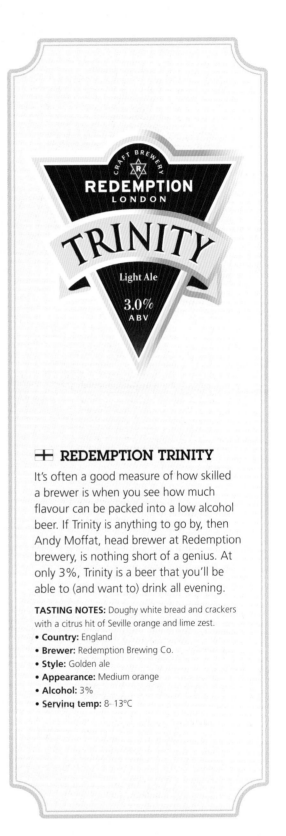

➕ REDEMPTION TRINITY

It's often a good measure of how skilled a brewer is when you see how much flavour can be packed into a low alcohol beer. If Trinity is anything to go by, then Andy Moffat, head brewer at Redemption brewery, is nothing short of a genius. At only 3%, Trinity is a beer that you'll be able to (and want to) drink all evening.

TASTING NOTES: Doughy white bread and crackers with a citrus hit of Seville orange and lime zest.
- **Country:** England
- **Brewer:** Redemption Brewing Co.
- **Style:** Golden ale
- **Appearance:** Medium orange
- **Alcohol:** 3%
- **Serving temp:** 8–13°C

✚ SAMBROOK'S RUSSIAN IMPERIAL STOUT

Duncan Sambrook was brewing beer in south-west London way before it was cool. In 2008 when Sambrook's began, London was a desert in brewing terms. But Duncan and his team have been pumping out beer of consistently high quality ever since. This Russian imperial stout is something of a departure from their usual line. Picking up 'Supreme Keg Champion' award in the 2016 SIBA Keg competition, this is an archetypical imperial stout in every sense.

TASTING NOTES: Perfect match with some vanilla ice cream or even a chocolate brownie.
- **Country:** England
- **Brewer:** Sambrook's Brewery
- **Style:** Russian imperial stout
- **Appearance:** Dark brown
- **Alcohol:** 10.4%
- **Serving temp:** 10–13°C

✚ WORTHINGTON'S WHITE SHIELD

The only pale ale still being made from the golden age of brewing in the 19th century, William Worthington's White Shield was first brewed to export to India and had to be highly hopped in order to survive the long journey. As a result, this traditional pale ale ages rather well in the bottle.

TASTING NOTES: Earthy hops and bitterness with a toffee, honeyed white bread from the malt.
- **Country:** England
- **Brewer:** Coors UK
- **Style:** IPA
- **Appearance:** Golden
- **Alcohol:** 5.6%
- **Serving temp:** 8–13°C

✚ WYLAM JAKEHEAD IPA

Wylam Brewery has brewed beer all over the north-east of England since 2000, at first in the sleepy countryside town of Heddon-on-the-Wall and later in Newcastle city centre in the stunning Palace of Arts in Exhibition Park. The only place it hasn't brewed is Wylam! Its latest incarnation has seen it turn from brewing purely traditional-style beers to more modern styles like this Jakehead IPA, which is darker than the average IPA to balance out the intense hop profile.

TASTING NOTES: Peachy hops with a warming malt backbone and a citrus finish.
- **Country:** England
- **Brewer:** Wylam Brewery
- **Style:** IPA
- **Appearance:** Amber
- **Alcohol:** 6.3%
- **Serving temp:** 4–7°C

✚ MARSTON'S PEDIGREE

Pedigree is the flagship brand of a brewing powerhouse, with sales hitting a peak of nearly 150,000 hectolitres in 2010. The traditional aromas from English hop varieties are teamed with Marston's yeast and fermented in a unique 19th-century system of huge oak barrels, called the Burton Union system.

TASTING NOTES: Caramel malts and hedgerow-like grassy hops with a smooth texture and easy-going finish.
- **Country:** England
- **Brewer:** Marston's
- **Style:** Bitter
- **Appearance:** Amber
- **Alcohol:** 4.5%
- **Serving temp:** 8–13°C

✚ FIVE POINTS RAILWAY PORTER

Former pub landlord Ed Mason began the highly-regarded Five Points brewery in Hackney back in 2013. Life on the other side of the bar suits him well and Five Points has become one of the East End's finest breweries. Railway Porter started life as a seasonal brew but quickly became a favourite around the many craft beer bars that have sprung up around London. Smooth, rich and yet somehow sessionable.

TASTING NOTES: Chocolate milkshake, salted caramel and a light hint of latte.
- **Country:** England
- **Brewer:** Five Points Brewing Co.
- **Style:** Porter
- **Appearance:** Dark brown
- **Alcohol:** 4.8%
- **Serving temp:** 8–10°C

✚ WILD BEER CO. WILD GOOSE CHASE

One of very few breweries in the UK to fully embrace wild fermentation, the Somerset-based Wild Beer Co. is pioneering a different way. Nearly every one of its many and varied beer styles undergoes a barrel-ageing process of some kind as well as a blending with older or younger versions of the same product. Wild Goose Chase is a great example – a tart, gooseberry-infused sour beer finished on vanilla pods in the ageing.

TASTING NOTES: A zingy gooseberry character but softened slightly by the ageing and the vanilla smoothness.
- **Country:** England
- **Brewer:** Wild Beer Co.
- **Style:** Fruit sour
- **Appearance:** Hazy yellow
- **Alcohol:** 4.5%
- **Serving temp:** 4–7°C

✚ THEAKSTON OLD PECULIER

Old Peculier owes its origin to the strong, dark stock beers that were brewed around 200 years ago in the cool winter months. These stock beers were kept to provide a base for the beers brewed in the summer months to give them stability in the warmer temperatures. It is still brewed using traditional methods in the Masham brewery in North Yorkshire, in an area known as Paradise Fields.

TASTING NOTES: Sweet bread pudding with rich fruit overtones of cherry and figs. Perfect paired with a dark stew.
- **Country:** England
- **Brewer:** T & R Theakston
- **Style:** Old ale
- **Appearance:** Deep ruby
- **Alcohol:** 5.6%
- **Serving temp:** 7–12°C

THE **WILD BEER** CO

Wild Goose Chase

Farmhouse Pale + Gooseberry + Zing

DRINK WILDLY DIFFERENT

Porter and stout were originally a murky brown colour, until the drum roaster was invented in 1817 by Daniel Wheeler. The black patent malt he created changed the colour and flavour of porter for ever.

✚ THORNBRIDGE JAIPUR

One of the most highly regarded brewers in the UK, Thornbridge was one of the first to take the exciting modern and hoppy beers of the USA and refine them with English sensibilities. The original brewery opened in the grounds of Thornbridge Hall, Derbyshire, in 2005; it has now been joined by a new, state-of-the-art brewery.

TASTING NOTES: Grapefruit and elderflower with a balance of white bread and honey. Perfect with a spicy Indian curry.
- **Country:** England
- **Brewer:** Thornbridge Brewery
- **Style:** IPA
- **Appearance:** Pale gold
- **Alcohol:** 5.9%
- **Serving temp:** 4–7°C

✚ BUXTON DOUBLE AXE

Buxton Brewery is well known for its excellent Axe Edge IPA. A tribute to the West Coast IPA style, Axe Edge is one of Buxton's flagship beers. Double Axe takes the Axe Edge recipe and literally doubles everything to create a true double IPA – twice the alcohol, twice the malt, twice the bitterness and twice the impact. Look out for the barrel-aged versions as they get released once per year.

TASTING NOTES: Sweet guava and passion fruit, sticky pine resin and honeydew and salted caramel popcorn.
- **Country:** England
- **Brewer:** Buxton Brewery
- **Style:** Double IPA
- **Appearance:** Hazy amber
- **Alcohol:** varies
- **Serving temp:** 4–7°C

✚ GREENE KING ABBOT ALE

Brewed atop the ruins of an ancient monastery, Greene King's Abbot Ale is a tribute to the brewing heritage of the Great Abbey in Bury St Edmunds. The cerevisiarii or ale brewers would brew on behalf of the Abbot of the monastery; they drew water from the same chalk wells still used today by the brewers at Greene King. They use only English ingredients, including the famous hop varieties Fuggles, Goldings and Challenger for an authentically English taste.

TASTING NOTES: Hints of elderflower and dark berries are subtly woven into a brown sugar rich malt background.
- **Country:** England
- **Brewer:** Greene King
- **Style:** Premium bitter
- **Appearance:** Amber
- **Alcohol:** 5%
- **Serving temp:** 8–12°C

✠ MEANTIME YAKIMA RED

Based on the cusp of the Greenwich Meridian, the Meantime brewery has gone from being a small-batch microbrewer to the definitive modern English brewery. This hoppy red ale gets its colour from a combination of German and English malts and is balanced with five of the fruitiest hops the Yakima Valley region of the USA can offer.

TASTING NOTES: Well-roasted malts and a plethora of hoppy fruit flavours make this a great match for crispy roast pork belly.
- **Country:** England
- **Brewer:** Meantime Brewing Co.
- **Style:** Amber ale
- **Appearance:** Dark amber
- **Alcohol:** 4.3%
- **Serving temp:** 4–7°C

✠ OAKHAM JHB

Named after the diminutive court jester Jeffrey Hudson, Oakham JHB is an award-winning bitter that was crowned Supreme Champion Beer of Britain 2001. This is traditional bitter with a modern twist. More hop-led than traditional-style bitters; it has a familiar buttery and biscuity-sweet malt base to give it real mass appeal.

TASTING NOTES: Pithy, citrus-infused hops at the forefront in both aroma and taste, with toasted malt afterthought.
- **Country:** England
- **Brewer:** Oakham Ales
- **Style:** Golden ale
- **Appearance:** Pale yellow
- **Alcohol:** 4.2%
- **Serving temp:** 6–10°C

✠ WINDSOR & ETON KNIGHT OF THE GARTER

Launched to mark the annual 'Ceremony of the Garter' at the royal residence of Windsor Castle in Berkshire. Awarded by the monarch, the Order of the Garter has only 24 members and is the most prestigious level of the honours system in England. Thankfully the beer is good enough to live up to its noble title.

TASTING NOTES: Lightly hoppy with a bready sweetness, making it perfect with roast chicken.
- **Country:** England
- **Brewer:** Windsor & Eton
- **Style:** Golden ale
- **Appearance:** Golden
- **Alcohol:** 3.8%
- **Serving temp:** 7–10°C

CRAFT BEER: ATLANTIC CROSSING

Great Britain has a great tradition of brewing that stretches back hundreds of years. In recent decades, this has been reinvigorated by an upsurge in interest from a new group of brewers. Step forward the craft brewer.

It is hard to pin down the definition of craft brewing and craft beer. For some people, it relates to the size of a brewery, with the use of the word 'craft' suggesting small and passionate teams producing low amounts of high-quality beer using the very best ingredients. Others see independence from large-scale brewing companies as one of the main criteria. Or maybe it relates to the type of beer that is being produced, typically taking existing styles and adding a dash of experimentalism.

In reality, craft brewing is probably a mix of all of these things, and some more besides. The roots of the movement can be traced to the United States, where in the 1970s and 80s pioneering brewers started to produce beers that provided drinkers with an alternative to the high-volume American lagers that dominated the marketplace.

Key names include Fritz Maytag, saviour of the Anchor Brewing Company, Jack McAuliffe, who started the first American microbrewery, the New Albion, Jim Koch, creator of Samuel Adams, and Ken Grossman, who founded the Sierra Nevada Brewing Company. They helped establish the framework for a new industry in the US, leading to an explosion of microbreweries and brewpubs. Where they led, breweries like Dogfish Head, Stone Brewing, New Belgium Brewing, Rogue Ales and many others have followed.

Although Europe has a more varied beer tradition, and one to which United States craft brewers have looked for inspiration, European brewers have not been immune to the charms of the United States. Indeed, America's craft beer movement has now become a model for a new generation of brewers.

Craft beer geeks in the United States have become experts at experimenting with somewhat side-lined beer types, such as fruit beers, barley wine and imperial stouts, producing imaginative results. Unusual recipes, seasonal specials and highly hopped versions of old favourites such as pale ale are all hallmarks of the craftbeer scene. UK brewers such as Dark Star, Meantime, Marble and BrewDog have paid homage to this approach.

The craft sector has also been a marketing success story. Although beer-obsessed cognoscenti will claim 'It's all about the beer', it's hard to deny that part of craft beer's allure is its cool, even sexy, status. It is brewed by young, hip guys for a well-heeled group of customers who see themselves as connoisseurs of beer rather than simply consumers.

Branding of beers by companies such as Thornbridge, St Peter's and the Camden Town Brewery is modern and intriguing. In the same way that New World wines made those of traditional winemakers seem dull, the iconography of craft beers makes them stand out in a crowded market.

Craft beer has also embraced kegs, which is another point of difference with real ale loyalists, who insist on cask conditioning as a badge of authenticity. Craft brewers have been more ready to use kegs to keep their beer fresh, as well as bottles and even cans.

A further reason that small-scale brewing has taken off in the United Kingdom is that the sliding scale of duty has made it more economically viable for producers with lower volumes to start up.

Whatever the reasons, craft beer is in the ascendancy. Established brewers such as Fuller's and Adnams have already collaborated with exponents of craft beer, both from the United Kingdom and the United States. Other brewers, such as Ringwood, have rebranded to emphasize that they too are brewing craft beer.

Only the future will tell if the title of craft beer still holds meaning, or whether the sector becomes part of a wider and more varied beer market.

✚ SAMUEL SMITH'S OATMEAL STOUT

The Samuel Smith brewery based in the small brewing town of Tadcaster in Yorkshire has always done things the old-fashioned way. This includes delivering beer to local venues by horse and cart, serving their product 'straight from the wood' where possible and using traditional Yorkshire slate square vessels to ferment their varied range of beers – including this silky oatmeal stout.

TASTING NOTES: Smooth, milky chocolate and roasted almonds are carried off with a thick and viscous texture in the mouth.
- **Country:** England
- **Brewer:** Samuel Smith Old Brewery
- **Style:** Oatmeal stout
- **Appearance:** Deep brown
- **Alcohol:** 5%
- **Serving temp:** 8–13°C

✚ ILKLEY MARY JANE IPA

'Tastes like happiness' is the byline for this transatlantic IPA from Ilkley in Yorkshire. Using their blonde ale Mary Jane as a base and traditional English hops for bittering, Mary Jane IPA includes floral and fragrant American hops from the Yakima Valley to give it a distinctly modern aroma and pleasantly sharp bitterness.

TASTING NOTES: Hints of orange blossom and pine resin together with elderflower and honey-enriched malt.
- **Country:** England
- **Brewer:** Ilkley Brewery
- **Style:** IPA
- **Appearance:** Hazy gold
- **Alcohol:** 6%
- **Serving temp:** 4–7°C

DID YOU KNOW?

Before the invention of thermometers brewers used their thumbs to estimate the right temperature at which to add yeast to their mix, thus giving rise to the phrase 'the rule of thumb'.

✚ MAGIC ROCK CANNONBALL

Magic Rock is a Yorkshire-based microbrewery set up in 2010 by two brothers with a love for beer, together with brewmaster Stuart Ross. Cannonball is one of Magic Rock's more restrained IPAs at 7.4%. The double IPA Human Cannonball weighs in at 9.2% while their 2013 Triple IPA Un-Human Cannonball is a massive 11%. This is a brewery that does everything but the ordinary.

TASTING NOTES: Tropical flavours of passion fruit and more resinous pine-like qualities balancing beautifully with a sweet malty backbone.
- **Country:** England
- **Brewer:** Magic Rock Brewing
- **Style:** IPA
- **Appearance:** Hazy amber
- **Alcohol:** 7.4%
- **Serving temp:** 4–7°C

✚ SHARP'S DOOM BAR

Doom Bar is Sharp's biggest-selling beer, accounting for nearly 90 per cent of all its sales. Named after a dangerous sandbank in North Cornwall that is notorious for getting sailors into tricky situations, Doom Bar is rather controversially sold in a clear bottle that offers very little protection from harmful UV rays in sunlight, but which shows off the beer's distinctive amber colour.

TASTING NOTES: Roasted caramel and honey with hints of orange blossom. A good match for roast chicken.
- **Country:** England
- **Brewer:** Sharp's Brewery
- **Style:** Bitter
- **Appearance:** Amber
- **Alcohol:** 4.3%
- **Serving temp:** 8–13°C

✚ CROUCH VALE BREWERS GOLD

In 2005, Brewers Gold became one of few beers ever to win the Supreme Champion Beer of Britain title, it was then awarded the exact same gong the very next year, further cementing its place in brewing history. Using 100 per cent Maris Otter barley and Brewers Gold hops, Crouch Vale also adds Hallertau hops to create a floral, almost Parma violet effect in this famous golden bitter.

TASTING NOTES: Parma violets and orange bitters with sweet biscuit finish.
- **Country:** England
- **Brewer:** Crouch Vale Brewery
- **Style:** Bitter
- **Appearance:** Golden
- **Alcohol:** 4%
- **Serving temp:** 10–13°C

⊞ ST AUSTELL KOREV

Proper lager should be stored for anything from one to five months in order for the lager yeast to do its job properly. Korev is a very well-made version from the St Austell brewery in Cornwall. Made with 100 per cent locally-grown barley and stored or 'lagered' at low temperatures for a lengthy maturation, Korev is easily distinguishable from most of the lagers you find in the average British pub. Full of fresh white bread aromas and a wonderfully crisp, bitter finish, it can pair nicely with a wide selection of dishes, from charcuterie to sushi.

TASTING NOTES: Doughy white bread, creamy marshmallow and a little lemony citrus fruit. Pure, clean and uncomplicated.
- **Country:** England
- **Brewer:** St Austell Brewery
- **Style:** Lager
- **Appearance:** Orange
- **Alcohol:** 4.8%
- **Serving temp:** 4–6°C

⊞ MARBLE DOBBER IPA

The bestselling beer in the Marble brewery's range is Dobber – a 5.9% IPA flavoured with hops native to New Zealand for an exotic taste that Mancunians and the rest of the United Kingdom are lapping up. This Manchester-based brewery also runs three brewpubs in the city – The Beerhouse, 57 Thomas Street and the Marble Arch. The latter was the inspiration for starting a brewery in the first place, in order to save a beloved local venue from extinction – though they nearly turned it into a karaoke bar instead.

TASTING NOTES: Ripe tropical fruits and buttery toffee caramel balanced with a dry, hoppy, bitter finish.
- **Country:** England
- **Brewer:** Marble
- **Style:** IPA
- **Appearance:** Hazy orange
- **Alcohol:** 5.9%
- **Serving temp:** 4–7°C

⊞ THE KERNEL TABLE BEER

Table beer was once a prominent style in Belgium and other parts of Europe. Table beer has a low alcoholic strength (traditionally only 1–2%) and is served up in large quantities at the dinner table. The Kernel's version is a little stronger – typically 2.7% – and uses plenty of American hops for a fresh aroma and bitter finish. Widely regarded as one of the best brewers in the British Isles for its artisanal and passionate approach to craft brewing.

TASTING NOTES: Considerable passion fruit aromas together with mandarins and peach, rounded off with a short sharp bitter finish.
- **Country:** England
- **Brewer:** The Kernel Brewery
- **Style:** Table beer
- **Appearance:** Hazy gold
- **Alcohol:** 2.7-3%
- **Serving temp:** 4–7°C

✕ BREWDOG PUNK IPA

Known for their brash marketing strategy, Scotland's 'punk' brewers BrewDog really caused a stir when they emerged, wild and restless, into the UK brewing scene in the early 2000s. Thankfully they weren't all mouth and no trousers. Punk IPA is still regarded as one of the best of the new wave of IPAs the United Kingdom has produced. All the exciting grapefruit and tropical flavour you'd expect from an American-style IPA, with a dry, mouth-puckering bitter finish to boot. Mohawk and nose rings not required to enjoy this one.

TASTING NOTES: Tropical fruit flavours from the blend of American and southern hemisphere hops.
- **Country:** Scotland
- **Brewer:** BrewDog
- **Style:** IPA
- **Appearance:** Light golden
- **Alcohol:** 5.6%
- **Serving temp:** 4–8°C

✕ ORKNEY RAVEN ALE

Based in a former schoolhouse, the Orkney Brewery was founded in 1988 by Roger White and still brews at the same site. This is its classic bitter, which is laced with intense grainy aromas – a result of the high-quality pale ale malt used in the brewing process. A very refreshing and easy drink.

TASTING NOTES: Sweet biscuit and light pine hoppiness in the aroma followed by more of the same on the palate.
- **Country:** Scotland
- **Brewer:** The Orkney Brewery
- **Style:** Blonde ale
- **Appearance:** Golden
- **Alcohol:** 3.8%
- **Serving temp:** 4–7°C

✕ TEMPEST BRAVE NEW WORLD

India pale ale doesn't get much better than this – classically American in attitude but using locally-grown Scottish barley alongside those Yakima Valley hops. Winner of the Gold medal in the Scottish Beer Awards 2016, this beer has a real claim to be one of the best out there. As with all great beers there has to be a balance between malt and hops and this one gets it spot on.

TASTING NOTES: Classic pine resin, tropical, grapefruit and pineapple with a lingering bitter finish.
- **Country:** Scotland
- **Brewer:** Tempest Brewing Co.
- **Style:** IPA
- **Appearance:** Hazy amber
- **Alcohol:** 7%
- **Serving temp:** 4–7°C

INNIS & GUNN ORIGINAL

Innis & Gunn was born when William Grant & Sons distillers requested help with breaking in some of their oak barrels. Creating a custom-made recipe, the founders of the brewery were eager to oblige and found that during its maturation time, the beer took on many characteristics of the whisky that previously occupied the barrels. Ever since, they've been creating barrel-aged beers like this Innis & Gunn Original.

TASTING NOTES: Aromas of vanilla and toffee, light citrus and a light and oaky finish.
- **Country:** Scotland
- **Brewer:** Innis & Gunn
- **Style:** Old ale
- **Appearance:** Honey-gold
- **Alcohol:** 6.6%
- **Serving temp:** 7–10°C

WEST ST MUNGO LAGER

Owned by German-born Petra Wetzel, the West brewery is located in the heart of Glasgow, and specializes in lagers and wheat beers. St Mungo Lager, the flagship brand of the company, follows the principles of the German purity law or Reinheitsgebot: only barley, hops and yeast are used for an authentic German-inspired flavour and character. A real taste of Bavaria via Scotland!

TASTING NOTES: Crisp and clean with a toffee note and equal parts of sweet fruits, toasted grain and nuttiness.
- **Country:** Scotland
- **Brewer:** West
- **Style:** Lager
- **Appearance:** Clear orange
- **Alcohol:** 4.9%
- **Serving temp:** 4–7°C

DID YOU KNOW?

In 2016, the Guinness World Record for the largest beer tasting took place at the The Publican Awards' annual ceremony in London with 1,236 participants.

HARVIESTOUN SCHIEHALLION

It's often hard to get excited about drinking a lager, but when it is as well made as Harviestoun's Schiehallion it becomes a little easier. First brewed in 1994, nobody envisioned the wild success of this Scottish favourite – now available all over the world – especially considering the tricky-to-pronounce name (pronounced 'She-hali-on'), which takes its name from a local mountain.

TASTING NOTES: Aromas of grass and caramelized apples with smaller hints of mango. A very crisp and fresh finish.
- **Country:** Scotland
- **Brewer:** Harviestoun Brewery
- **Style:** Lager
- **Appearance:** Yellow
- **Alcohol:** 4.8%
- **Serving temp:** 4–7°C

🏴󠁧󠁢󠁳󠁣󠁴󠁿 BLACK ISLE ORGANIC BLONDE

David Gladwin, head brewer and founder of Black Isle, began work in 1998 with a simple idea in mind that's still rare to find in the modern brewing world. Every ingredient he uses in his award-winning beers is organically farmed, in some cases in his own backyard. This blonde ale is simple, crisp and refreshing and embodies the spirit of highland living.

TASTING NOTES: Grassy hops, meadow spice and a sweet biscuit body.

- **Country:** Scotland
- **Brewer:** Black Isle Organic
- **Style:** Blonde
- **Appearance:** Golden
- **Alcohol:** 4.5%
- **Serving temp:** 7–10°C

⚔ ORKNEY
DARK ISLAND RESERVE

Ageing its award-winning Dark Island ale for three months at low temperatures in old Orkney whisky casks, the Orkney Brewery works some serious magic into this highly decorated beer. It is made in limited quantities and will age very nicely at home, so be in no great rush to drink it.

TASTING NOTES: Soft peaty notes with a touch of oak and plenty of bitter chocolate and coffee.
- **Country:** Scotland
- **Brewer:** The Orkney Brewery
- **Style:** Barley wine
- **Appearance:** Deep brown
- **Alcohol:** 10%
- **Serving temp:** 8–15°C

⚔ ARRAN BLONDE

On one of Scotland's many small but beautiful islands there is a brewer that positions itself at the centre of the local community. Arran Blonde is drunk at Highland games, in small folk clubs and along the many hiking trails of Arran. Thankfully, the island doesn't keep all the supply of this wonderful golden ale to itself.

TASTING NOTES: Brown bread with notes of honey, peppery bitterness and a herbal grassy hop finish.
- **Country:** Scotland
- **Brewer:** Isle of Arran Brewery
- **Style:** Golden ale
- **Appearance:** Golden
- **Alcohol:** 5%
- **Serving temp:** 4–7°C

⚔ WILLIAMS BROTHERS
FRAOCH HEATHER ALE

Described by the brewers Williams Brothers as the 'Original Craft Beer', Fraoch is based on an ancient Gaelic recipe for heather ale – a recipe that dates back over 4,000 years. Williams Brothers is the only brewery that produces this rarity and distributes it worldwide. The brewery is noted for many other interesting styles, including a Scots pine ale, a tayberry beer and a chocolate seaweed ale.

TASTING NOTES: Herbal, honey flavours combine with bready malts and a slight spicy ginger finish.
- **Country:** Scotland
- **Brewer:** Williams Brothers
- **Style:** Heather ale
- **Appearance:** Golden
- **Alcohol:** 5%
- **Serving temp:** 8–13°C

⚌ FYNE ALES JARL

One of the first beers in the United Kingdom to demonstrate the potential of the vibrant Citra hop, Jarl is a very drinkable session beer. The Nordic name refers to the Norwegian Earls (Jarls) who, in the 12th century, claimed much of the land that now surrounds the Fyne Ales brewery in Argyll.

TASTING NOTES: Citrus and grassy hop flavours are at the forefront, with a light and quickly diminishing finish.
- **Country:** Scotland
- **Brewer:** Fyne Ales
- **Style:** Blonde ale
- **Appearance:** Golden
- **Alcohol:** 3.8%
- **Serving temp:** 4–7°C

⚌ EDEN MILL ROCK LIQUOR

Making the most of their combined skillsets, Eden Mill is so much more than just a great brewer. As well as distilling high-quality spirits the team are also excellent mixologists creating cocktails that utilize their beers and spirits. Rock Liquor is their Scotch ale and is filled to the brim with caramelized dark sugar flavours. Surprisingly smooth for such a strong beer with all the alcohol very well masked by the taste.

TASTING NOTES: Sticky toffee pudding, hints of star anise and more subtle hints of soy.
- **Country:** Scotland
- **Brewer:** Eden Mill
- **Style:** Scotch Ale
- **Appearance:** Mahogany red
- **Alcohol:** 9.2%
- **Serving temp:** 10–13°C

⚌ ALECHEMY CITRA BURST

Yet another brewer with a scientific background, James Davies cut his teeth in industrial sciences before turning his hand to brewing. Alechemy Brewery is family owned and turns out handcrafted real ales and bottles using locally-produced barley like this Citra-hopped APA. Originally a one-off, it became such a popular brew that Alechemy had to start brewing it all year round to meet demand.

TASTING NOTES: Citra hop imparting pine resin and orange bitterness.
- **Country:** Scotland
- **Brewer:** Alechemy
- **Style:** Pale ale
- **Appearance:** Light gold
- **Alcohol:** 5.4%
- **Serving temp:** 7–10°C

▮ ▮ ELBOW LANE ANGEL STOUT

A relative newcomer to the world of microbrewing, Elbow Lane produced its first beer, Angel Stout, in 2012, soon followed by Elbow Lager and Wisdom Ale. In the wonderful Angel Stout, brewed with dark burnt malts and the strong Herkules hop variety, Elbow Lane has created a truly authentic taste of Irish dry stout.

TASTING NOTES: Thick bitter chocolate, coffee and a firm, spicy hop profile.
• **Country:** Ireland
• **Brewer:** Elbow Lane
• **Style:** Dry stout
• **Appearance:** Deep brown
• **Alcohol:** 5%
• **Serving temp:** 8–13°C

▮▮ FARMAGEDDON IPA

Farmaggeddon was founded by seven friends who came together via a mutual passion for martial arts, punk rock and of course top quality beer. With four core beers and a seasonal released every six weeks or so, all the beers produced are made without finings or other fish products to ensure vegan drinkers get a share of the love as well. This is their core IPA – American hopped with a distinctive cloudy appearance.

TASTING NOTES: Floral hops, orange bitterness and rose hips.
- **Country:** Northern Ireland
- **Brewer:** Farmageddon Brewing Co-op
- **Style:** IPA
- **Appearance:** Cloudy gold
- **Alcohol:** 5.5%
- **Serving temp:** 4–7°C

DID YOU KNOW?

To pour a perfect pint of Guinness you need to let it rest for exactly 119.5 seconds between the first pour and the top-up – a period called the surge and settle.

▮▮ TROUBLE BREWING DARK ARTS PORTER

Trouble Brewing, based in County Kildare, brewed its first beers in 2010. Using an open-source computerized system to control its brewing mechanism, it is able to be precise about every detail of the brewing process. This easy-drinking porter is made with a low and sessionable alcohol content, while keeping the flavour intense and in balance. Dark Arts Porter is one of the regular beers, joined by seasonal specials at different times of the year. The first brewery in Ireland to accept payment in Bitcoins.

TASTING NOTES: Long-lasting fresh coffee and bitter chocolate without being heavy. Easy-drinking porter.
- **Country:** Ireland
- **Brewer:** Trouble Brewing
- **Style:** Porter
- **Appearance:** Deep brown
- **Alcohol:** 4.4%
- **Serving temp:** 8–13°C

▌▌ METALMAN PALE ALE

Like many microbreweries, Metalman was set up when its founders became disillusioned with lack of choice, lack of flavour and the same old beers over and over again. This American-style pale ale is its only permanent beer, but it releases seasonal beers every few weeks to keep its range as interesting as possible. The pale ale manages to keep a fairly low alcohol content, while still offering a large array of citrus fruit and tropical hops with a deliciously bitter aftertaste. Perfect with a curry of any kind.

TASTING NOTES: Grapefruit and tinned mandarins from the hops, with a spicy bitter finish.
- **Country:** Ireland
- **Brewer:** Metalman Brewing Co.
- **Style:** American pale ale
- **Appearance:** Dark gold
- **Alcohol:** 4.3%
- **Serving temp:** 4–7°C

▌▌ HARP LAGER

Marketed with the Brian Boru harp as its logo, a can of Harp could, at a glance, be confused with Guinness. Unlike Guinness though, this is a pale lager and not nearly as widely available as the famous Irish stout. Known for being the default lager option in many Irish pubs, its taste will be familiar to any Irish lager lover. Crisp, clean with a dry finish.

TASTING NOTES: Easy to drink with light malts, fresh fruity citrus hints on the nose and a very smooth aftertaste.
- **Country:** Ireland
- **Brewer:** Dundalk Brewery
- **Style:** Pale lager
- **Appearance:** Yellow
- **Alcohol:** 4.3%
- **Serving temp:** 2–5°C

▌▌ GUINNESS

Guinness is as famous around the world as it is in its native Ireland. With its distinctive thick tan head and matt black body, it has a reputation for being a meal in a glass – yet surprisingly it is lighter in calories than most lagers. Guinness is known for its exceptionally creamy taste. The archetypal Irish stout.

TASTING NOTES: Creamy beige head with aromas of coffee, dark chocolate and sugar. Uncomplicated bliss.
- **Country:** Ireland
- **Brewer:** Guinness Brewery
- **Style:** Dry stout
- **Appearance:** Matt black
- **Alcohol:** 4.1%
- **Serving temp:** 7–12°C

▌▌ GALWAY BAY BURIED AT SEA

Buried at Sea from Galway Bay brewery is a sweet milk stout made with added lactose (milk sugar). Since lactose can't be consumed by yeast during fermentation, it remains in the beer and gives a sweetish taste. The sweetness works brilliantly with the chocolatey flavours of a stout. A real after-dinner treat for grown-ups.

TASTING NOTES: Surprisingly light with hints of hazelnut, dark chocolate and milk. Prime candidate for a scoop of vanilla ice cream.
- **Country:** Ireland
- **Brewer:** Galway Bay Brewery
- **Style:** Milk stout
- **Appearance:** Deep brown
- **Alcohol:** 4.5%
- **Serving temp:** 7–12°C

▌▌ MURPHY'S IRISH STOUT

Known simply as Murphy's to drinkers around Ireland, Murphy's Irish Stout was intended to be lighter and less bitter than its famous compatriot Guinness. However, Murphy's has a textbook dry stout finish. The lively rivalry between the two is famous in recent Irish folk history.

TASTING NOTES: Strong hints of chocolate and coffee suggest a milky cappuccino flavour.
- **Country:** Ireland
- **Brewer:** Heineken Ireland
- **Style:** Dry stout
- **Appearance:** Black
- **Alcohol:** 4%
- **Serving temp:** 4–7°C

▌▌ BOUNDARY IMBONGO

Another co-operative brewery from Belfast is the Boundary Brewery. Completely community-owned it fuses the American-style brewing techniques with their heavy use of powerful hops with more European French and Belgian techniques. Imbongo began as a seasonal beer that was loved so much it was promoted to a core product.

TASTING NOTES: Lychee notes with additional tropical fruit and orange rind.
- **Country:** Northern Ireland
- **Brewer:** Boundary Brewing
- **Style:** IPA
- **Appearance:** Pale straw
- **Alcohol:** 5.5%
- **Serving temp:** 4-7°C

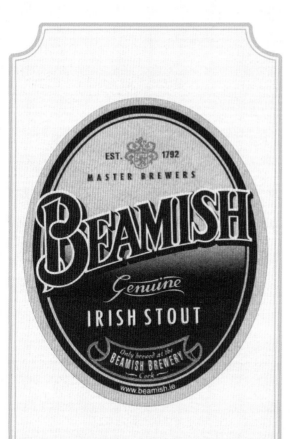

DID YOU KNOW?

The patron saint of Ireland, St Patrick, evangelized pagan Ireland in the 5th century. Having a brewmaster in his missionary team may have helped as he wooed the tribal chieftains with his tasty beer.

 BEAMISH IRISH STOUT

The flagship beer of Cork-based brewery Beamish and Crawford, Beamish Stout is a traditional Irish stout. In a similar vein to Ireland's most famous and bestselling dry stout, Guinness, Beamish has a drier flavour and is noted for its large creamy head that laces the glass to the last drop. Great with a hearty Irish stew.

TASTING NOTES: Slightly smoky in the nose with notes of burnt coffee, Beamish has an oily texture and a quick, dry finish.
- **Country:** Ireland
- **Brewer:** Heineken Ireland
- **Style:** Dry stout
- **Appearance:** Dark brown
- **Alcohol:** 4.1%
- **Serving temp:** 6–10°C

PORTERHOUSE OYSTER STOUT

Traditionally, oysters were not seen as the luxurious aphrodisiac they are perceived as today. On the contrary, they were so cheap and plentiful, they'd be added to pies and stews to bulk them out. Oysters and stout are a great pairing. Here, oysters are added to the conditioning tank for a subtle savoury touch.

TASTING NOTES: Roasted malt aroma with a smooth, salty and bread-like flavour. Unsuitable for vegetarians!
- **Country:** Ireland
- **Brewer:** Porterhouse Brewing Co.
- **Style:** Oyster stout
- **Appearance:** Black
- **Alcohol:** 5.2%
- **Serving temp:** 8–13°C

🏴 BRAINS BITTER

Usually requested by drinkers with the sentence 'A pint of Brains, please!' this long-standing flagship brew sells at a rate of 12 pints per minute. Not surprisingly it's the Brains brewery's – and indeed Wales's – biggest-selling cask beer. It's made with a smart mix of those classic British hops, Goldings and Fuggles – though they are harvested not in Kent, but in the heartlands of Wales.

TASTING NOTES: Soft peach and apple orchard fruits combined with pale, bready malt.
- **Country:** Wales
- **Brewer:** Brains
- **Style:** Bitter
- **Appearance:** Light brown
- **Alcohol:** 3.7%
- **Serving temp:** 8–13°C

🏴 OTLEY MOTLEY BREW

The Otley brewery believes strongly in bottle-conditioned beers and this double IPA is no exception. When the beer is bottled, all the yeast is left in so the beer continues to ferment and mature in the bottle. As it ferments, carbon dioxide is produced, which gives the beers their carbonation. It's this 100 per cent natural quality that makes good ale, 'real ale'.

TASTING NOTES: Fruit salad sweets, orange, grapefruit and hints of pine.
- **Country:** Wales
- **Brewer:** Otley Brewing
- **Style:** Imperial IPA
- **Appearance:** Cloudy amber
- **Alcohol:** 7.5%
- **Serving temp:** 4–7°C

🏴 BLUESTONE BEDROCK BLONDE

Bluestone Brewery is a family-run operation brewing in the picturesque setting of Pembrokeshire in Wales. If you can make the journey to go and visit they'll let you pitch in and help around the brewery – even paying you with free beer. You might perhaps get a bottle of this smooth and easy-drinking Bedrock Blonde ale, brewed with grassy Saaz and Hallertau hops.

TASTING NOTES: Leafy hops flavours, sweet stone fruits and a gentle light bitterness.
- **Country:** Wales
- **Brewer:** Bluestone Brewing Co.
- **Style:** Golden ale
- **Appearance:** Golden
- **Alcohol:** 4%
- **Serving temp:** 4–7°C

🏴 TOMOS WATKIN OSB

Resurrected in 1995 by Simon Buckley – having been out of business for over a century – Tomos Watkin quickly became one of the fastest-growing brands in Wales. Buckley left the company in 2002 and went on to open Evan Evans, while Tomos Watkin has gone from strength to strength and now brews a wide range of beers, including OSB, or Old Style Bitter.

TASTING NOTES: Light orange and grassy hop aromas quickly give way to butterscotch and caramel, with an oily texture.
- **Country:** Wales
- **Brewer:** Tomos Watkin
- **Style:** Bitter
- **Appearance:** Clear amber
- **Alcohol:** 4.5%
- **Serving temp:** 8–13°C

🏴 CRAFTY DEVIL ROCK 'N' ROLL STAR

The American brewing industry has been the source of inspiration for many a burgeoning craft brewer around the world and nowhere more so than in the United Kingdom. This young Welsh microbrewer uses almost entirely American hops for those bold flavours. It calls this pale ale 'the king of beers' in tribute to the king of rock and roll – loud, brash and in-your-face with flavour, and at this strength best in small doses!

TASTING NOTES: Caramel malt tones and passion fruit juiciness.
- **Country:** Wales
- **Brewer:** Crafty Devil Brewing Co.
- **Style:** APA
- **Appearance:** Hazy amber
- **Alcohol:** 6.2%
- **Serving temp:** 4–7°C

🏴 TINY REBEL HADOUKEN

Tiny Rebel is a very modern and accomplished brewery that is causing quite a stir in its native Wales and beyond. Hadouken was brewed in collaboration with a famous craft beer bar in London and is named for the finishing move of a 1990s' arcade game. A true American-style, hoppy IPA and one of Tiny Rebel's most famous creations.

TASTING NOTES: Big caramel and biscuit malt flavour with a pine resin, oily hop counterbalance.
- **Country:** Wales
- **Brewer:** Tiny Rebel Brewing Co.
- **Style:** IPA
- **Appearance:** Hazy amber
- **Alcohol:** 7.4%
- **Serving temp:** 4–7°C

FELINFOEL DOUBLE DRAGON

In the 1830s, David John bought a pub in the village of Felinfoel. He brewed his own beer, as did most pubs of the time. The difference? His was just that much better. Soon he was selling his beer to all the pubs in the region and was able to build an imposing brewhouse on the river Lliedi. Double Dragon is still brewed there today.

TASTING NOTES: Lots of toffee and malty notes in the flavour with a slightly floral hop note and a thin body.

- **Country:** Wales
- **Brewer:** Felinfoel Brewery Co.
- **Style:** Bitter
- **Appearance:** Amber
- **Alcohol:** 4.2%
- **Serving temp:** 8–13°C

UNTAPPED EMBER

Founded by a pair of friends whose friendship blossomed in Cardiff over many glasses of fine wine, Untapped brewery has been producing small batch brews since 2009. Brewed to stave off the harsh Welsh winters, Ember is warmth by name and warmth by nature. A mixture of the best Kentish First Gold hops and the more modern multi-talented hop Cascade goes into making this rich and decadent winter ale.

TASTING NOTES: Orange rind, hazelnut and mild coffee alongside a deeper hint of red berries.

- **Country:** Wales
- **Brewer:** Untapped Brewing Co.
- **Style:** Old ale
- **Appearance:** Dark ruby
- **Alcohol:** 5.2%
- **Serving temp:** 10–13°C

DID YOU KNOW?

Felinfoel Brewery was the first outside the USA to commercially can beer, in 1931. During World War II it was a major supplier to the armed forces as cans saved space and weight.

🏴 PIPES SMOKED LAGER

Pipes takes inspiration from the world-renowned brewing and smoking techniques of the Schlenkerla brewery in Bamberg. Smoking the malt adds another dimension of flavour before the mashing-in process to create flavours not normally associated with pale lager. This smoked lager is a great match with old steaks and roasted meat and is completely additive-free. It is also suitable for vegans because the brewery eschews finings in its products.

TASTING NOTES: Lychee notes with additional tropical fruit and orange rind.
- **Country:** Wales
- **Brewer**: Pipes Brewery
- **Style:** Smoked lager
- **Appearance:** Copper
- **Alcohol:** 5.4%
- **Serving temp:** 4–7°C

🏴 PURPLE MOOSE MADOG'S ALE

Purple Moose Brewery named this crisp red session bitter after architectural pioneer William Alexander Madocks. Multi award-winning since it began life in 2005, the brewery is now a 40 bbl plant and this is one of its flagship products. Sessionable, easy-going and light enough for a pint to slip down easier than you'd think with its dry and bitter finish leaving you wanting another pint immediately.

TASTING NOTES: Dry and peppery with hints of walnut and orange bitters.
- **Country:** Wales
- **Brewer:** Purple Moose Brewery
- **Style:** Bitter
- **Appearance:** Burnt orange
- **Alcohol:** 3.7%
- **Serving temp:** 10–13°C

🏴 EVAN EVANS CWRW

The Buckley family began brewing beer in 1767 and the Evan Evans brewery in Llandeilo is run by Simon and James Buckley, the seventh and eighth generations of the family – still flying the flag for traditional Welsh beer. Cwrw, the Welsh word for beer, has won a string of awards in the Best Bitter category.

TASTING NOTES: Malty backbone is complemented by gentle but very definite earthy hop flavours.
- **Country:** Wales
- **Brewer:** Evan Evans
- **Style:** Bitter
- **Appearance:** Amber
- **Alcohol:** 4.2%
- **Serving temp:** 8–13°C

HIMBURGS BRAUKUNST KELLER BAVARIAN DRY HOP LAGER

Another brewer looking for influences from around the world is the excellent Braukunst Keller in Munich. The lager style is one that's been frequently overdone but here it is given a modern twist with the addition of Citra and Simcoe hops to the mix post-fermentation. The result is more of an 'India' lager with more emphasis on hops that work so well with the soft Bavarian water.

TASTING NOTES: Sweet peach, grapefruit and nectarine with a grassy edge to the finish.
- **Country:** Germany
- **Brewer:** Himburgs Braukunst Keller
- **Style:** India lager
- **Appearance:** Gold
- **Alcohol:** 5.3%
- **Serving temp:** 4–7°C

BERLINER PILSNER

Here we have a good example of a traditional German Pilsner. The differences between Czech and German-style Pilsners are subtle but important. While Czech Pilsners use Saaz hops to impart an earthy, herbal aroma that needs balancing with more malt, German styles are lighter in hops and use harder water, which results in a much longer-lasting bitter finish.

TASTING NOTES: Crisp, refreshing with a long bitter finish. Very light, with high carbonation.
- **Country:** Germany
- **Brewer:** Berliner Kindl Schultheiss
- **Style:** Pilsner
- **Appearance:** Golden
- **Alcohol:** 5%
- **Serving temp:** 3–5°C

RIEDENBURGER DOLDEN SUD IPA

The IPA has undergone many a rebirth in cities all over the world ranging from the more modern American hopped versions to the old-world IPAs that were exported from the British Isles to India. This one lies somewhere in-between – a great balance of the old and the new with some interesting flavours that add another dimension to the ever-popular style and its evolution through the ages.

TASTING NOTES: Hints of lemongrass and popcorn as well as the expected tropical fruits and big base malt.
- **Country:** Germany
- **Brewer:** Riedenburger Brauhaus
- **Style:** IPA
- **Appearance:** Orange-gold
- **Alcohol:** 6.5%
- **Serving temp:** 4–7°C

■ AUGUSTINER HELLES

The Augustiner brewery is certainly one of the most distinguished in Germany. When people speak of Augustiner, they generally refer to this extremely popular Helles (pale) lager. This drink is given a secondary fermentation over a long period to allow its superb liquid bread character to develop fully. A perfect example of how bready and wholesome the Helles style can be.

TASTING NOTES: Pure liquid bread! Aromas of proving dough dominate the nose, with a smooth, light bitter aftertaste.
- **Country:** Germany
- **Brewer:** Augustiner-Bräu München
- **Style:** Helles
- **Appearance:** Golden
- **Alcohol:** 5.2%
- **Serving temp:** 4–6°C

■ CAMBA BLACK SHARK

A highly-decorated craft brewer from Seeon, Bavaria, Camba brewery began life with far better equipment than most fledgling upstarts. Taking a pilot kit with modern technology from a large scale brewer which no longer needed it, it was able to produce top-quality beer consistently from the get-go. This luxurious black IPA is one of its more modern styles bursting with American hops.

TASTING NOTES: Nose of rhubarb and gooseberry with a flavour of aromatic coffee and cocoa.
- **Country:** Germany
- **Brewer:** Camba
- **Style:** Imperial Black IPA
- **Appearance:** Black
- **Alcohol:** 8.5%
- **Serving temp:** 11–13°C

DID YOU KNOW?

The beer purity law was adopted in Germany in 1516. It stated that to improve the quality of beer, only water, malt, hops and yeast may be used as ingredients. This law is followed today.

■ BRLO PORTER

A brewery with some kooky ideas about its water supply (energized with gemstones apparently), BRLO has, however, unquestionably noble ethics around sourcing ingredients from sustainable and ecologically-sound suppliers. This English-style porter has so much power that it's really halfway to being an imperial stout but is none the worse for that. Drink with a rich dish of pork knuckle and potatoes for the ultimate Sunday afternoon experience.

TASTING NOTES: Dark caramel, spicy hops and a very roasty, toasty finish.
- **Country:** Germany
- **Brewer:** BRLO
- **Style:** Porter
- **Appearance:** Deep brown
- **Alcohol:** 7%
- **Serving temp:** 10–13°C

▬ AYINGER JAHRHUNDERT

The Ayinger brewery prides itself on its absolute mastery of the brewing process. Aware that the smallest change in temperature can affect the extraction of sugar from the malt, it uses the most up-to-date equipment and techniques to produce this superb Dortmund-style Helles. First brewed in 1978 to celebrate the 100th anniversary of the Ayinger brewery.

TASTING NOTES: Bready malts, sweet brown bread and hints of honey and grains.
- **Country:** Germany
- **Brewer:** Ayinger
- **Style:** Dortmund Helles
- **Appearance:** Straw
- **Alcohol:** 5.2%
- **Serving temp:** 4–6°C

▬ FLENSBURGER PILSENER

Today the Flensburger brewery is still owned by the two families who founded it in 1888, the Petersens and the Dethleffsens. Back then, the brewers needed to take huge blocks of ice from frozen lakes in the winter to keep underground storage facilities cool in summer. Today's Flensburger Pilsener is fermented at cool temperatures using modern refrigeration methods.

TASTING NOTES: A very traditional German Pilsner with low malt and hop profiles and a long crisp finish.
- **Country:** Germany
- **Brewer:** Flensburger Brauerei
- **Style:** Pilsner
- **Appearance:** Light yellow
- **Alcohol:** 4.8%
- **Serving temp:** 3–5°C

DID YOU KNOW?

Germany's Veltins-Arena stadium has a beer pipeline that connects the many bars and supplies thirsty soccer fans with roughly 11,000 gallons/52,000 litres of beer on match days.

▬ FLESSA BRÄU MANDARINA RED LAGER

As you might suspect, there's something of the mandarin about this deep-red, Vienna-style lager, though it's not due to the addition of citrus fruit at any point in the brewing process. The aptly-named Mandarina hop imparts the most vivid orange flavours making this one of the more interesting beers in Flessa Bräu's fairly conservative range.

TASTING NOTES: Satsuma, tangerine and mandarin with a light bitter finish.
- **Country:** Germany
- **Brewer:** Flessa Bräu
- **Style:** Weiss beer
- **Appearance:** Amber
- **Alcohol:** 5%
- **Serving temp:** 4–7°C

ERDINGER DUNKEL

Erdinger Dunkel is a great example of a dark wheat beer. Dunkelweizen (dark wheat) uses dark malted wheat as well as malted barley. The Reinheitsgebot of 1516 decreed that barley was the only grain brewers could use – but wheat beer, made in royal breweries, was exempt. Royal control was loosened in the 1870s, and brewers such as Erdinger began to make wheat beers.

TASTING NOTES: Very light hints of malted wheat make it through rich and sweet banana flavours.
- **Country:** Germany
- **Brewer:** Erdinger Weissbräu
- **Style:** Dunkelweizen
- **Appearance:** Dark brown
- **Alcohol:** 5.3%
- **Serving temp:** 8–10°C

FRANZISKANER HEFE-WEISSBIER

This is a great example of the light German wheat beer style called Hefeweizen. Made with pale malted wheat and malted barley, the yeast flavour breaks through, revealing spiced notes of clove and soft fruits – most notably banana. The Franziskaner is loaded with both spice and fruit and is certainly one of the best Hefeweizens on the market.

TASTING NOTES: Banana, cloves and very light malty wheat. Little hints of citrus in the aroma.
- **Country:** Germany
- **Brewer:** Spaten-Bräu Franziskaner
- **Style:** Hefeweizen
- **Appearance:** Hazy yellow
- **Alcohol:** 5%
- **Serving temp:** 3–5°C

FRÜH KÖLSCH

Kölsch is one of the more interesting beers to come out of Germany – specifically Cologne. It is first fermented like an ale at a warm 13–21°C, and then cold-matured or lagered. The result is the best of both the lager and the ale styles. Früh Kölsch has a very light golden colour with aromas of grassy hops and a slightly sour hint. A medium-bodied beer, much like bready ale, with the long bitter finish you'd expect from a good lager. Delicious with cold meat.

TASTING NOTES: Mild malt, faint grassy hops and a sweet bready corn flavour. Long bitter finish.
- **Country:** Germany
- **Brewer:** Cölner Hofbräu
- **Style:** Kölsch
- **Appearance:** Clean gold
- **Alcohol:** 4.8%
- **Serving temp:** 3–5°C

OKTOBERFEST: THE FESTIVAL OF BEER

There are many beer festivals around the world, but perhaps the most famous is Munich's Oktoberfest.

Every year, more than six million people attend the event, which is held in Munich's vast Theresienwiese parkland. It is spread over 16–18 days, depending on which day German Unification Day falls, and actually begins in late September.

To understand Oktoberfest you need to know a little history. Oktoberfest commemorates the celebrations that were held in October 1810 for the marriage of Bavaria's Prince Ludwig and Princess Therese of Saxe-Hildburghausen. In honour of the union, a huge party was held for the Munich citizens, featuring a parade, horse racing and beer drinking.

The time of year also coincided with the recommencement of brewing following the summer lay-off. Before refrigeration, summer was not a good time to brew German beers, which require cold fermentation. Instead, producers brewed a surplus of beer in spring, known as Märzen (March beers), to last until fresh brews were made in the cooler autumn.

The teaming of a royal wedding and the new season ale was such a winning combination that the good burghers of Munich decided to make it an annual event. It has been that way ever since, with a few missed years due to war and cholera outbreaks.

Over the years the date slipped to a September start to take advantage of the last of the summer weather. The event gradually evolved to include a carnival and a parade as well as horse racing, although this activity was dropped in 1960.

Oktoberfest kicks off at noon on the first Saturday, with the Lord Mayor of Munich opening the first barrel of beer and making the traditional Bavarian announcement 'O'zapft is' meaning 'It has been tapped'.

The following day, a parade marks the ceremonial opening, with a procession of the Oktoberfest staff and breweries. The parade, which started in 1887, is led by the Münchner Kindl, or Munich Child, who features on the city's emblem holding a mug of beer and a radish. Following are horse-drawn coaches and drays adorned with flowers, the bands of the festival tents, waitresses on decorated carriages and up to 9,000 people in folk costume.

Inside the festival visitors drink officially designated Oktoberfest Beer. This must conform to the Reinheitsgebot purity laws and is quite strong, at about 6% alcohol by volume. The beer must also be brewed within the city limits by six breweries: Spaten, Löwenbräu, Augustiner-Bräu, Hofbräu-München, Paulaner or Hacker-Pschorr.

Drinkers consume it in huge steins by the litre or 'Maß', although a smaller half litre, or 'Halbe' is on offer. Originally a dark Märzen lager, Oktoberfest beer has become progressively lighter and is now golden in colour. Each of the breweries has its own tent and in total there are 14 large tents, which can seat up to 6,000 drinkers, as well as a number of smaller tents. Entry to the tents and showground is free but it is advisable to get there early as tables are usually full with carousing festivalgoers before noon.

Dressing in traditional Bavarian costume of lederhosen and dirndl dresses is not obligatory, but thousands of foreign visitors take the opportunity to channel their inner German.

As well as becoming an item on many people's bucket lists, Oktoberfest has also spawned celebrations around the world, with around 2,000 spin-offs globally. However, there is only one original.

▬ VAGABUND SZECHUAN SAISON

The saison style is given an oriental kick by Vagabund brewery which brews out of a tiny nanobrewery in Berlin. The beauty of so much small batch production is that the brewers can afford to experiment and experimentation often yields great things! This saison is infused with the spicy peppercorns of the Far East which complement the naturally funky yeast flavours perfectly.

TASTING NOTES: Pepper spice and hints of radish and herbs. A great match with a pepperoni pizza.
- **Country:** Germany
- **Brewer:** Vagabund Brauerei
- **Style:** Saison
- **Appearance:** Hazy gold
- **Alcohol:** 5.2%
- **Serving temp:** 4–7°C

DID YOU KNOW?

In the drinking game Stiefeltrinken sips of beer are taken in turns from a glass boot; as the level drops you must avoid splashes by twisting the boot, or the next round's on you!

▬ PLANK DUNKLER WEIZENBOCK

Strong, dark and made with high proportions of malted wheat, this Weizenbock's malt flavours take centre stage. Though the Weizenbock (wheat bock) style is often noted for high levels of esters, which provide fruity flavours, Michael Plank's wholesome version is all about the malted grains in a very smooth, silky beer, which aims to warm your heart rather than refresh.

TASTING NOTES: Bread, pepper with light hints of raisin and toasted pecans. Pair with apple strudel for a pleasant combination.
- **Country:** Germany
- **Brewer:** Brauerei Plank-Laaber
- **Style:** Weizenbock
- **Appearance:** Dark red
- **Alcohol:** 7.5%
- **Serving temp:** 8–10°C

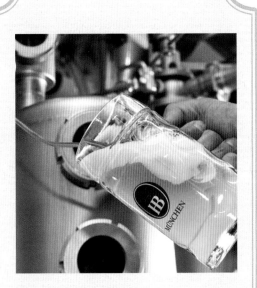

■ HOFBRÄU MÜNCHNER WEISSE

For many years, the purity law forbade brewing wheat beer in order for the government to control grain supplies. However, certain noble families were allowed to break the rules! The Hofbräuhaus (Royal Court Brewery) relished this freedom, holding a monopoly on wheat beer in Bavaria for 200 years. The sheer quality of this beer speaks of its history.

TASTING NOTES: Bananas, cloves, citrus and malted wheat in perfect balance.
- **Country:** Germany
- **Brewer:** Hofbräu München
- **Style:** Hefeweizen
- **Appearance:** Hazy yellow
- **Alcohol:** 5.1%
- **Serving temp:** 4–7°C

■ BECK'S

The world's best-selling German beer, Beck's is instantly recognizable: it was the first beer in Germany to use a green glass bottle. A brewing powerhouse, Beck's is sold in around 90 countries as well as its native Germany; the largest markets are the United Kingdom and the USA. The 'key' logo is derived from the Bremen city coat of arms.

TASTING NOTES: Light malt with a very subtle hop aroma. Very easy to drink with a relaxed flavour profile.
- **Country:** Germany
- **Brewer:** Beck's
- **Style:** Pale lager
- **Appearance:** Golden
- **Alcohol:** 4.8%
- **Serving temp:** 1–2°C

■ GÄNSTALLER BRÄU AFFUMICATOR

A beer for the bold hearted, this smoked lager takes inspiration from the renowned beers of Bamberg and the Schlenkerla brewery. It uses smoked malt for an intense and unusual flavour in a lager that reminds the palate of meaty, savoury foods. This makes it a fantastic match for smoked meat like ribs and smoked salmon with black bread. Certainly not a session beer for casual drinking!

TASTING NOTES: Smokey bacon, toffee and lighter hints of milk chocolate and dried fruits.
- **Country:** Germany
- **Brewer:** Gänstaller
- **Style:** Smoked lager
- **Appearance:** Dark brown
- **Alcohol:** 9.5%
- **Serving temp:** 4–7°C

■ WEIHENSTEPHANER PILSNER

Even the world's oldest brewery has to follow trends to some extent. But as long as it takes the same care and attention to brew the ubiquitous Pilsner that it does with the rest of its historic beers, it still retains every inch of the integrity it has become famous for. A perfectly rounded and traditionally-made Pilsner.

Tasting notes: Brewer's mash, light caramel and hints of honey and lemon.
• **Country:** Germany
• **Brewer:** Bayerische Staatsbrauerei Weihenstephan
• **Style:** Pilsner
• **Appearance:** Light yellow
• **Alcohol:** 5.1%
• **Serving temp:** 3–5°C

■ LÖWENBRÄU ORIGINAL

Löwenbräu beers have been served at every single Oktoberfest in Munich since 1810. Along with five other breweries that operate in Munich, the brewery produces a special Oktoberfestbier to go alongside its regular range. The most recognizable beer from Löwenbräu though is its Original Helles lager – brewed in accordance with the famous purity law of 1516. The brewery traces its history back to 1524, so you're drinking a small part of German brewing history when you open a Löwenbräu Original.

TASTING NOTES: Fresh notes of citrus, lemony bubbles and a healthy dose of sweet grains and cereal.
• **Country:** Germany
• **Brewer:** Löwenbräu Munich
• **Style:** Helles
• **Appearance:** Light yellow
• **Alcohol:** 5.2%
• **Serving temp:** 3–5°C

DID YOU KNOW?

A heat-damaged but still-sealed bottle of Löwenbräu, taken from the wreckage of the German airship Hindenburg in 1937, reached over $16,000 at auction in 2009, setting a record for the most expensive bottle of beer.

■ HACKER-PSCHORR WEISSE

Hacker-Pschorr uses 60 per cent malted wheat and 40 per cent malted barley in the mash. After the grains have released their sugars, hops are added and the beer is fermented. It undergoes a secondary fermentation in the bottle, resulting in a yeasty sediment, so pour it carefully or you'll get a mouthful of yeast.

TASTING NOTES: Mild yeast, banana and a hint of citrus and spice. Great to pair with Chinese food like shrimp chow mein.
- **Country:** Germany
- **Brewer:** Hacker-Pschorr
- **Style:** Hefeweizen
- **Appearance:** Cloudy yellow
- **Alcohol:** 5.5%
- **Serving temp:** 3–5°C

■ ALTENBURGER SCHWARZES

The Altenburger brewery has been in operation since 1871 at its present location in the Kauerndorf district of Altenburg. Altenburger Schwarzes is a black beer, a style of lager that is always deep brown to black in colour, with low sweetness and bitterness and very little fruitiness. The flavours are fairly subdued, making it an easy drink that is consumed in large quantities at mealtimes in the beer halls of Germany. Eat with dark and sticky pretzels and sauerkraut to get the full effect.

Tasting notes: Bready flavours, with notes of chocolate and a nutty aroma. A smooth and subtle caramel finish.
- **Country:** Germany
- **Brewer:** Altenburger
- **Style:** Schwarzbier
- **Appearance:** Dark brown
- **Alcohol:** 4.9%
- **Serving temp:** 8–13°C

■ CAMBA OAK AGED MILK STOUT – BOURBON

The old enforcers of the Reinheitsgebot would not be best pleased to see this sort of thing hit the shelves of Germany – and more fool them! Barley, hops, yeast and water are of course the base ingredients of this beer but the addition of rolled oats and lactose give a full body that isn't achievable by adhering to tradition alone. A long ageing in bourbon-soaked barrels finishes this gorgeous milk stout to perfection.

TASTING NOTES: Creamy chocolate milk, iced latte and bourbon truffle.
- **Country:** Germany
- **Brewer:** Camba Bavaria
- **Style:** Imperial stout
- **Appearance:** Deep black
- **Alcohol:** 9%
- **Serving temp:** 10–13°C

▬ ALE-MANIA GOSE MANIA

The Gose style was a recipe that defied the Reinheitsgebot, often using at least 50 per cent wheat in the mash and adding aromatics such as coriander and lemon peel, topped with a healthy dose of added salt, or for real authenticity the salty water that surrounds the town of Goslar in Northern Germany. Ale-Mania places serious emphasis on the coriander aspect in this delicious love letter to the Gose style.

TASTING NOTES: Herbal coriander, tangy citrus and a salty finish.
- **Country:** Germany
- **Brewer:** Ale-Mania
- **Style:** Gose
- **Appearance:** Pale gold
- **Alcohol:** 5%
- **Serving temp:** 4–7°C

DID YOU KNOW?

The Guinness World Record for the most beer steins carried over 40 metres (131 feet) was set by Oliver Struempfel in Germany in 2014 when he carried 25 steins across the finish line.

▬ LÜBZER PILS

All Pilsners are bottom-fermented. This means the yeast used in the brew sinks to the bottom of the fermintation tank and has minimal contact with the air outside. The long fermentation time produces more carbon dioxide and gives the beer a beautiful foamy head that will last all the way down. Enjoy with light food such as steamed clams or chicken.

TASTING NOTES: Sweet, mellow grain flavours, herbal hoppy notes and a long-lasting bitterness in the finish.
- **Country:** Germany
- **Brewer:** Mecklenburgische Brauerei Lübz
- **Style:** Pilsner
- **Appearance:** Clear gold
- **Alcohol:** 4.9%
- **Serving temp:** 3–5°C

▬ RADEBERGER PILSNER

This classic Pilsner has something of a distinguished history. Elevated to 'Kanzier-Brau' (Chancellor-brew) in 1887 by the first German Chancellor, Otto Von Bismarck, the beer also became the favourite drink of King Frederick Augustus III of Saxony in 1905. In the early 21st century, however, the beer had a rather less noble following – being the beer of choice for Charlie Sheen's character in the TV series *Two and a Half Men* doesn't have quite the same ring to it! A fantastic example of a good Pilsner nonetheless.

Tasting notes: Easy-going malty flavour, toasted sweet grains with a slightly buttery finish.
- **Country:** Germany
- **Brewer:** Radeberger Exportbierbrauerei
- **Style:** Pilsner
- **Appearance:** Medium yellow
- **Alcohol:** 4.8%
- **Serving temp:** 3–5°C

▬ MAISEL'S WEISSE ORIGINAL

One of the proudest family brewers in all of Germany. Founded in 1887 by two brothers, the brewery remains in the family to this day largely due to the success of this fantastic Hefeweizen, Maisel's Weisse Original. The beer is one of the archetypal examples of the style, which literally translates as 'yeast wheat' – the two main flavour components of the beer.

TASTING NOTES: Bananas, bubblegum, vanilla and cloves. A very refreshing drink in hot weather.

- **Country:** Germany
- **Brewer:** Brauerei Gebruder Maisel
- **Style:** Hefeweizen
- **Appearance:** Hazy gold
- **Alcohol:** 5.4%
- **Serving temp:** 3–5°C

■ RIEGELE NOCTUS 100

Starting life in 1386 as 'The Golden Horse Brewery', Riegele Brewery is certainly among the oldest breweries in the world. Its Golden Horse emblem is still visible on every beer it makes as a nod to the past, but this Noctus 100 is a beer born very much of modern times. A huge alcohol percentage compared to most other German beers, it also uses an Irish yeast strain similar to that used in a certain famous Irish stout.

TASTING NOTES: Roasted caramel flavours, hot chocolate and Coco Pops.
- **Country:** Germany
- **Brewer:** Brauhaus Riegele
- **Style:** Imperial stout
- **Appearance:** Black
- **Alcohol:** 10%
- **Serving temp:** 10–13°C

■ CREW REPUBLIC FOUNDATION 11

Crew Republic brewery in Munich is one of the more modern producers of beer in Germany. Mario and Timm are mere babies on the German beer scene having only been brewing since 2011, but their mission is simple: to bring new hop flavours to Germany and combine them with the best of what is grown locally to produce distinctively modern German beers. This Foundation 11 pale ale does exactly that – combining the best of German and American produce.

TASTING NOTES: Hoppy lemons and candied orange with light biscuit finish.
- **Country:** Germany
- **Brewer:** Crew Republic
- **Style:** Pale ale
- **Appearance:** Hazy gold
- **Alcohol:** 5.6%
- **Serving temp:** 4–7°C

■ PAULANER SALVATOR

One of the older beers to come out of the Paulaner brewery, the name Salvator means 'saviour' in Latin. The name may suggest that the Paulaner monks who established the brewery would drink this strong beer instead of food in times of fasting. The recipe is little changed since Brother Barnabus, the most famous Paulaner monk, first brewed this beer in the 18th century.

TASTING NOTES: Strong malty flavours, with traces of honey, caramel and bread dough.
- **Country:** Germany
- **Brewer:** Paulaner Brauerei
- **Style:** Doppelbock
- **Appearance:** Cloudy brown
- **Alcohol:** 7.9%
- **Serving temp:** 8–10°C

■ SCHNEIDER AVENTINUS

The archetypal Weizenbock, Schneider has been brewing this strong, dark wheat beer since 1907. The beer takes its name from the 16th-century historian Johannes Aventinus. Schneider was sold the right to brew wheat beers in 1872. Before that, only the royal family and those with special permission were allowed to use wheat – an ingredient prohibited in beer by the Reinheitsgebot. Schneider is largely credited with saving wheat beer from extinction in the face of competition from golden lager.

TASTING NOTES: Sweet plums, ripe soft banana with hints of spice and raisins.
- **Country:** Germany
- **Brewer:** G. Schneider & Sohn
- **Style:** Weizenbock
- **Appearance:** Dark brown
- **Alcohol:** 8.2%
- **Serving temp:** 8–10°C

■ HOLSTEN PILSENER

First brewed in accordance with the beer purity law, Holsten Pilsener was created in 1953 and became a big success in Germany. Since then, the Holsten business has expanded steadily – it now owns seven breweries in Germany. The name Holsten derives from an old Germanic tribe who lived in the north of Germany in a region now called Holstein.

Tasting notes: Lightly baked crackerbreads, cereal and hints of earthy, peppery hops.
- **Country:** Germany
- **Brewer:** Holsten Brauerei
- **Style:** Pilsner
- **Appearance:** Clear yellow
- **Alcohol:** 4.8%
- **Serving temp:** 3–5°C

■ WEIHENSTEPHANER HEFEWEISSBIER

Ancient documents from AD 768 refer to a hop garden in the Freising district of Bavaria. Many take this as proof of the claim that Weihenstephan, the location of the Weihenstephan monastery is the world's oldest operational brewery. What is certain is the quality of Weihenstephan Hefeweissbier – a perfect example of cloudy German wheat beer at its best.

TASTING NOTES: Banana, cloves, pepper and hints of orange. A great match for Weisswurst sausage.
- **Country:** Germany
- **Brewer:** Bayerische Staatsbrauerei Weihenstephan
- **Style:** Hefeweizen
- **Appearance:** Cloudy yellow
- **Alcohol:** 5.4%
- **Serving temp:** 3–5°C

◼ KOSTRITZER SCHWARZBIER

The Köstritzer Schwarzbierbrauerei has always been famed for its black beer – with the first recorded example being brewed in 1543. The style almost died out, but when the Bitburger brewery bought Köstritzer in 1991, this beer was reintroduced to great critical acclaim. Drink with blackened pork loin or washed-rind cheeses.

TASTING NOTES: Lots of roasted malt aroma, berries and light smoke. All this is evident in the taste too with a peppery background.
- **Country:** Germany
- **Brewer:** Köstritzer Schwarzbierbrauerei
- **Style:** Schwarzbier
- **Appearance:** Black
- **Alcohol:** 4.8%
- **Serving temp:** 4–7°C

DID YOU KNOW?

In medieval Bavaria official beer bouts could be ordered by the Burgermeister (mayor) to settle disputes; the contesting parties drank for three hours without standing up, and the steadiest at the end was the winner.

◼ SCHLENKERLA RAUCHBIER MÄRZEN

Famous among German beer enthusiasts, Schlenkerla Märzen is known for its pungent aroma, achieved by smoking the barley malt before adding it to the mash tun. Distinctive, almost meaty, flavours emerge as a result and it's not something many enjoy on first taste. In Bamberg they say that before you decide whether you like or dislike the flavour of the Rauchbier, you must first drink your own bodyweight in it – though presumably not all in one sitting.

TASTING NOTES: Bacon, smoke and sweet malt. Try boiling some bratwurst in this beer for 10 minutes before grilling them.
- **Country:** Germany
- **Brewer:** Brauerei Heller
- **Style:** Smoked beer
- **Appearance:** Dark brown
- **Alcohol:** 5.1%
- **Serving temp:** 8–10°C

JEVER PILSENER

The word lager is German for storeroom, and derives from the long period of maturation, or storage, that lagers traditionally underwent. In the case of Jever Pilsener, this maturation period is a massive 90 days. The word 'Herb' on the label does not mean it contains herbs: herb is the German word for dry or bitter, and this is a particularly hoppy Pilsner.

TASTING NOTES: Herby hop aromas with light biscuit-like malt flavours. Great with a salad or sushi.
- **Country:** Germany
- **Brewer:** Jever
- **Style:** Pilsner
- **Appearance:** Clear yellow
- **Alcohol:** 4.8%
- **Serving temp:** 3–5°C

OETTINGER HEFEWEISSBIER

Many beer purists would say that unless the yeast strain *Torulaspora delbrueckii* is used, then the beer shouldn't be called a Hefeweizen. It's this specific strain of yeast that imparts the banana, bubblegum and clove flavours that are evident in this example from Oettinger. A good one to drink with Chinese dim sum.

TASTING NOTES: Lightly spiced banana with hints of bubblegum, clove and a bubbly malted wheat finish.
- **Country:** Germany
- **Brewer:** Oettinger Brauerei
- **Style:** Hefeweizen
- **Appearance:** Hazy gold
- **Alcohol:** 4.9%
- **Serving temp:** 3–5°C

SPATEN OKTOBERFEST

One of the six breweries that provide beer for the Munich Oktoberfest, the Spaten-Franziskaner brewery brews this Märzen (March) beer in the spring to allow it to mature in time for autumn. 'Spaten' literally translates as spade in German – a tool all brewers are familiar with after shifting tons of malt around all day. This Oktoberfest beer is a great example of the style.

TASTING NOTES: Flavoursome lager. Sweet bready malts give way to a crisp, clean aftertaste with a touch of spice.
- **Country:** Germany
- **Brewer:** Spaten-Franziskaner Bräu
- **Style:** Märzen
- **Appearance:** Medium yellow
- **Alcohol:** 5.9%
- **Serving temp:** 4–5°C

▮▮ ABBAYE DES ROCS BRUNE

Steak-lovers everywhere rejoice! There is a beer to rival red wine when it comes to matching your favourite dinner and it comes in the form of this Abbaye Des Rocs beer. This fruity, woody and hugely flavoursome beer has all the body, colour and rich dark colour you need with a robust meaty dish. The brewmasters created such a complex taste by using seven types of malt and three different hop varieties. One of the most underrated beers in Belgium.

TASTING NOTES: Some dark fruits, oaky wood and caramel flavours. Savour with dark, bloody meat.
• **Country:** Belgium
• **Brewer:** Abbaye Des Rocs
• **Style:** Belgian strong ale
• **Appearance:** Deep ruby
• **Alcohol:** 9%
• **Serving temp:** 8–13°C

▮▮ 3 FONTEINEN OUDE GEUZE

One of the all-time great Lambic beers. Usually a blend of the last three consecutive years' batches, 3 Fonteinen is always then aged in the bottle with its own yeast for at least one year before release. Look out for a sparkle not unlike champagne and a hint of oak from the barrels it sits in. Even the hops in this beer get aged until they are perfectly ripe and slightly cheesy. This is a classic that will never die.

TASTING NOTES: Zesty orange and kumquat, tart apple, light vanilla and oak with a refreshing sour finish.
• **Country:** Belgium
• **Brewer:** Brouwerij 3 Fonteinen
• **Style:** Gueuze
• **Appearance:** Bright gold
• **Alcohol:** 6%
• **Serving temp:** 4–7°C

▮▮ AFFLIGEM TRIPEL

The tiny Flemish village of Opwijk is the home of this luxurious Abbey-style tripel. Affligem Tripel gets a second fermentation in the bottle so it carries on maturing after it's bottled. This makes it a prime candidate for storage to allow its flavours to develop further. High alcohol content but somehow still fantastically refreshing.

TASTING NOTES: Candyfloss, banana and cane sugar. Serve with a plate of ham and Brie.
• **Country:** Belgium
• **Brewer:** Brouwerij Affligem
• **Style:** Tripel
• **Appearance:** Light amber
• **Alcohol:** 9.5%
• **Serving temp:** 8–10°C

▪▪ BOON KRIEK

While some sour cherry Lambics include a measure of sweetness to make them more approachable, Boon Kriek is a more 'serious' brew. With a much more subtle and complex flavour, Boon Kriek retains all the sourness with slightly less sugar. Still very drinkable – especially alongside a piece of dark chocolate or vanilla ice cream – but definitely one for the more experienced Lambic lover.

TASTING NOTES: Sour barnyard-type aromas with sweet black cherries and acidic lemon juice.
- **Country:** Belgium
- **Brewer:** Brouwerij Boon
- **Style:** Kriek
- **Appearance:** Deep red
- **Alcohol:** 4%
- **Serving temp:** 4–7°C

Belgium has six of the eight Trappist breweries in Europe: Chimay, Orval, Rochefort, Westmalle, Westvleteren and Achel. They are famous for strong ales produced using centuries-old methods.

▪▪ DE DOLLE STILLE NACHT

Called a Christmas beer by many, De Dolle Stille Nacht is a fabulous beer in its own right without any seasonal gimmicks needed to make it stand out. It has an unusually high density of texture owing to its long boil time (five hours) and added candy sugar. There is also an interesting sourness that develops as the beer matures. Keep this one in the cellar for a year or two.

TASTING NOTES: Sweet candyfloss, sour yeast and a hop balance for bitterness. A perfect flavour triangle.
- **Country:** Belgium
- **Brewer:** De Dolle Brouwers
- **Style:** Belgian strong ale
- **Appearance:** Dirty brown
- **Alcohol:** 12%
- **Serving temp:** 8–10°C

▋▋ GRIMBERGEN BLONDE

Grimbergen Abbey, north of Brussels, was founded in 1128. Over the centuries it was destroyed by fire and rebuilt several times, hence the phoenix emblem. Only the finest Gatinais barley is used for the mash as the hop profile is so light. A lovely yeast flavour rounds this beer off nicely.

TASTING NOTES: Light citrus fruits, hints of spice from the yeast and a creamy and fast-collapsing head.
- **Country:** Belgium
- **Brewer:** Alken-Maes
- **Style:** Belgian blonde
- **Appearance:** Clear gold
- **Alcohol:** 6.7%
- **Serving temp:** 3–5°C

▋▋ ROCHEFORT 8

Sold in order to support the resident monks at the Abbey of Notre-Dame de Saint Rémy, Rochefort 8 makes up approximately 80 per cent of the brewery's output; it has an enthusiastic following around the world. To round off this beer, a small amount of demi-sec (medium dry wine) is added to give acidity. Serve in a champagne glass.

TASTING NOTES: Long-lasting aromas of plums and red berries pair nicely with gentle chocolate and raisins.
- **Country:** Belgium
- **Brewer:** Brasserie de Rochefort
- **Style:** Trappist
- **Appearance:** Deep brown
- **Alcohol:** 9.2%
- **Serving temp:** 8–10°C

▋▋ BRUGSE ZOT

For many, Brugse Zot is the archetypal Belgian blonde beer. The only beer to be both brewed and matured in the centre of Bruges, this crisp, refreshing, pale blonde ale is labelled with its affectionate tribute to the people of Bruges – a city once dubbed 'one big fools' house' by the Emperor of Austria. This explains the literal translation: the Bruges Fool.

TASTING NOTES: Light lemon, with subtle spices and orange and a long and defined malty sweetness.
- **Country:** Belgium
- **Brewer:** Huisbrouwerij De Halve Maan
- **Style:** Belgian blonde
- **Appearance:** Golden
- **Alcohol:** 6%
- **Serving temp:** 4–7°C

▮▮ HET ANKER GOUDEN CAROLUS NOEL

A long tradition of brewing this Christmas special was put to rest by Het Anker brewery in the 1960s after a decline in demand for the style. Happily, after over 35 years, Het Anker brewery brought it back to life and it tastes as good as ever. Six different herbs and spices and three types of hop ensure complexity, depth and a memorable drinking experience for those winter nights.

TASTING NOTES: Figs, plum jam and red fruits with a hint of marzipan.
- **Country:** Belgium
- **Brewer:** Het Anker
- **Style:** Quadrupel
- **Appearance:** Ruby red
- **Alcohol:** 10.5%
- **Serving temp:** 10–13°C

▮▮ BLANCHE DE BRUXELLES

Blanche de Bruxelles is a Belgian-style wheat beer, also known as a witbier, or white beer. These differ from the more restrained German wheat beers because brewers in Belgium can use other ingredients besides just malt, hops, water and yeast. Blanche de Bruxelles is made with a combination of malted wheat and barley with coriander and orange peel thrown in for good measure.

TASTING NOTES: Light, bubbly and very refreshing with notes of lemon and very light spice. Perfect with mussels and fries.
- **Country:** Belgium
- **Brewer:** Brasserie Lefebvre
- **Style:** Witbier
- **Appearance:** Hazy yellow
- **Alcohol:** 4.5%
- **Serving temp:** 4–7°C

▮▮ DE LA SENNE TARAS BOULBA

Started by Yvan De Baets and Bernard Leboucq, Brasserie de la Senne is known as a quality producer of unfiltered and unpasteurized beers free of additives and using only the best ingredients. Unusually for a Belgian ale, Taras Boulba is a mere 4.5% making it light enough to drink as a session ale. Look for the complex yeasty flavours as well as the more obvious citrus notes.

TASTING NOTES: Grassy citrus, earthy tones and an extremely light and zesty mouthfeel.
- **Country:** Belgium
- **Brewer:** Brasserie de la Senne
- **Style:** Belgian ale
- **Appearance:** Hazy yellow
- **Alcohol:** 4.5%
- **Serving temp:** 4–7°C

▌▌ BELLE-VUE KRIEK

Even for the most ardent beer haters, Kriek, or cherry Lambic, styles are extremely drinkable. With their inviting, deep fruity colours and sweet/sour balance, you could be forgiven for thinking you'd opened a particularly tangy fruit juice rather than a beer. Belle-Vue Kriek is a great example of the style. Made with whole cherries, this is a beer that anyone can enjoy.

TASTING NOTES:
Sour cherries, lemon and a tangy mouth-puckering finish. Try with a piece of dark chocolate.

- **Country:** Belgium
- **Brewer:** Belle-Vue
- **Style:** Kriek
- **Appearance:** Deep ruby
- **Alcohol:** 5.2%
- **Serving temp:** 4–7°C

DID YOU KNOW?

Belgian brewery Brasserie Ellezelloise produces a world-classic Russian stout named after the famous Belgian detective Hercule Poirot — however, Poirot himself never drank beer, preferring herbal tisanes and blackcurrant cassis.

▌▌ WESTVLETEREN 12

When the brewers of Westvleteren 12 first began brewing this beer, they limited buyers to ten crates at a time. But as the beer increased in popularity, buyers were permitted less and less until in 2009, they were allowed one crate only. Priced at €40 per crate of 24 bottles, the abbey prohibits any resale of the beer, meaning if you want to buy it then you must go to Belgium to the abbey café. This scarcity of supply has only increased its popularity. In 2005 it was voted Best Beer in the World and given worldwide press attention – much to the annoyance of the monks who brew it!

TASTING NOTES: A perfect balance of toffee, bitter, sweet, spice, vanilla, oak, berries and dried fruit. The best beer ever created.

- **Country:** Belgium
- **Brewer:** Westvleteren Abdij St Sixtus
- **Style:** Trappist quadrupel
- **Appearance:** Deep brown
- **Alcohol:** 10.2%
- **Serving temp:** 8–10°C

HOLY ORDERS

Monasteries have been involved in brewing since the Middle Ages, when they began to recognize it as a useful method of raising money and also serving their local communities.

This process continues today in the Trappist breweries of Belgium, the Netherlands and Austria. The monks at the eight authentic Trappist breweries produce some of the most exquisite beers available.

The Trappists are a branch of the Cistercians who broke away from the main order in the 17th century to pursue a more devout version of the faith. Their name comes from the abbey of La Grande Trappe in Normandy, France, which began to institute reforms in 1664.

Beer was an important part of monastic life for several reasons. In medieval times, water quality was not always good, so beer was a better bet as a daily drink.

Monasteries were places where travellers could find shelter, food and drink, so beer was a saleable product. Trappist monks were among the most active brewers, with many monasteries producing their own beer.

Over the years, the monks built up an impressive knowledge of beer-making, especially the ability to brew stronger beers. There was no way of measuring the alcoholic strength of beer, but monks realized that by doubling or tripling the ingredients, they could make stronger beer. This led to the enkel, dubbel and tripel (single, double and triple) naming system, which indicates progressively stronger brews.

Trappist beers became increasingly popular in

Belgium, where most of the brewing monasteries are located, especially when spirits were banned in bars in 1919. Drinkers in search of a stronger drink turned to the high-alcohol Trappist beers, and production increased to keep pace with demand.

However, the popularity of Trappist beer led to other brewers launching their own 'Trappist' beers. These were not brewed according to Trappist principles, and in 1962 a Ghent brewer was sued for passing off his beer as Trappist.

In 1997, the Trappist abbeys of Belgium (Orval, Chimay, Westvleteren, Rochefort, Westmalle and Achel), Koningshoeven in the Netherlands and Mariawald in Germany formed the International Trappist Association (ITA) to safeguard the Trappist name. Trappist abbeys can use a logo on bottles of beer and other products such as cheese and wine to show their authenticity. Trappist beer must be brewed within the walls of the abbey, either by the monks or under their control. The economic purpose of the brewery must be directed towards charity and not towards financial profit.

This guidance relates to how the beer is produced, but the type of beer is not described. Consequently, there are a number of different beer styles under the Trappist umbrella. Most are top-fermented and bottle-conditioned, but the beers range from blonde through amber to very dark ales. Alcohol content is similarly varied, although most Trappist beers are much stronger than normal 'session' beers. Rochefort's 10 beer has 11.3% alcohol.

The monasteries also sometimes brew a lower-strength beer for consumption by the monks. Known as patersbier, this is usually only available at the abbey.

Since the introduction of the ITA designation, non-Trappist beers are sometimes called abbey beers. They can be similar in style to monastic beers, but are produced by a non-Trappist monastery or by a commercial brewery under an arrangement with an existing monastery. Some have no connection to existing religious orders.

The newest Trappist brewery only received its ITA affiliation in 2012. Stift Engelszell in Austria was founded in the 13th century but the monastery was dissolved by the Emperor in the 18th century. Refounded in the 20th century, it has recently started brewing after the monastery teamed up with a local, family-run brewer, Brauerei Hofstetten. It produces two beers, both using the abbey's own honey.

Stift Engelszell was not to be the last of the Trappist breweries as other monasteries have started to add brewing capacity. Abdij Maria Toevlucht in the Netherlands revived a brewing tradition that dated back to 1899 when it commenced producing Zundert Trappist beer in 2013. Meanwhile, St Joseph's Abbey in Massachusetts launched the first American Trappist beer in early 2014.

It seems the Trappist tradition is set to continue.

■ ■ VEDETT EXTRA BLOND

It's no coincidence that Vedett Extra Blond comes in the same shape bottle as Duvel. The same brewer makes this easy-going 5.2% premium lager and it has gained a loyal cult following in the Antwerp-Brussels region since 1945. Made with a percentage of rice and extra hops, it has a very crisp and clean taste.

TASTING NOTES: Moderate amounts of hay, toast and grains in the aroma with a bubbly, carbonated character.
- **Country:** Belgium
- **Brewer:** Duvel Moortgat
- **Style:** Pale lager
- **Appearance:** Pale yellow
- **Alcohol:** 5.2%
- **Serving temp:** 3–4°C

■ ■ CANTILLON KRIEK

Making Kriek is a great way of using up all the cherries that grow in Belgium. Take an 18-month-old Lambic beer, add a vast quantity of cherries, and their natural sugars and yeast kick-start fermentation as well as imparting flavour. Cantillon Kriek is made in the old-fashioned way with oak barrels and decades of know-how.

TASTING NOTES: Acidic, lemon juice, sour cherry and subtle farmyard-like aromas. Drink with brown bread and white cheese.
- **Country:** Belgium
- **Brewer:** Cantillon
- **Style:** Kriek
- **Appearance:** Cherry red
- **Alcohol:** 5%
- **Serving temp:** 4–7°C

DID YOU KNOW?

Monastic brewers were prevented from using hops, which the church deemed the 'fruit of the devil', although the ban was most likely because the bishops had a monopoly over the 'gruyt' (herbs and spices) used instead.

■■ MALHEUR BIÈRE BRUT

Rarely seen outside Belgium, Malheur's champagne beer range is one some raise an eyebrow at. Using the same method as is used for champagne, the beer is fermented and bottled; it undergoes a second fermentation in the bottle, after which the processes of remuage and disgorgement remove the residual yeasts before the beer is bottled in a thick glass bottle. This secondary fermentation in the bottle is what gives champagne (and Malheur Bière Brut) its trademark sparkle and theatrical pop when the cork is removed.

TASTING NOTES: Light peach, orchard fruits and sour yeasts combine beautifully to mask a fairly high alcohol content.
• **Country:** Belgium • **Brewer:** Malheur
• **Style:** Champagne beer
• **Appearance:** Golden • **Alcohol:** 11%
• **Serving temp:** 4–7°C

■■ WESTMALLE TRAPPIST DUBBEL

Since 1856, the monks of the Trappist Abbey of Westmalle brewery have brewed a dark reddish-brown dubbel beer to go alongside their low-alcohol 'table beers'. The recipe has been modified over the years to make it stronger but the style remains the same. Skilfully blended malts, punchy sour yeast and soft, fruity, heartwarming flavour.

TASTING NOTES: Doughy, yeasty aromas of proving wholemeal bread. Sweet chocolatey body and a smooth caramel finish.
• **Country:** Belgium
• **Brewer:** Brouwerij der Trappisten van Westmalle
• **Style:** Trappist dubbel
• **Appearance:** Murky brown
• **Alcohol:** 7%
• **Serving temp:** 8–10°C

■■ CELIS WHITE

Pierre Celis, a milkman from the village of Hoegaarden, revived the Belgian wheat beer or witbier (white beer) style in the 1960s using a recipe that included coriander and orange peel. When a fire forced him to sell off his brewery to AB InBev (owners of today's Hoegaarden), he moved to Austin, Texas, to brew Celis White. He granted this brewery the right to make it in Belgium.

TASTING NOTES: Fresh grassy wheat with notes of orange peel and coriander. A great match for any seafood.
• **Country:** Belgium
• **Brewer:** Brouwerij Van Steenberge
• **Style:** Witbier
• **Appearance:** Hazy gold
• **Alcohol:** 5%
• **Serving temp:** 4–7°C

▪▪ PAUWEL KWAK

This fruity Belgian ale comes with its own masterful glass and stand – a commodity that many people took to stealing after a night on the Kwak. To combat the problem, some pub landlords asked drinkers to part with their shoes before using the glass and stand. Drinkers would drop their footwear in a basket, which was then winched up to the ceiling out of reach.

TASTING NOTES: Lots of malty caramel, roasted nuts and a hint of spice make this perfect with a spicy kebab.
• **Country:** Belgium
• **Brewer:** Brouwerij Bosteels
• **Style:** Belgian strong ale
• **Appearance:** Amber
• **Alcohol:** 8%
• **Serving temp:** 8–10°C

▪▪ DELIRIUM TREMENS

With its trademark white speckled bottle, you might be forgiven for mistaking Delirium Tremens for a funky bottle of salad dressing. Thankfully, a masterfully smart but very potent blend of spice, boozy apples and three tangy types of yeast await you when you pop the lid. Given the 1998 World Beer Championship gold medal, it has a reputation fully deserved.

TASTING NOTES: Apples, orange and grape in the nose with a sharp citrus tang in the taste. Great with spicy seafood dishes.
• **Country:** Belgium
• **Brewer:** Brouwerij Huyghe
• **Style:** Belgian strong ale
• **Appearance:** Hazy yellow
• **Alcohol:** 8.5%
• **Serving temp:** 4–7°C

▪▪ RODENBACH GRAND CRU

The Rodenbach brewery is famous for its well-loved Flemish red-style beers. Usually barrel-aged for months at a time in oak barrels, this style of beer has a lot in common with wine or sherry. Once aged it can be blended with younger ales or bottled unblended – as is the case with Rodenbach's wonderful Grand Cru.

TASTING NOTES: Winey aromas, acidity and berry-like fruits make this a great match for fresh shrimp and other seafood.
• **Country:** Belgium
• **Brewer:** Brauwerij Rodenbach
• **Style:** Flemish red
• **Appearance:** Red-brown
• **Alcohol:** 6%
• **Serving temp:** 8–10°C

■■ LINDEMANS PECHERESSE

All Lambic beers ferment in shallow open vats, to let natural yeasts enter and start fermentation. Fruit Lambic beers are then boiled with fresh fruit – most commonly cherries. But here, peaches are used to give a refreshing, fruity taste you'll never forget.

TASTING NOTES: Vivid flavours of peach combined with a sour tang and a bubbly refreshing aftertaste. Serve in a champagne glass!
- **Country:** Belgium
- **Brewer:** Lindemans
- **Style:** Fruit Lambic
- **Appearance:** Golden
- **Alcohol:** 2.5%
- **Serving temp:** 4–5°C

■■ ST FEUILLIEN BLONDE

The St Feuillien brewery is built on the site of the Abbey of St Feuillien, named after an Irish monk – Feuillien, who passed through the forest in the 7th century. After he was martyred, his disciples built a chapel, which later became a prosperous abbey. The abbey was destroyed after the French Revolution, but St Feuillien's name lives on in this strong Belgian blonde.

TASTING NOTES: Candied oranges, spices and hops. A clever balance of sour, bitter and sweet.
- **Country:** Belgium
- **Brewer:** Brasserie St Feuillien
- **Style:** Belgian blonde
- **Appearance:** Hazy gold
- **Alcohol:** 7.5%
- **Serving temp:** 4–7°C

■■ ST BERNARDUS ABT 12

The only thing stopping this beer from gaining the same mythical status as the famous Westvleteren is the term Trappist. St Bernardus is not a Trappist brewery but its Abt 12 is surely one of the highest-regarded beers in the world. Based on an original Westvleteren recipe, it's brewed in the classic quadrupel style. Perfect with a wild game dish.

TASTING NOTES: Dark fruits, liquorice and sticky toffee malts. Serve with wild boar or roasted venison.
- **Country:** Belgium
- **Brewer:** St Bernardus
- **Style:** Quadrupel
- **Appearance:** Murky brown
- **Alcohol:** 10.5%
- **Serving temp:** 8–10°C

▮▮ CHIMAY BLUE

To be deemed a Trappist ale, the beer must be made within the walls of the monastery by a member of the monastic community. In addition, the proceeds from any sales must go towards providing for the community or other local charitable projects. Monks at Notre-Dame de Scourmont Abbey, near the town of Chimay, began brewing in 1862. The range includes Chimay Red (7% alcohol), best enjoyed within a year, and Chimay Blue, their most famous and highly-rated beer, which can mature for several years.

TASTING NOTES: Malty caramels, boozy raisins and toffee apple with just a hint of bitterness. Matures with age.

- **Country:** Belgium
- **Brewer:** Chimay
- **Style:** Belgian strong ale
- **Appearance:** Muddy brown
- **Alcohol:** 9%
- **Serving temp:** 8–10°C

DID YOU KNOW?

There are over 800 beers made in Belgium, so it's not surprising the world's first beer academy opened in Herk-de-Stad, in the Belgian province of Limburg, in 1999.

▮▮ TRIPEL VAN DE GARRE

Just off the main square of Bruges, a small, centuries-old beer café has been serving up this local brew for decades. Brewed exclusively for the Staminee de Garre, Tripel Van De Garre is made by the Van Steenberge brewery - the same people who brew Gulden Draak. At 11.5%, it's not really a session beer, more one to sip and savour.

TASTING NOTES: A hazy orange colour and swirling white cream foam. Flavours of orange, alcohol and yeast.

- **Country:** Belgium
- **Brewer:** Brouwerij Van Steenberge
- **Style:** Tripel
- **Appearance:** Hazy orange
- **Alcohol:** 11.5%
- **Serving temp:** 4–7°C

■■ LA CHOUFFE

Strong, bubbly and thoroughly easy to drink, La Chouffe has been a firm favourite since its inception in 1982. Brewed in the green heartlands of the Belgian Ardennes, it's easy to spot a bottle as each one comes complete with a cheeky elf – a favourite character in many myths and legends of the Ardennes. La Chouffe is the flagship beer in the range, and like many Belgian ales, it's dangerously easy to drink despite its high alcohol content. Handle this one with care.

TASTING NOTES: Light fragrance of apple, orange and floral hops with an extremely bubbly yet soft finish.

- **Country:** Belgium
- **Brewer:** Brasserie d'Achouffe
- **Style:** Belgian strong ale
- **Appearance:** Light orange
- **Alcohol:** 8%
- **Serving temp:** 4–7°C

▪▪ CORSENDONK PATER

The name refers to the Priory of Corsendonk, which was in operation from 1398 to 1784 and was rebuilt as a hotel complex in the 1960s. The dubbel abbey beer style usually means a strong, rich brown ale. This example is extremely complex owing to its blend of multiple hops and malts; the less pronounced yeast flavours allow the malts to take centre stage.

TASTING NOTES: Light spice and caramel malts with a solid fruity flavour. A great beer for roasted game dishes like venison.
- **Country:** Belgium
- **Brewer:** Brasserie Du Bocq
- **Style:** Abbey dubbel
- **Appearance:** Rusty brown
- **Alcohol:** 7.5%
- **Serving temp:** 8–10°C

▪▪ LEFFE BRUNE

Leffe Abbey survived many disasters over the centuries, and was finally abandoned after the French Revolution. In the early 20th century the monks returned and restored the buildings, but suffered further setbacks during the two world wars. In the 1950s, in order to resolve the abbey's financial problems, the abbot decided to renew ancient brewing traditions and licensed a local brewery to make beer under the Leffe name.

TASTING NOTES: Delicate flavours of coffee, vanilla, cloves and heavy caramel malts. Great with caramelized onion soup.
- **Country:** Belgium
- **Brewer:** AB InBev
- **Style:** Abbey dubbel
- **Appearance:** Dark brown
- **Alcohol:** 6.5%
- **Serving temp:** 5–6°C

▪▪ TRIPEL KARMELIET

Voted World's Best Ale in the 2008 World Beer Awards, Tripel Karmeliet owes its smooth body to a mixture of pale malt, wheat and a good percentage of oats. One of the most famous Belgian blonde ales for its full flavour, the addition of oats makes the body creamy and silky, while the limited use of hops allows yeast flavours to come through.

TASTING NOTES: Banana, vanilla with some citrus fruits. Perfect for robust seafood dishes like fish pie.
- **Country:** Belgium
- **Brewer:** Brouwerij Bosteels
- **Style:** Belgian blonde
- **Appearance:** Hazy gold
- **Alcohol:** 8.4%
- **Serving temp:** 4–7°C

■■ DE KONINCK

Not all Belgian beers are going to blow your head off with a high alcohol content and sickly richness. De Koninck keeps things pretty restrained in this beer, the flagship beer of its range. Brewed with barley malt, water, yeast and hops, this is a 100 per cent natural product with a smart hoppy finish from the Czech-sourced Saaz hops. A good beer to start the evening.

TASTING NOTES: Easy-going with notes of sweet malts, a little sourness and a subtle bitter finish from the hops.
- **Country:** Belgium
- **Brewer:** De Koninck
- **Style:** Belgian ale
- **Appearance:** Dark copper
- **Alcohol:** 5.2%
- **Serving temp:** 4–5°C

■■ ORVAL

Orval Abbey is a Trappist monastery brewery, and its beer Orval is special in many ways. Its bottle is one of a kind, shaped like a skittle from a ten-pin bowling alley. Its cloudy colouring and large foamy head also mark it out. But the best part is the perfectly balanced dry, hoppy finish – a result of Orval's special yeasts combined with the use of dry hopping techniques in the maturation process.

TASTING NOTES: Long-lasting creamy head with citrus in the nose and banana in the taste. Try with honey-roast duck.
- **Country:** Belgium
- **Brewer:** Brasserie d'Orval
- **Style:** Trappist
- **Appearance:** Copper
- **Alcohol:** 6.9%
- **Serving temp:** 8–10°C

DID YOU KNOW?

Dutch influence on Belgian beer persists in the use of spices, originally imported from the East Indies — Belgium was part of the Netherlands before a revolution in the 1830s, sparked partly by taxes on beer.

■■ FANTÔME

The Fantôme brewery produces several variations of the saison style. Originally created for farm workers to drink in the summer months, saisons were traditionally very refreshing, with complex earthy and herbal notes developing from their yeasts. Fantôme's flagship product is a tribute to this style but a little stronger – not just in its alcohol content – but also in its very intense flavours and pronounced sourness. Not for the faint of heart.

TASTING NOTES: Strong peach, strawberry and bitter orange flavours with a pronounced sourness.
- **Country:** Belgium
- **Brewer:** Brasserie Fantôme
- **Style:** Saison
- **Appearance:** Hazy yellow
- **Alcohol:** 8%
- **Serving temp:** 4–7°C

■ ■ DE RYCK AREND TRIPEL

A mother and daughter team is one you find all too rarely in the world of brewing. The De Ryck brewery has been family-run for several generations and is now in the hands of An De Ryck, with a fantastic range of beers. This abbey tripel is very well balanced with a gorgeous sweet but sour flavour.

TASTING NOTES: Alcohol and orchard fruit in the aroma are rounded off with a sweet, sour and spicy taste.
- **Country:** Belgium
- **Brewer:** Brouwerij De Ryck
- **Style:** Abbey tripel
- **Appearance:** Hazy gold
- **Alcohol:** 8%
- **Serving temp:** 4–7°C

■ ■ LIEFMANS GOUDENBAND

Made in large open-topped vats, Liefmans Goudenband is then left to mature for up to 12 months before being blended with a younger version of itself to restart fermentation. This is a beer you can store for many years as in essence it's really already gone off! Sour beers are a special product: refreshing, complex, but something of an acquired taste.

TASTING NOTES: Sour rhubarb, cherries and brown sugar. Delicate palates may pick up on woody notes. Acidic finish.
- **Country:** Belgium
- **Brewer:** Liefmans
- **Style:** Flemish Brown
- **Appearance:** Dark brown
- **Alcohol:** 8%
- **Serving temp:** 5–6°C

■ ■ DUVEL

This strong golden pale ale is exported to more than 40 countries around the world. The name comes from the Flemish word *duivel* which translates as devil. There's certainly a devilish aspect to Duvel as despite its 8.5%, it's extremely easy to drink – making it a dangerous beer indeed. Handle with care.

TASTING NOTES: Smooth, crisp and refreshing with a dry finish. Great with soft creamy cheeses.
- **Country:** Belgium
- **Brewer:** Duvel Moortgat
- **Style:** Belgian strong ale
- **Appearance:** Clear yellow
- **Alcohol:** 8.5%
- **Serving temp:** 4–5°C

■■ GULDEN DRAAK

Belgian brewers are noted for their willingness to experiment and innovate. Gulden Draak (golden dragon) uses a wine yeast in its secondary fermentation – giving it a unique flavour and also making it very versatile in cooking. Try using a bottle in a bordelaise sauce or a rich stew and you'll be astounded. Pure indulgence as an aperitif or with dessert.

TASTING NOTES: Very sweet with notes of berries, yeast and alcohol. A dry hoppy ending.
- **Country:** Belgium
- **Brewer:** Brouwerij Van Steenberge
- **Style:** Belgian barley wine
- **Appearance:** Deep brown
- **Alcohol:** 10.5%
- **Serving temp:** 8–10°C

■■ JUPILER

Generally speaking, the people of Belgium have escaped the dominance of pale lager in the latter part of the 20th century. Traditional methods and beers prevailed. Jupiler is something of an exception to the rule and has become the biggest-selling beer in Belgium, according to the brand owners AB InBev. Sometimes, a simple crisp lager is all you need.

TASTING NOTES:
Refreshing, carbonated and crisp pale malts give way to a dry but only lightly bitter finish.
- **Country:** Belgium
- **Brewer:** Brasserie Piedboeuf
- **Style:** Pale lager
- **Appearance:** Golden
- **Alcohol:** 5.2%
- **Serving temp:** 3–5°C

▬ BEAVER BREWING BUSHES OF LOVE

Beaver Brewing is one the newer brewers to hit Austria and it places just as much emphasis on traditional American food as on a modern take on brewing. This delicious and refreshing golden ale is given an extra element during brewing with the addition of hand-picked elderflowers from nearby Hollabrunn. The result is suitably floral, zingy and truly memorable.

TASTING NOTES: Elderflowers, rose hips and zesty West Coast US hops.
- **Country:** Austria
- **Brewer:** Beaver Brewing Co.
- **Style:** Golden ale
- **Appearance:** Yellow-gold
- **Alcohol:** 4.5%
- **Serving temp:** 4–7°C

▬ BEVOG KRAMAH IPA

This young Austrian microbrewer is hugely influenced by Great Britain and the traditional real ales, porters and IPAs that originated there. Kramah IPA takes the IPA style into the 21st century by using hops that are higher in alpha acids. These varieties are invariably fruitier and more aromatic than English hops and make for a vibrant citrus and tropical flavour.

TASTING NOTES: Fruity aromas of lychee, citrus and mango are carried on to the palate. Like biting into a juicy, boozy grapefruit!
- **Country:** Austria
- **Brewer:** Bevog Brewery
- **Style:** IPA
- **Appearance:** Clear amber
- **Alcohol:** 7%
- **Serving temp:** 4–7°C

▬ 1516 BLACK & TAN

Blending beers used to be extremely common and the practice is still alive and well in many places around Northern Europe. The 1516 Brewing Company brews a variety of interesting beers but is famous for this mixture of half blonde ale and half black ale which results in the best of both worlds. Rich yet citrus and roasted yet subtle. This is one for those who just can't decide what they want!

TASTING NOTES: Varies depending on the mix but caramel toffee and butter will always feature.
- **Country:** Austria
- **Brewer:** 1516 Brewing Co.
- **Style:** Blend
- **Appearance:** Amber
- **Alcohol:** 5%
- **Serving temp:** 4–7°C

PRIMÁTOR DOUBLE 24

The higher the Plato rating, the fuller the body of the beer. Here, the Plato scale rating is 24 and this well-balanced doppelbock does not disappoint. Very smooth and dark, with a turbocharged 10.5%, this beer is packed with flavours of prunes, caramel, brown bread and hints of honey. Sip it alongside a piece of barbecued meat to enjoy it at its best.

TASTING NOTES: Caramel, butter, prunes, hints of honey and a nice boozy hit of banana at the end.
- **Country:** Czech Republic
- **Brewer:** Pivovar Nachod
- **Style:** Doppelbock
- **Appearance:** Dark brown
- **Alcohol:** 10.5%
- **Serving temp:** 8–10°C

BERNARD CELEBRATION LAGER

The Bernard brewery was bought by three investors in 1991. It is an operation that oversees the ingredients of its beer from start to finish and it produces around 6,700 tons of Pilsner malt per year in its own malt house. Bernard Celebration Lager uses this excellent supply of malt and is one of the most-decorated beers in the country. The secret to its taste is the secondary fermentation it receives in the bottle so don't be surprised to find a light sediment in the bottom of your glass.

TASTING NOTES: Toasted grains, doughy bread-like note with a floral earthy hop aroma and dry bitter finish.
- **Country:** Czech Republic
- **Brewer:** Bernard
- **Style:** Pilsner • **Appearance:** Golden
- **Alcohol:** 5%
- **Serving temp:** 3–5°C

PILSNER URQUELL

The name Urquell in German translates to 'the original source' and that's exactly what this beer is in the world of brewing. The first Pilsner ever to be produced, approximately 90 per cent of the beer drunk in the world today is inspired by this original recipe. The inventor, Josef Groll, used large amounts of Saaz hops and the palest malts possible (in those days dark and smoked malts were the norm). The golden lager beer that resulted went on to become the most popular style in the world.

TASTING NOTES: Lots of earthy aromatics from the Saaz hops and a long-lasting trademark bitter finish.
- **Country:** Czech Republic
- **Brewer:** Plzensky Prazdroj
- **Style:** Pilsner
- **Appearance:** Golden yellow
- **Alcohol:** 4.4%
- **Serving temp:** 3–5°C

DID YOU KNOW?

The Czech Republic consumes more beer per capita than any other country in the world. The country drinks, on average, about 283 pints (161 litres) of beer per person each year.

🏴 STAROPRAMEN PREMIUM LAGER

The flagship product of the Staropramen brewery in Prague, this is one of the most famous beers to come out of the Czech Republic, being popular across much of Europe and the United Kingdom. The name Staropramen translates as 'old spring' and refers to the brewery's water source – an attribute it is fiercely proud of. Along with all the other Czech breweries, Staropramen was nationalized after World War II. It is now owned by brewing behemoth Molson Coors and has become the second most-popular beer in the Czech Republic.

TASTING NOTES: Delicately floral hops, light malt and a long bitter finish.
- **Country:** Czech Republic
- **Brewer:** Staropramen Breweries
- **Style:** Pale lager
- **Appearance:** Yellow
- **Alcohol** 5% • **Serving temp:** 3–5°C

🏴 BOHEMIA REGENT PREZIDENT

There can surely be no better place to drink a Pilsner than the Czech Republic and this classic example from Bohemia Regent will have any Czech-born beer lover weeping patriotically into his glass after one sip. Noted for its rich gold colour and extensive use of the locally grown Saaz hop, this crisp and bitter lager boasts a huge amount of flavour. The Regent brewery is one of the oldest in the world dating back to 1379, and now has a beerhouse in the courtyard, where you can drink the beers.

TASTING NOTES: Floral, earthy hop aromas from the Saaz hops and a freshly baked bread flavour on the palate.
- **Country:** Czech Republic
- **Brewer:** Bohemia Regent
- **Style:** Pilsner
- **Appearance:** Golden
- **Alcohol:** 6%
- **Serving temp:** 3–5°C

BUDWEISER BUDVAR

Not to be confused with the American Budweiser, this Czech Pilsner has been the subject of a trademark dispute for many years. The term Budweiser describes something (or someone) from the city of Budweis in Bohemia, which the company believes cannot apply to an American beer. However, Anheuser-Busch created their beer in the late 19th century, after a visit to Budweis.

TASTING NOTES: A wonderful Saaz hop aroma with grass, flowers and a slightly peppery note. Dominated by hops.
- **Country:** Czech Republic
- **Brewer:** Budejovický Budvar
- **Style:** Pilsner
- **Appearance:** Golden
- **Alcohol:** 5%
- **Serving temp:** 3–5°C

SVATY NORBERT IPA

An excellent example of what a modern India pale ale should taste like. Using two of the most flavoursome American hops, Amarillo and Cascade, the historic Strahov brewery has shown how it can move with the times. Closed in 1907 after a 600-year history, in 2000 it was reopened and refurbished to accommodate 350 people in its restaurant and brewhouse.

TASTING NOTES: Relatively mild-mannered with strong hints of orange blossom, perfumed hops and a very bitter finish.
- **Country:** Czech Republic
- **Brewer:** Klášterni Pivovar Strahov
- **Style:** IPA
- **Appearance:** Hazy amber
- **Alcohol:** 6.3%
- **Serving temp:** 4–7°C

MATUŠKA HELLCAT IMPERIAL IPA

Founded by Martin Matuska on Easter Monday 2009, the Matuska brewery is one of the more modern in the Czech Republic. The Hellcat Imperial IPA is a serious flavour bomb. With its use of American hops, big citrus flavours are achieved, including grapefruit, lemon peel and orange blossom. This heavy flavour profile is typical of the double IPA style, as is the refreshing green hoppy bitterness. This works fantastically well with jerk chicken to put out the fire.

TASTING NOTES: A range of tropical and citrus fruits, including tangerine, grapefruit, lemons and limes, with a toffee finish.
- **Country:** Czech Republic
- **Brewer:** Pivovar Matuška
- **Style:** Double IPA • **Appearance:** Hazy orange
- **Alcohol:** 8.4% • **Serving temp:** 4–7°C

🏴 BIRRIFICIO DI MONTEGIOCO RUNA

Often working alongside local farmers, bakers and cheesemongers, Birrificio di Montegioco takes a lot of influence from Belgium in its production and philosophy. It believes beer to be just as good as wine when it comes to food matching and it brews Runa with this in mind. Crisp and golden with hints of white bread, Runa is one of the more versatile beers to match food with.

TASTING NOTES: Bready notes with a nose of fresh pear, herbal hops and light apricot.
- **Country:** Italy
- **Brewer:** Birrificio di Montegioco
- **Style:** Belgian ale
- **Appearance:** Golden
- **Alcohol:** 4.8%
- **Serving temp:** 3–5°C

DID YOU KNOW?

Before becoming President, the young Václav Havel was a dissident playwright. Finding himself short of money he worked in a brewery, rolling barrels and filtering beer, and based an absurdist play on his experiences.

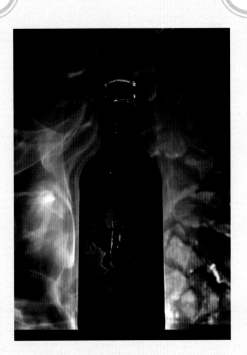

🏴 REVELATION CAT BLACK KNIGHT

Some of the most critically acclaimed beers in Italy come from the Revelation Cat brewery in Rome. With his evil-looking logo, Anglo-Italian head brewer Alex Liberati makes modern-style beers with big flavour and personality. This one is the first imperial stout from the brewery and was aged for one year before being bottled in 2012. The release is being staggered over three years as there are a limited number of this fantastically boozy creation. Be sure to age this one to mellow the flavours before drinking.

TASTING NOTES: Chocolate, cherries, bourbon and vanilla. Pours a thick, oily black with a dense, tan head.
- **Country:** Italy
- **Brewer:** Revelation Cat Craft Brewing
- **Style:** Imperial stout
- **Appearance:** Black
- **Alcohol:** 14%
- **Serving temp:** 12–16°C

▐▌ BIRRIFICIO INDIPENDENTE ELAV GRUNGE IPA ALLE PESCHE

The American IPA rears its head once again, this time in the heart of Northern Italy just outside of Milan. Elav brewery goes to great lengths to make a faithful rendition of the style but in this version it has also added fresh peaches to the mix to ensure a more obvious fruit overtone is apparent. Juicy, bold and delightfully different, this beer embodies the experimental spirit of Italy.

TASTING NOTES: Ripe peach, apricot and lemony citrus.
- **Country:** Italy
- **Brewer:** Birrificio Indipendente Elav
- **Style:** IPA
- **Appearance:** Orange
- **Alcohol:** 6.3%
- **Serving temp:** 4–7°C

▐▌ BIRRIFICIO DEL DUCATO SALLY BROWN

This young and thriving microbrewery is located in a small village in Parma province – home to the famous Parma ham and sparkling wines like Lambrusco. Taking its name from a Laurel Aitkins song, Sally Brown is a masterpiece, using a blend of 11 different malts all skilfully woven together into one smooth, complex beer.

TASTING NOTES: Comforting aromas of coffee, cocoa beans and campfires. Pair with dry smoked salmon or oysters.
- **Country:** Italy
- **Brewer:** Birrificio del Ducato
- **Style:** Stout
- **Appearance:** Ebony black
- **Alcohol:** 5.2%
- **Serving temp:** 8–13°C

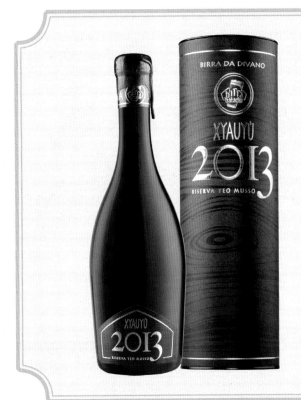

🇮🇹 XYAUYÙ

Open in 1996 as a brewpub, Baladin is today a farm brewery in the sleepy Italian village of Piozzo – opened by a local and a young French dancer. They brewed this superb barley wine in the spirit of experimentation to surprise their regulars with an unfamiliar taste and accidentally created one of the best – but least known – beers in all of Italy.

TASTING NOTES: Caramel, dates, banana, bread. Goes superbly well with aged cheese.
- **Country:** Italy
- **Brewer:** Baladin
- **Style:** Barley wine
- **Appearance:** Deep red
- **Alcohol:** 14%
- **Serving temp:** 8–13°C

🇮🇹 BIRRIFICIO ITALIANO TIPOPILS

Birrificio Italiano Tipopils is a simple, light and refreshing beer with no frills and no gimmicks. Sold as a Pilsner, the beer isn't matured for nearly as long as a standard lager – being bottle-ready in a little over two weeks after its primary fermentation. The short maturation means the flavours are strong, but uncomplicated.

TASTING NOTES: Sweet caramel, citrus hops and a dry bitter finish. Exactly what you want from a lager.
- **Country:** Italy
- **Brewer:** Birrificio Italiano
- **Style:** Pilsner
- **Appearance:** Clear yellow
- **Alcohol:** 5.2%
- **Serving temp:** 4–7°C

🇮🇹 CR/AK BREWING PERFECT CIRCLE

Another more experimental take on an American invention can be found in a tiny microbrewery just outside Venice. This area has become a hotbed of young breweries emulating and expanding upon beer styles from across the globe and one of them is CR/AK brewery with its formidable double IPA. An explosion of hops with the usual resinous pine and citrus is given a new lease of life with the introduction of agave nectar.

TASTING NOTES: Blood orange, butterscotch, sweet pink grapefruit and hints of spice.
- **Country:** Italy
- **Brewer:** CR/AK Brewing
- **Style:** Double IPA
- **Appearance:** Clear orange
- **Alcohol:** 7.5%
- **Serving temp:** 4–7°C

▮▮ BREWFIST 24K

A truly modern Italian brewery, Brewfist is rewriting the rules on beer within its home country. Founded in 2010, it has already built up a good core range: one of the most popular beers is this British-style golden ale, 24k. Rich in biscuit flavour and light citrus in the finish, it's one meant for drinking all evening.

TASTING NOTES: Biscuity malt, sweet and buttery with a note of honey. Pairs well with tempura prawns.
- **Country:** Italy
- **Brewer:** Brewfist
- **Style:** Golden ale
- **Appearance:** Golden
- **Alcohol:** 4.6%
- **Serving temp:** 4–7°C

▮▮ BARLEY BREWERY TOCCADIBÒ

Barley Brewery has been operating in Italy since 2006 and has become well known in its locale of Sardinia, specializing in modern twists on European classics and pairing beers with food with as much reverence as that accorded to wine. This strong golden ale is Belgian in style with the trademark Brussels lace and plenty of high alcohol notes.

TASTING NOTES: Apricots, peach and hints of chive with a very distinct touch of almond liqueur.
- **Country:** Italy
- **Brewer:** Barley Brewery
- **Style:** Golden strong ale
- **Appearance:** Golden
- **Alcohol:** 8.4%
- **Serving temp:** 4–7°C

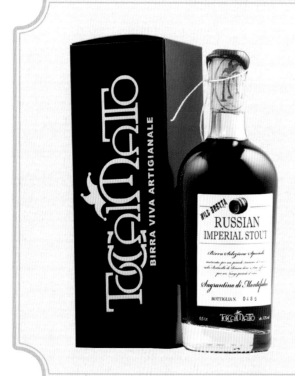

▮▮ TOCCALMATTO WILD BRETTA RUSSIAN IMPERIAL STOUT

A very special seasonal beer from the Toccalmatto brewery in Emilia-Romagna. Barrel-ageing is becoming more and more widespread in craft brewing, with high prices being paid for different ageing vessels. Whisky, bourbon and sherry casks have all become popular to impart flavour. The Wild Bretta Russian Imperial Stout is aged in barrels that previously contained a premium Italian wine made with 100 per cent Sagrantino grapes from the province of Perugia.

TASTING NOTES: Sherry, tannins, liquorice and vanilla. Superb with vanilla ice cream or as an all-evening beer. Serve just below room temperature.
- **Country:** Italy • **Brewer:** Toccalmatto
- **Style:** Imperial stout • **Appearance:** Black • **Alcohol:** 12%
- **Serving temp:** 13–16°C

▮▮ NASTRO AZZURRO PERONI

Peroni is certainly the most recognizable brand in the country, having been dominant since the 1960s. The name Nastro Azzurro means 'blue ribbon' in honour of the Blue Riband won by the Italian ocean liner SS *Rex* in 1933. Nastro Azzurro is the company's flagship premium lager and extremely successful worldwide – not just in its native Italy.

TASTING NOTES: Aromas of grass, malt and earthy hops with a lightly sweet, slightly metallic flavour.
- **Country:** Italy
- **Brewer:** Birra Peroni
- **Style:** Pale lager
- **Appearance:** Golden yellow
- **Alcohol:** 5.1%
- **Serving temp:** 1–2°C

▮▮ BIRRA DEL BORGO ETRUSCA

Owned by macrobrewers AB InBev, Birra del Borgo has taken brewing to new heights with this ancient style. Inspired by some of the earliest beers ever created, Etrusca is made with natural tree resins, honey and pomegranates as sugar sources and then left to ferment spontaneously in terracotta vessels. The end result is quite unlike any beer in the world and a true taste of the past.

TASTING NOTES: Ripe red fruits, sour cherry and hints of honey and heather.
- **Country:** Italy
- **Brewer:** Birra Del Borgo
- **Style:** Ancient amber
- **Appearance:** Amber
- **Alcohol:** 9.3%
- **Serving temp:** 10–13°C

▮▮ MENABREA 1846

Lots of beers pride themselves on using only four ingredients: barley, hops, yeast and water. Other grains like maize or rice can be added for extra sweetness or a lower cost and this is the case with Menabrea 1846. A fairly easy-going beer, its flavours do not dominate the palate, meaning it's good to drink as a session beer.

TASTING NOTES: Light flavours of malt, sweetcorn and a thin body. One to drink for refreshment rather than mind-blowing flavour.
- **Country:** Italy
- **Brewer:** Menabrea
- **Style:** Pale lager
- **Appearance:** Golden yellow
- **Alcohol:** 4.8%
- **Serving temp:** 1–2°C

DID YOU KNOW?

In the 4th century, the Roman Emperor Julian composed an epigram mocking the beer of the Celts and claiming that a wine-drinker smells of nectar while a beer-drinker smells like a goat!

▮▮ BAPBAP TOAST

BapBap brewery takes its production methods very seriously, being one of the few microbreweries that takes the extra step of milling its own grain. 'Brewed in Paris, drunk in Paris' is its byline and so everything is kept small batch. This is its version of an English porter and the brewery takes the trouble to import the finest East Kent Goldings hops to go alongside its blend of roasted malts. Light enough to drink as a session beer.

TASTING NOTES: Breakfast in a bottle. Golden toast and fresh coffee.
- **Country:** France
- **Brewer:** Brasserie BapBap
- **Style:** Porter
- **Appearance:** Black
- **Alcohol:** 4.5%
- **Serving temp:** 7–10°C

▌▌ METEOR PILS

With a nod to the aromatic and bitter qualities of Czech-style Pilsners, the Brasserie Meteor has created a fitting tribute to those historic beers in its own version – Meteor Pils. Made with the same Saaz hops that the Czechs use, the earthy yet lightly floral aroma makes it flavoursome while still being wonderfully refreshing – as golden lagers should be.

TASTING NOTES: Slightly sweeter than most Czech Pilsners but with the same bitter aftertaste and aroma.
- **Country:** France
- **Brewer:** Brasserie Meteor
- **Style:** Pilsner
- **Appearance:** Clear yellow
- **Alcohol:** 5%
- **Serving temp:** 1–2°C

▌▌ PANAME L'OEIL DE BICHE

The Belle Époque or 'Beautiful Era' was a period of optimism and peace in Western Europe at the end of the 19th century. However, there was at that time a small band of criminal outlaws known as the Apaches whose membership was marked by a tattoo known as the doe eyes or *l'oeil de biche*, after which Paname names its flagship pale ale!

TASTING NOTES: A blend of five American hops provides light refreshing citrus notes.
- **Country:** France
- **Brewer:** Paname Brewing Co.
- **Style:** Pale ale
- **Appearance:** Hazy straw
- **Alcohol:** 4.6%
- **Serving temp:** 4–7°C

▌▌ FROG WHITE LIGHT

A melding of beer styles is often a great way of innovating and many great beers are invented in such a way. White Light is a mixture of the classic Belgian style Witbier or bierre blanche and the powerful hoppy notes of an American IPA. The result is smoother than an IPA with a softer body but with all the interesting hoppy flavours so beloved by the Americans.

TASTING NOTES: Herbal, smooth, light banana and tropical fruits in the finish.
- **Country:** France
- **Brewer:** Frog Brewery
- **Style:** White IPA
- **Appearance:** Hazy yellow
- **Alcohol:** 4.7%
- **Serving temp:** 4–7°C

▐▐ KRONENBOURG 1664

France's bestselling beer by a long way and the second-biggest premium lager across the channel in the United Kingdom. Kronenbourg 1664 is made from malted barley, malted wheat and maize for extra sweetness, and one of the few hops that grow in the Alsace region: Strisselspalt. This earthy hop gives the beer its distinct aroma. Caramel colouring is added for extra depth in the appearance.

TASTING NOTES: Moderate flavours of corn, malt and hints of toasted grain. Serve ice cold.

- **Country:** France
- **Brewer:** Kronenbourg
- **Style:** Pale lager
- **Appearance:** Yellow
- **Alcohol:** 5.5%
- **Serving temp:** 1–2°C

▐▐ DENISE PALE ALE

As 'Brasseurs du Grand Paris', Anthony and Fabrice created their first beers in a makeshift brewery on the fifth floor of an office block and wherever they could find space in other breweries. They now finally have their own permanent brewery and have officially become Brasserie du Grand Paris. This is their fruity APA which was originally brewed at Brasserie Rabourdin in their days as fledgling gypsy brewers.

TASTING NOTES: Toffee popcorn, lemon peel and a hint of spicy meadow hops.

- **Country:** France
- **Brewer:** Brasserie du Grand Paris
- **Style:** APA
- **Appearance:** Hazy yellow
- **Alcohol:** 5.5%
- **Serving temp:** 4–7°C

▐▐ DECK & DONOHUE INDIGO IPA

Many a friendship was formed over beer. Mike Donohue and Thomas Deck met in the beer-rich environment of Georgetown University, Washington. After over a decade of experimenting in the United States, the pair crossed the Atlantic to set up Deck & Donohue in 2013 and never looked back – except perhaps when they made this typically American IPA!

TASTING NOTES: Tropical fruit aromas, peachy on the palate and delightfully bitter.

- **Country:** France
- **Brewer:** Deck & Donohue
- **Style:** IPA
- **Appearance:** Amber
- **Alcohol:** 6.5%
- **Serving temp:** 4–7°C

▌▌ 3 MONTS

The *bière de garde* (literally a 'beer for keeping') style of beer was originally brewed in French farmhouses during the colder months and kept until summer, when farmworkers would drink it as payment or part payment. The reason for this long storage was because it was so difficult to brew in summer, when higher temperatures had an unpredictable effect on yeast. The long maturation period allows the beer to develop pronounced flavours.

TASTING NOTES: Freshly baked white bread in both taste and aroma. Wonderfully simple and perfect with cheese and ham.
- **Country:** France
- **Brewer:** Brasserie de St Sylvestre
- **Style:** Bière de garde
- **Appearance:** Clear gold
- **Alcohol:** 8.5% • **Serving temp:** 4–7°C

▌▌ BRASSERIE LA GOUTTE D'OR CHÂTEAU ROUGE

Opening in late 2012, Brasserie La Goutte d'Or was one of the first breweries in Paris for several years. Located deep in the African quarter of Paris, it likes to add flavour to its beers with the addition of unconventional ingredients – in the case of Château Rouge, chilli peppers. The spice flavour adds character without being overwhelming as well as a slight sweetness that only pepper can give.

TASTING NOTES: Caramel and red fruits with hints of spice and herbs.
- **Country:** France
- **Brewer:** Brasserie La Goutte d'Or
- **Style:** Chilli beer
- **Appearance:** Deep mahogany
- **Alcohol:** 6.5%
- **Serving temp:** 7–10°C

▌▌ CASTELAIN CH'TI AMBRÉE

Another *bière de garde*, but Ch'ti Ambrée is a little different to the 3 Monts. Slightly lower in alcohol but still with bags of flavour, it demonstrates the variety in French farmhouse ales. This amber-coloured *bière de garde* bears a strong resemblance to the saison beers of Belgium but has a much more pronounced malt profile over the yeast.

TASTING NOTES: Strong flavours of toffee, caramel and brown bread. Good with a hard, mature cheese.
- **Country:** France
- **Brewer:** Brasserie Castelain
- **Style:** Bière de garde
- **Appearance:** Amber
- **Alcohol:** 5.9%
- **Serving temp:** 7–9°C

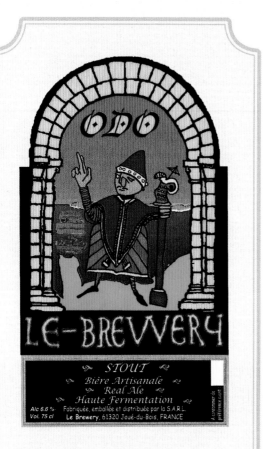

■■ BELZEBUTH PUR MALT

Named after the devil himself, this beer varies in alcohol content depending on which batch you are drinking but it never strays much below 12% – it is devilishly strong. Depending on which year it was brewed it may be labelled Pur Malt, Blonde or Extra Strong. The Grain d'Orge brewery just can't seem to make up its mind on this one.

TASTING NOTES: Devilish flavours of warming brandy, honey and faint traces of elderflower.
- **Country:** France
- **Brewer:** Brasserie Grain d'Orge
- **Style:** Belgian strong ale
- **Appearance:** Amber
- **Alcohol:** 13%
- **Serving temp:** 8–13°C

■■ LE BREWERY ODO

It would be fair to say the French and the English have had a slightly chequered history. In Le Brewery's Odo, though, the two countries meet to superb effect. The milk stout style made popular by the English in the years following World War I is done extremely well by the Normandy-based brewery founded by Englishman Steve Skews in 2001.

TASTING NOTES: Sweet, creamy chocolate with hints of coffee, milk and light liquorice.
- **Country:** France
- **Brewer:** Le Brewery
- **Style:** Milk stout
- **Appearance:** Dark ruby
- **Alcohol:** 6.6%
- **Serving temp:** 8–13°C

DID YOU KNOW?

In his book *Studies on Fermentation* in 1876, French chemist Louis Pasteur revolutionized the scientific understanding of the beer-making process, changing the course of brewing and paving the way for modern brewers.

🇨🇭 BFM √225 SAISON

The Belgian saison style is not necessarily the most popular in the world but when done properly it has a taste you'll never forget. BFM, the Brasserie des Franches-Montagnes, makes one of the most perfect examples you'll ever try. Extremely refreshing with tart apple, pear and grape flavours, it pairs well with almost any food but especially a simple loaf of bread and soft cheese.

TASTING NOTES: Slightly sour with yeasty, lemony and floral notes in the aroma.
- **Country:** Switzerland
- **Brewer:** BFM
- **Style:** Saison
- **Appearance:** Clear gold
- **Alcohol:** 5%
- **Serving temp:** 4–7°C

🇨🇭 1936 BIÈRE

Set in the spectacular surroundings of the Swiss Alps, 1936 is a family-run brewery with a close eye on its environmental impact. Taking water from a beautifully pure source in the Alps, malt grown at 1,650 metres/5,400 feet above sea level and organic hops, this is pale lager with a touch of class.

TASTING NOTES: Lemony citrus hops, with a pale malt taste to match and a nice bitter finish.
- **Country:** Switzerland
- **Brewer:** 1936 Bière
- **Style:** Premium lager
- **Appearance:** Gold
- **Alcohol:** 4.7%
- **Serving temp:** 2–5°C

🇨🇭 TROIS DAMES SAISON HOUBLON

The best saisons are thirst-quenchers at heart and are always fermented at slightly higher ambient temperatures than normal ales in line with their history. Trois Dames has added an extra dimension to this version by dry hopping – thereby increasing the aromatic qualities to complement the slightly spicier elements achieved by ambient fermentation. This is one of the best saisons you'll ever try.

TASTING NOTES: Herbaceous and spicy with a more pronounced citrus edge than normal for this style.
- **Country:** Switzerland
- **Brewer:** Brasserie Trois Dames
- **Style:** Saison
- **Appearance:** Golden
- **Alcohol:** 6.8%
- **Serving temp:** 4–7°C

🇨🇭 LOCHER APPENZELLER HANFBLÜTE

As well as hops, the brewers at Locher add a close relative of hops, hemp. Using both the flowers and leaves from this pungent plant imparts aromas of ginger, pepper and spice as well as the distinctive aroma of hemp.

TASTING NOTES: Hemp aromas, hemp flavours, with hints of chilli, ginger and other spices thrown in for good measure.
- **Country:** Switzerland
- **Brewer:** Brauerei Locher
- **Style:** Hemp beer
- **Appearance:** Yellow orange
- **Alcohol:** 5.2%
- **Serving temp:** 8–10°C

DID YOU KNOW?

The Swiss have the highest concentration of breweries per capita in the world; however, they are moderate drinkers and consider it tacky to become drunk.

OKULT NO.1 BLANCHE

A tribute to the Belgian witbier style revived by Pierre Celis at Hoegaarden in the 1960s, Okult No.1 Blanche is laced with fragrances of orange peel and coriander and is brewed with pale wheat instead of barley. The beer uses 100 per cent organically farmed ingredients. Look out for its hazy light-yellow appearance – there is yeast still in the bottle.

TASTING NOTES: Zesty citrus aromas, bitter orange blossom and a light spice towards the end.
- **Country:** Luxembourg
- **Brewer:** Brasserie Simon
- **Style:** Witbier
- **Appearance:** Hazy yellow
- **Alcohol:** 5.4%
- **Serving temp:** 4–7°C

OEDIPUS THAI THAI

The wacky brewing professors at Oedipus brewery give their zany take on the beloved Belgian tripel style. Belgian beers are noted for the addition of extra ingredients and coriander, citrus zest and peppercorns can be quite common. Oedipus takes this a step further with galangal, chilli flakes and orange to create a Belgian tripel like no other.

TASTING NOTES: Spice from the chilli, softer heat from the galangal with orange blossom and floral rose hips.
- **Country:** The Netherlands
- **Brewer:** Oedipus
- **Style:** Tripel
- **Appearance:** Dark yellow
- **Alcohol:** 8%
- **Serving temp:** 4–7°C

DE MOLEN HEL & VERDOEMENIS

De Molen's Hel & Verdoemenis (literally translating to 'Hell and Damnation') is a Belgian-style imperial stout. Brewed to a strength similar to the stouts that were exported to Russia from London in the 18th and 19th centuries, this super flavoursome stout is one of the crown jewels of De Molen's highly-rated selection. Like many artisanal breweries, the first brews were made in head brewer Menno Olivier's kitchen and then, after a year, in his garage. These humble beginnings soon gave way to some of the best beers in all of Europe.

TASTING NOTES: Lots of sweet chocolate malt with spices, smoke and a hint of peat. Great with a berry dessert.
- **Country:** The Netherlands
- **Brewer:** Brouwerij de Molen
- **Style:** Imperial stout
- **Appearance:** Red/brown
- **Alcohol:** 10% • **Serving temp:** 8–13°C

AMSTEL LAGER

One of the more famous brands of the Netherlands, Amstel Lager was first brewed in Amsterdam in 1870 and is named after the Amstel River. As well as giving this beer its name, the Amstel River also provided refrigeration as brewers used the winter ice build-up to keep their purpose-built double-walled cellars cold enough for lagering.

TASTING NOTES: Pale malt flavours with hints of canned sweetcorn and light crisp hops.
- **Country:** The Netherlands
- **Brewer:** Amstel Brouwerij
- **Style:** Pale lager
- **Appearance:** Pale yellow
- **Alcohol:** 5%
- **Serving temp:** 2–3°C

DID YOU KNOW?

A beer called Kwispelbier, advertised as 'a beer for your best friend' and made with beef extract and malt, was created by pet-shop owner Gerrie Berendsen for her dogs to enjoy after hunting.

HEINEKEN

A dominant worldwide brand, this is the bestselling beer in all of the Netherlands. When the papers announced the end of Prohibition in America, a shipload of Heineken was sent across the Atlantic to wait patiently off the East Coast until 5pm on April 11, 1933. After a 14-year wait, the Americans could finally taste Heineken again – just after they clocked off work for the day.

TASTING NOTES: Pale malt imparts a light white breadiness in the aroma. Low hop bitterness.
- **Country:** The Netherlands
- **Brewer:** Heineken Nederland
- **Style:** Pale lager
- **Appearance:** Golden
- **Alcohol:** 5%
- **Serving temp:** 2–3°C

LA TRAPPE QUADRUPEL

De Koningshoeven is one of only two Trappist breweries outside of Belgium. La Trappe Quadrupel is the strongest in its range at 10% and gets its banana and almond-like aromas from its second fermentation, which happens after it is bottled. Consequently, the longer you keep this in the cellar the more it matures and the flavours develop. Serve this wonderful beer at cellar temperature with a dense sweet dessert like a plum pudding with crème anglaise.

TASTING NOTES: Ripe, boozy plums, with sweet spices, hints of cinnamon and big caramel malt backbone.
- **Country:** The Netherlands
- **Brewer:** De Koningshoeven
- **Style:** Quadrupel
- **Appearance:** Cloudy amber
- **Alcohol:** 10%
- **Serving temp:** 8–10°C

GROLSCH PREMIUM LAGER

The Grolsch Brewery is the second largest in all of the Netherlands (after Heineken) with more than three million hectolitres brewed every year. The name Grolsch literally means 'of Grolle' – the name of the town where Grolsch was first brewed. Its premium lager is its flagship product and is often sold in the old-fashioned swing-top bottles.

TASTING NOTES: Toasted grains, brown bread with a sweet malt aftertaste. Crisp and clean on the palate.
- **Country:** The Netherlands
- **Brewer:** Grolsch Brewery
- **Style:** Premium lager
- **Appearance:** Pale yellow
- **Alcohol:** 5%
- **Serving temp:** 2–3°C

DID YOU KNOW?

In 1983, brewery heir Alfred 'Freddy' Heineken, was kidnapped for three weeks until a ransom of 35 million Dutch guilders was paid. A Hollywood film version of the events was released in 2015.

GARAGE BEER CO. W.A.R

Started by an expat Englishman and an Italian ex-marketing manager, Garage Beer Co. is situated slap in the middle of Barcelona and offers a taproom with eight handles, a seasonal programme and some of the finest beer Spain has to offer. This Mojito Berliner Weisse fuses fresh mint, limes and redcurrants to a malt bill that's heavy on wheat.

TASTING NOTES: Lightly sour with hints of mint and rosewater and citrus.
- **Country:** Spain
- **Brewer:** Garage Beer Co.
- **Style:** Berliner Weisse
- **Appearance:** Ruby
- **Alcohol:** 5.1%
- **Serving temp:** 3–5°C

CRUZCAMPO

Founded by Roberto and Agustin Osborne in 1904, the Cruzcampo brewery was named after the La Cruz del Campo (The Cross of the Field), which still stands in a nearby field. It is the biggest beer producer in Spain and this 4.8% lager is the flagship product of the brewery. Like many other brewers, it uses the legendary brewing king Gambrinus on its logo.

TASTING NOTES: Slightly metallic with hints of corn, peppery hops and a very slight fruity note.
- **Country:** Spain
- **Brewer:** Cruzcampo
- **Style:** Pale lager
- **Appearance:** Pale yellow
- **Alcohol:** 4.8%
- **Serving temp:** 2–3°C

DOUGALL'S 942 IPA

The craft beer revolution that swept America is still young in Spain. But nevertheless a growing proportion of the country's beer producers are taking influence from across the pond. DouGall's brewery is one such producer. This modern American-style IPA is hard to find in Spain unless you visit the brewery pub in Liérganes near Santander.

TASTING NOTES: Grapefruit aroma with a caramel note to match. Well balanced with a long and very bitter finish.
- **Country:** Spain
- **Brewer:** DouGall's
- **Style:** IPA
- **Appearance:** Deep gold
- **Alcohol:** 7%
- **Serving temp:** 4–7°C

🏳 NÔMADA TU JARDÍN

Nômada Brewing likes to challenge the status quo with all of its beers, rarely sticking to well-tried commercial styles and favouring the unusual. Tu Jardín is a saison with a twist in that blackberries and rose petals are added to the beer post-fermentation to give an extra floral and slightly juicy fruit note. Quite a unique beer and unlike any other in this book.

TASTING NOTES: Lychee, blackberry and herbal hops.
- **Country:** Spain
- **Brewer:** Nômada Brewing Co.
- **Style:** Saison
- **Appearance:** Caramel
- **Alcohol:** 7.2%
- **Serving temp:** 4–6°C

🏳 REINA ORO

Not a beer often found in mainland Spain, Reina Oro is most often found in the Canary Islands where tourists and locals quaff it down for its refreshing and thirst-quenching qualities. A standard pale lager in every respect, it has a few characteristics of a German-style Pilsner with slight bready overtones and little hop aroma.

TASTING NOTES: Light and slightly bready malt flavours with only a hint of bitterness at the end.
- **Country:** Spain
- **Brewer:** Cervezas Anaga
- **Style:** Pale lager
- **Appearance:** Pale yellow
- **Alcohol:** 5.5%
- **Serving temp:** 2–3°C

DID YOU KNOW?

Gambrinus is a legendary European culture hero celebrated as an icon of beer and brewing. Traditional songs, poems and stories describe him as a king, duke or count of Flanders and Brabant.

🏳 LAUGAR FIBONATXI 0

The first in their artisanal and slightly more experimental range, Fibonatxi 0 takes the idea of a saison and turns it on its head. The addition of rye malt for a spice kick is accentuated even more by infusing the wort with ginger. The dry finish is akin to ginger ale whilst remaining very much a farmhouse-style beer which is bursting with refreshing citrus tones.

TASTING NOTES: Ginger spice, hints of anise and lemon.
- **Country:** Spain
- **Brewer:** Laugar
- **Style:** Ginger saison
- **Appearance:** Cloudy orange
- **Alcohol:** 4.9%
- **Serving temp:** 3–5°C

≡ SKOVLYST BØGEBRYG BROWN ALE

If you ever get bored with the conventional beers of the world, remember to try BøgeBryg Brown Ale. Translating as 'Beech Brew', this American-style brown ale is unusual because of the addition of beech wood twigs from the nearby forest, which impart a woodsmoke aroma.

TASTING NOTES: Floral hops, smoky campfire and roasted toffee. Eat with a nutty aged Gouda cheese or smoky grilled lamb.
- **Country:** Denmark
- **Brewer:** Bryggeri Skovlyst
- **Style:** Brown ale
- **Appearance:** Deep brown
- **Alcohol:** 5.2%
- **Serving temp:** 8–13°C

≡ EVIL TWIN EVEN MORE JESUS

Imperial stouts are a favourite among craft beer enthusiasts. Famous for their huge flavour profiles, their thick, viscous texture and high alcohol content, beers like Evil Twin's Even More Jesus can be intimidating. Beers like this should be treated more like fine wine. Sip slowly and make them last.

TASTING NOTES: Toffee, chocolate fudge and a hefty whack of coffee compete with alcohol and muscovado sugar.
- **Country:** Denmark
- **Brewer:** Westbrook Brewing
- **Style:** Imperial stout
- **Appearance:** Black
- **Alcohol:** 12%
- **Serving temp:** 8–13°C

≡ FUGLSANG HVID BOCK

Bock is a style of beer that has long been associated with times of celebration – particularly religious festivals. During long periods of fasting, Bavarian monks would use this strong, flavoursome lager as a form of nourishment to stave off a rumbling belly. Though bocks are usually very dark, this one is brewed with light malt from Fuglsang's own maltings.

TASTING NOTES: Doughy flavours with aromas of proving bread and toasted grains. Great with Mexican cuisine.
- **Country:** Denmark
- **Brewer:** Bryggeriet S.C. Fuglsang
- **Style:** Bock
- **Appearance:** Hazy honey
- **Alcohol:** 7.6%
- **Serving temp:** 4–7°C

🇩🇰 MIKKELLER
BEER GEEK BREAKFAST

Mikkeller has two loves: beer and coffee. As well as its Koppi (coffee IPA) and its Beer Geek Brunch Weasel, the beer it is most famous for is the Beer Geek Breakfast. Brewed with oats for that silky smooth texture and a good helping of the brewer's favourite coffee, this one is guaranteed to wake you up with a bang. It uses a complex blend of malts – Pilsner, oat, smoked, caramunich, brown, and two types of chocolate malt – and roasted barley and flaked oats also make an appearance.

TASTING NOTES: Espresso aromas, lightly smoky with a pleasant and interesting pine resin hop flavour on the palate. Drink with (or for) breakfast.

- **Country:** Denmark • **Brewer:** Mikkeller
- **Style:** Stout
- **Appearance:** Deep brown
- **Alcohol:** 7.5% • **Serving temp:** 8–13°C

HORNBEER THE FUNDAMENTAL BLACKHORN

Hornbeer brews every beer with artistry. This supercharged imperial stout has been given a heavier dose of hops than is usual for the style. It is then aged in walnut and oak casks. A powerful flavour profile of liquorice and dark chocolate, with hints of oak and honey, awaits you in every bottle.

TASTING NOTES: Try this one with rich chocolate desserts, vanilla ice cream or aged blue cheese.
- **Country:** Denmark
- **Brewer:** Westbrook Brewing
- **Style:** Imperial stout
- **Appearance:** Black
- **Alcohol:** 11%
- **Serving temp:** 8–13°C

NØRREBRO BRYGHUS RAVNSBORG ROD

Beginning its brewing story in 2003, the Nørrebro Bryghus was founded by an ex-brewmaster of Carlsberg. With an established reputation for brewing a wide variety of American-influenced beers, the brewery has grown to become a sizeable regional brewer. This classic British-style red ale is given the American treatment with spicy Amarillo hops and lots of dark roasted malt.

Tasting notes: Dark fruits, lots of spice and warm caramels.
Country: Denmark
Brewer: Nørrebro Bryghus
Style: Red ale
Appearance: Red
Alcohol: 5.5%
Serving temp: 10–13°C

TO ØL LIQUID CONFIDENCE

To Øl brewery's founders were dreaming of better beers while they were still studying their ABCs in high school back in 2005. Tore Gynther and Tobias Emil Jensen might not have their own premises yet, preferring instead to stick to gypsy brewing, but they have certainly proved they know what they're doing with this chilli-infused imperial stout.

TASTING NOTES: Ancho and chipotle chillies give this chocolatey stout an interesting kick.
- **Country:** Denmark
- **Brewer:** To Øl
- **Style:** Imperial stout
- **Appearance:** Black
- **Alcohol:** 12.2%
- **Serving temp:** 10–13°C

🇩🇰 ØRBÆK FYNSK FORÅR

On first taste, you could be forgiven for thinking that Ørbæk Fynsk Forår was a strange type of shandy. Brewed with elderflowers, a fragrant sweetness is revealed. Freshly pressed apple notes appear with hints of cider – you'll have to double check the label to make sure it's definitely a beer you just opened.

TASTING NOTES: Concentrated elderflower flavours in both the aroma and taste, with hints of fermented apple.
• **Country:** Denmark
• **Brewer:** Ørbæk Bryggeri
• **Style:** Blonde ale
• **Appearance:** Cloudy yellow
• **Alcohol:** 5%
• **Serving temp:** 4–7°C

🇩🇰 AMAGER WOOKIEE IPA

Founded by a couple of homebrewers in 2007, the Amager brewery is named for the island it sits on which is south of central Copenhagen. Collaborating with Port Brewing from California, it has produced this potent West Coast IPA. Creaking with hops including Sorachi Ace for a herbal touch, this is a beer only for true hopheads.

TASTING NOTES: Marmalade jam, ripe red fruits and a butterscotch malt base.
• **Country:** Denmark
• **Brewer:** Amager Bryghus
• **Style:** IPA
• **Appearance:** Light amber
• **Alcohol:** 7.2%
• **Serving temp:** 4–7°C

🇩🇰 WARPIGS KICKED TO SLEEP

Warpigs Brewpub offers authentic Texas barbecue food in the middle of Copenhagen! This smokehouse and brewery is a joint venture between local heroes Mikkeller and American brewery Three Floyds. Kicked to Sleep is one of the crown jewels of their brewing venture. Thick, dark and savoury – it goes superbly with smoky ribs.

TASTING NOTES: Hints of marzipan, butterscotch and dark burnt sugars.
• **Country:** Denmark
• **Brewer:** Warpigs Brewpub
• **Style:** Imperial stout
• **Appearance:** Black
• **Alcohol:** 11.5%
• **Serving temp:** 10–13°C

⚏ BREWSKI MANGOFEBER DIPA

Despite being the first-ever brew produced by the good folks at Brewski Brewery, this mango-infused imperial IPA uses a recipe that continues to be refined and improved upon. Brimming with tropical fruit flavours and sweet, ripe sticky mango, this is not for the faint of heart – it's strictly for hop lovers only. Enjoy with some pineapple upside-down cake.

TASTING NOTES: Overly ripe mango with boozy fruit flavours and pine resin.
- **Country**: Sweden
- **Brewer**: Brewski
- **Style**: Double IPA
- **Appearance**: Hazy orange
- **Alcohol**: 8%
- **Serving temp**: 4–7°C

⚏ OMNIPOLLO NOA PECAN MUD CAKE – BOURBON

Henok Fentie, head brewer at Omnipollo, used to harbour dreams of being a pastry chef, and this decadent, sweet imperial stout is by his own admission a slight nod to what could have been. Overtly flavoured with chocolate, coffee and nutty sweetness, this childhood dessert in a bottle is then aged on well-seasoned bourbon barrels for an extra hit of booze and spice.

TASTING NOTES: Marmalade jam, ripe red fruits and a butterscotch malt base.
- **Country:** Sweden
- **Brewer:** Omnipollo
- **Style:** Imperial stout
- **Appearance:** Dark brown
- **Alcohol:** 12%
- **Serving temp:** 10–13°C

⚏ CARNEGIE STARK PORTER

Carnegie Porter was first brewed in 1836 and is officially the oldest registered trademark still in use today. There are two versions: one at 3.5% and this Stark ('strong') version. It has true national status in the same way Guinness does in Ireland. Currently owned and brewed by Carlsberg Sverige, there are plans alongside Brooklyn Brewery in the USA to open a microbrewery in the Hammarby area in Sweden to make this beer.

TASTING NOTES: Chocolate, bitter coffee and toffee. The flavour mellows as it ages so try to cellar a bottle if possible.
- **Country:** Sweden
- **Brewer:** Carlsberg Sverige
- **Style:** Porter
- **Appearance:** Dark brown
- **Alcohol:** 5.5%
- **Serving temp:** 8–13°C

≡≡ NILS OSCAR GOD LAGER

The Nils Oscar brewery is named after a young Swede who in the 19th century travelled to America four or five times to learn farming and agricultural skills. His Swedish farming empire is managed by his descendants today and they grow the oats, wheat and barley that go into this beautiful golden lager. A genuinely traditional Swedish product from grain to bottle.

TASTING NOTES: Pure, unadulterated liquid bread in a bottle. Goes nicely with any food you throw at it.
- **Country:** Sweden
- **Brewer:** Nils Oscar
- **Style:** Helles
- **Appearance:** Golden
- **Alcohol:** 5.3%
- **Serving temp:** 4–7°C

≡≡ STIGBERGETS AMAZING HAZE

One of the rising stars of Swedish brewing, Stigbergets has been making serious waves since its arrival on the Gothenburg beer scene in 2012. Amazing Haze is the flagship beer of the brewery, not only selling huge amounts in its native Sweden but also across the sea in Western Europe. Hop forward in attitude and insanely drinkable for a 6.5% beer.

TASTING NOTES: Moderate to heavy hops with peach and light pineapple and some tropical notes.
Country: Sweden
Brewer: Stigbergets Bryggeri
Style: IPA
Appearance: Hazy yellow
ABV: 6.5%
Serving temp: 4–7°C

DID YOU KNOW?

The Swedish government has a monopoly on alcohol sales – only Systembolaget outlets are allowed to sell spirits, wine and full-strength beer, and they are only open certain hours and not on Sundays.

≡≡ NORRLANDS GULD EXPORT

One of the most popular beers in Sweden and one instantly recognizable to any Swedish native, Norrlands Guld is advertised as the beer for the most laid-back people. The principal on-screen advocate since the early 1990s is the relaxed Ingemar, who comes from the peaceful Norrland province. A classic pale lager.

TASTING NOTES: Light malt, toasted grains and an easy-going crisp finish. A drink free from all pretension.
- **Country:** Sweden
- **Brewer:** Spendrups Bryggeri
- **Style:** Pale lager
- **Appearance:** Golden
- **Alcohol:** 5.3%
- **Serving temp:** 4–7°C

🇸🇪 JÄMTLANDS HELL

If you want to brew a truly great beer, ask the people who drink the most for some help. This premium lager was made in collaboration with two pubs – The Akkurat and the Oliver Twist – in the heart of Stockholm. Undoubtedly the crown jewel of the Jämtlands collection, it packs more flavour than all the other lagers in Sweden put together. Highly hopped for maximum bitterness without going overboard. Serve with flash-fried chilli-flecked squid or mild cheddar to get the full, crisp cleansing effect.

TASTING NOTES: Aromatic hops, dried fruit and bitter orange in the nose. Bitter hops, honey and citrus on the tongue. Perfect lager.
- **Country:** Sweden
- **Brewer:** Jämtlands Bryggeri
- **Style:** Lager
- **Appearance:** Medium orange
- **Alcohol:** 5.1%
- **Serving temp:** 8–10°C

🇸🇪 NYNÄSHAMNS BÖTET BARLEY WINE JAMAICAN RUM CASK

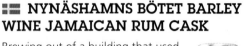

Brewing out of a building that used to supply electricity and power to the entire region, the Nynäshamns brewery uses the same region to name most of its beers. A boat trip around the local coastline will take you past the names of every beer in the portfolio. The added time this barley wine gets in Jamaican rum casks gives an extra intensity of banana, clove and oak spice.

TASTING NOTES: Heavy on caramel and vanilla, with dark oak and sticky figs.
- **Country:** Sweden
- **Brewer:** Nynäshamns Ångbryggeri AB
- **Style:** Barley wine
- **Appearance:** Dark ruby
- **Alcohol:** 11%
- **Serving temp:** 10–13°C

🇸🇪 DUGGES JASMINE DRAGON

Brewery founder Mikael Dugge Engström takes inspiration for his beers from all over the world. In 2014 he went on a trip to China and brought back to the brewery a bag of jasmine flowers, used mostly for tea in the East. Whole blossom flowers were then added to the brew in much the same way hops are used to create a unique and floral flavour.

TASTING NOTES: Orange blossom, subtle parma violets and perfume.
- **Country:** Sweden
- **Brewer:** Dugges Bryggeri
- **Style:** Sour
- **Appearance:** Hazy orange
- **Alcohol:** 3.5%
- **Serving temp:** 3–5°C

⬛ HANSA BORG BAYER

Dunkel ('dark') is the term used to describe many types of dark German-style beers. They are typically brewed using dark Munich malts, a proportion of which may have been boiled to a higher temperature to extract more starch and impart a deeper malty flavour. This is a classic example of the style from the Hansa Borg brewery.

TASTING NOTES: Deep, sweet salty caramel and roasted malt. Liquorice flavours dominate the finish.
- **Country:** Norway
- **Brewer:** Hansa Borg Bryggerier
- **Style:** Dunkel lager
- **Appearance:** Dark amber
- **Alcohol:** 4.5%
- **Serving temp:** 4–7°C

⬛ HAANDBRYGGERIET HAANDBUKK

Brewed several years before its release, the first batch of Haandbukk spent several years ageing in oak barrels to intensify and add extra complexity. After initially using a fairly conventional base yeast strain, as it's added to the barrel several wild yeasts are introduced to impart sourness in the style of the Flemish reds popularized in Belgium.

TASTING NOTES: Lots of interesting wild oaky aromas with a vinous, tart and sour flavour.
- **Country:** Norway
- **Brewer:** Haandbryggeriet
- **Style:** Flemish red
- **Appearance:** Dark mahogany
- **Alcohol:** 8%
- **Serving temp:** 7–10°C

DID YOU KNOW?

The Norse word 'beserk' means 'bare shirt' and comes from the Viking habit of stopping mid-battle for a beer break, drinking huge quantities, and then returning to fight without their armour or shirts!

⬛ KINN JULEFRED

Christmas beers are especially common in Scandinavia and here we have a fine example. Julefred ('Christmas peace') is brewed every year and always to a slightly different recipe, ranging from 4.5% to 6.7%. Often very spice-led, Kinn's Julefred is subtle in its use of spice, with dark fruit and caramel taking the lead. A consistently well-made Christmas seasonal.

TASTING NOTES: Raisins, plums and dried figs with hints of coffee, candy sugar and butterscotch
- **Country:** Norway
- **Brewer:** Kinn Bryggeri
- **Style:** Christmas seasonal ale
- **Appearance:** Hazy brown
- **Alcohol:** 6.5%
- **Serving temp:** 8–10°C

🇳🇴 AASS BOCK

As one of the only breweries left in the region of Drammen, Norway, the Aass brewery takes its responsibility very seriously. In its humble beginnings in 1834, it sold beer with no packaging to people who brought along their own bins or buckets to fill up. Aass Bock is a dark strong lager and one of the closest things to a pint of liquid brown bread you can drink. Strong, doughy and versatile – it pairs well with a wide range of foods.

TASTING NOTES: Doughy brown bread and yeast aromas. Very comforting and warming to drink.
- **Country:** Norway
- **Brewer:** Aass Bryggeri
- **Style:** Bock
- **Appearance:** Deep red
- **Alcohol:** 6.5%
- **Serving temp:** 4–7°C

🇳🇴 LERVIG/WAY BEER 3 BEAN STOUT

Lervig has fast become one of the most championed brewers in Norway putting together many a collaborative beer with friends to be sold alongside its core range. Way Beer is based in Brazil and during a trip to Norway the brewers brought with them three type of beans – Vanilla, Cocoa and Tonka, which add a huge array of diverse flavours to this imperial stout. Goes well with porridge!

TASTING NOTES: Vanilla, cinnamon and crème brûlée with hints of chocolate.
- **Country:** Norway
- **Brewer:** Lervig/Way Beer
- **Style:** Imperial stout
- **Appearance:** Black
- **Alcohol:** 13%
- **Serving temp:** 10–13°C

🇳🇴 ABC BREWING HENRIK IMPERIAL AMBER

One of the most legendary gypsy brewers in Norway! After homebrewing for over 25 years, Gahr Smith-Gahrsen and Kim Odland decided to take the plunge and begin commercially cuckooing at several breweries around Norway. This imperial amber style was brewed with their good friends at Lervig brewery but the recipe is all theirs. A cross between an American amber and a double IPA – this is not for the faint of heart.

TASTING NOTES: Salted caramel with hints of blueberry, carrot cake and soft tropical fruits.
- **Country:** Norway
- **Brewer:** ABC Brewing
- **Style:** Imperial amber
- **Appearance:** Amber
- **Alcohol:** 8.5%
- **Serving temp:** 7–10°C

⚎ BERENTSENS ROGALANDS PILS

The Berentsens brewery is famous for producing all kinds of drinks, including apple juice and mineral water, alongside a wide range of beers. By far its most popular brew is this Pilsner lager. Nice as a light aperitif, served very cold with a bowl of salty mixed nuts.

TASTING NOTES: Pale yellow in colour with very light, dusty malt notes and a carbonated finish.
- **Country:** Norway
- **Brewer:** Berentsens Brygghus
- **Style:** Pilsner
- **Appearance:** Light yellow
- **Alcohol:** 4.7%
- **Serving temp:** 1–2°C

⚎ NØGNE Ø INDIA PALE ALE

One of the best-respected breweries in Norway, Nøgne Ø's mastery of brewing extends to brown ales, imperial stouts and beyond. This is their perfectly-balanced IPA. A combination of American Cascade and Chinook hops lead to the pungent and resinous nose before the caramel malts take over on the palate.

TASTING NOTES: Strong pine resins, sweet grapefruit and hints of lime dominate this perfectly-executed IPA. Try it with spicy jerk chicken.
- **Country:** Norway
- **Brewer:** Nøgne Ø
- **Style:** IPA
- **Appearance:** Orange
- **Alcohol:** 7.5%
- **Serving temp:** 8–10°C

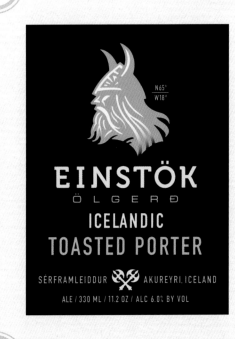

⚎ EINSTÖK ICELANDIC TOASTED PORTER

The Einstök brewery makes much of its location – just 97 km/60 miles south of the Arctic Circle. The water is claimed to be perfect for brewing beer, having filtered down through ancient lava flows and mountain glaciers. This toasted porter is made with well-toasted and chocolate malts to give its deep, dark and silky black colour.

TASTING NOTES: Strong notes of espresso and dark chocolate. Perfect with well-charred meat.
- **Country:** Iceland
- **Brewer:** Einstök Ölger
- **Style:** Porter
- **Appearance:** Dark brown
- **Alcohol:** 6%
- **Serving temp:** 8–13°C

FAT LIZARD SWEET MARY 390

Double IPAs are often viewed as an indulgence; something to partake in now and then rather than as session beers. This is due to their strength in both flavour and alcohol. None deserve this indulgent reputation quite so much as Fat Lizard's Sweet Mary 390. Brewed with saffron (the world's most expensive spice), the hop notes are given an extra depth and power which oozes class and makes this luxurious style feel even more premium.

TASTING NOTES: Sweet spice from the saffron and with a honey and 'of the sea' type edge.
- **Country:** Finland
- **Brewer:** Fat Lizard Brewing Co.
- **Style:** Double IPA
- **Appearance:** Orange
- **Alcohol:** 8.3%
- **Serving temp:** 4–7°C

BEER HUNTERS MUFLONI SAISON DE RANDONNEUR

The farmhouse saison gets another incarnation with this gorgeous grainy version from the Beer Hunters. Utilizing not only barley but also wheat and a small amount of rye for extra body and spice, this modern saison remains fresh and bready and a perfect match to seafood dishes, salads and soft white cheeses. A very refreshing beer and perfect for the summer months.

TASTING NOTES: Peppery spice, light honey and rye bread with an exceptionally light and bubbly mouthfeel.
- **Country:** Finland
- **Brewer:** Beer Hunters
- **Style:** Black IPA
- **Appearance:** Amber
- **Alcohol:** 7%
- **Serving temp:** 5–7°C

HIISI PLÄKKI

The black IPA style is one that's often rather vague, and some are more akin to American IPAs without the pale colour, focusing purely on hops and citrus vibrancy. This version from Hiisi is very much the other end of the spectrum with a strong dark toasty malt base with a slight heat and spice. The finish allows the hops to come through a little more with soft, orchard fruits playing a part.

TASTING NOTES: Black bread and plums with a liquorice hint and dark coffee finish.
- **Country:** Finland
- **Brewer:** Hiisi
- **Style:** Black IPA
- **Appearance:** Black
- **Alcohol:** 6.3%
- **Serving temp:** 10–13°C

✚ LAITILAN KIEVARI IMPERIAALI

Brewed for the 15th anniversary of the brewery in Laitila, Finland, Laitilan Kievari Imperiaali is an imperial-style stout. In a celebration of the age of the brewery, it has a 15-month maturation process, which allows its strong alcohol flavours to mellow and broaden. Keep a bottle in the cellar to take this process further.

TASTING NOTES: Malty brown bread, roasted coffee and strong liquorice. Pairs excellently with coffee ice cream.
- **Country:** Finland
- **Brewer:** Laitilan Wirvoitusjuomatehdas
- **Style:** Imperial stout
- **Appearance:** Dark brown
- **Alcohol:** 9.2%
- **Serving temp:** 8–13°C

✚ HARTWALL LAPIN KULTA

The brand name Lapin Kulta is used for a variety of different strength lagers, including a 2.7%, a 4.5% and a 5.2%. The bestseller is the 4.5% premium lager, which is one of the most popular bottled beers in Finland. Its extremely light flavour profile is easy to drink and can go with a wide variety of food.

TASTING NOTES: Very light maltiness with very little bitterness and a soft finish.
- **Country:** Finland
- **Brewer:** Hartwall
- **Style:** Pale lager
- **Appearance:** Pale yellow
- **Alcohol:** 4.5%
- **Serving temp:** 1–2°C

✚ MALMGÅRD BARLEY WINE

Situated near the lush fields of the Malmgård Estate, the Malmgård brewery was set up after its founders were inspired by the abundance of grains all around. With a focus on speciality malts like spelt and emmer, this is a brewery that doesn't simply load up the copper with kilos and kilos of hops but places the noble grain at centre stage. This barley wine is a great example of that ethos.

TASTING NOTES: Dates, plum and sweet wooden notes with a light fruity finish.
- **Country:** Finland
- **Brewer:** Malmgård
- **Style:** Barley wine
- **Appearance:** Mahogany red
- **Alcohol:** 10.4%
- **Serving temp:** 11–14°C

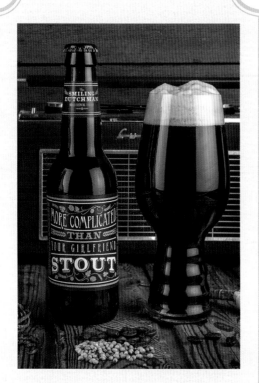

✚ TEERENPELI JULMAJUHO

The Teerenpeli brewery takes its food as seriously as its brewing, with restaurants all around Finland matching beers carefully with food. This is a beer that would pair wonderfully with a smoky meat dish like ribs or cured fish as the barley itself undergoes a smoking process before being used at the mashing-in stage.

TASTING NOTES: Notes of tobacco, wood smoke and tar with a liquorice and woody finish.
- **Country:** Finland
- **Brewer:** Teerenpeli
- **Style:** Smoked porter
- **Appearance:** Dark brown
- **Alcohol:** 7.7%
- **Serving temp:** 10–13°C

✚ THE FLYING DUTCHMAN NOMAD MORE COMPLICATED THAN YOUR GIRLFRIEND STOUT

A high-density stout full of dark and toasty flavours, this beer has an ingredients list almost as long as its name! It is brewed in the conventional way but finished and aged on a variety of flavourful additions. Coffee beans, cocoa nibs, two types of vanilla beans and American oak chips infused with 'Devils cut' bourbon are what give this beer its unique character. Truly more complicated than anyone's girlfriend (or boyfriend).

TASTING NOTES: Thick tan head, floral perfumed oak with notes of chocolate fudge and caramel.
- **Country:** Finland
- **Brewer:** Flying Dutchman Nomad Brewing Company
- **Style:** Imperial stout
- **Appearance:** Dark brown
- **Alcohol:** 8%
- **Serving temp:** 10–13°C

✚ SINEBRYCHOFF KOFF PORTER

Founded in 1819 in Helsinki by a Russian-born trader, the Sinebrychoff brewery is now one of the largest in Finland. Its most famous product is predictably its pale lager but this Baltic-style porter is by far its best product. Made with a slightly higher amount of hops than most Baltic porters for an added flavour dimension.

TASTING NOTES: Mild smoke, light alcohol, roasted malt and smooth bitter chocolate and coffee.
- **Country:** Finland
- **Brewer:** Sinebrychoff
- **Style:** Baltic porter
- **Appearance:** Clear black
- **Alcohol:** 7.2%
- **Serving temp:** 8–13°C

ROCKMILL JUICY MELODY

Rockmill brewery consists of another crew of enthusiastic homebrewers who take lots of influence from America. Their Juicy Delight IPA is a relatively easy-going straightforward American hopped beer. Juicy Melody expands on the theme with a higher dose of hops and dry hopping process post-fermentation. The result is a double IPA of considerable power.

TASTING NOTES: Peachy and grapefruity with pine needles, papaya and doughy malt backbone.
- **Country:** Poland
- **Brewer:** Browar Rockmill
- **Style:** Double IPA
- **Appearance:** Dark gold
- **Alcohol:** 7.8%
- **Serving temp:** 4–7°C

DID YOU KNOW?

Poles often enjoy their beer flavoured with raspberry or blackcurrant juice (piwo z sokiem) and drunk through a straw, while in winter they drink hot beer with cloves and cinnamon, sweetened with honey (piwo grzane).

TYSKIE GRONIE

Commanding nearly 20 per cent of the Polish beer market, Tyskie is one of the country's leading brands. Since the EU opened its doors to Poland, Tyskie has become more available in other countries, especially in the United Kingdom where many Polish people chose to settle in the mid 2000s. An easy-going yet flavoursome pale lager to knock back as a thirst quencher.

Tasting notes: Light citrus aromas from the hops and a sweet bready malt to match.
- **Country:** Poland
- **Brewer:** Tyskie Brewery
- **Style:** Pale lager
- **Appearance:** Yellow
- **Alcohol:** 5.5%
- **Serving temp:** 3–5°C

BURA BREW TORNADO

Balance is the key to making great beer, and too many bold hop flavours will only get you so far. Bura Brew mixes the feisty Amarillo and Chinook hops with mellow East Kent Goldings from the United Kingdom. The mix goes into a base of three lightly roasted malts giving a strong contrast to the potent hops and an easy marriage with the easy-going East Kent Goldings. A classy example of an American IPA.

TASTING NOTES: Biscuit malt base with a juicy citrus nose and clean bitter finish.
- **Country:** Croatia
- **Brewer:** Bura Brew
- **Style:** IPA
- **Appearance:** Deep amber
- **Alcohol:** 6.3%
- **Serving temp:** 4–7°C

BALTIKA NO.4

Based in St Petersburg, Russia, the baltika brewery is the largest in Eastern Europe. Its No. 4 Dunkel was first brewed in 1994 and uses maltose syrup and rye alongside other brewing ingredients, and has a fairly low hop profile.

TASTING NOTES: Burnt caramel, nutty and metallic flavours come through with a slightly artificial sugar taste.
- **Country:** Russia
- **Brewer:** Baltika Brewery
- **Style:** Dunkel
- **Appearance:** Dark amber
- **Alcohol:** 5.6%
- **Serving temp:** 8–13°C

TOMISLAV TAMNO

A warming and comforting Baltic-style porter, this beer is brewed with a high amount of sugar extracted from the double malted barley. This extra sugar content eventually ferments into the strongest beer in Croatia at 7.3%. The alcohol is masked well by treacle, chocolate and rich hints of coffee and dates.

TASTING NOTES: Dried fruit, toast and caramel with chocolate and syrupy sugar notes.
- **Country:** Croatia
- **Brewer:** Zagrebacka Pivovara
- **Style:** Baltic porter
- **Appearance:** Dark brown
- **Alcohol:** 7.3%
- **Serving temp:** 8–10°C

◼ BIRRA TIRANA

This pale lager is named after the capital city of Albania, where the beers are brewed at the Birra Malto brewery. Albanians took a while to catch on to beer, their traditional drinks being wine and brandy. Today, the brewery produces 150,000 hectolitres per year.

Tasting notes: Light corn-like malts and very little bitterness. Extremely easy to drink as an aperitif.
- **Country:** Albania
- **Brewer:** Birra Malto
- **Style:** Pale lager
- **Appearance:** Light yellow
- **Alcohol:** 4%
- **Serving temp:** 1–2°C

Belgrade Beer Fest is an annual festival of beer in Belgrade, Serbia. It started in 2003 and has rapidly grown in size, now attracting over 900,000 visitors.

◼ ZAJEČARSKO SVETLO

Serbian beer is not known for its wide variety. The dominant style of beer is pale lager, with a few darker lagers being produced in small quantities. This is a Pilsner-style beer with its roots more in the mellow Pilsners of Germany than in those of the Czech Republic. Serve ice cold as an aperitif.

Tasting notes: Bready and full bodied yet light in the finish and very drinkable.
- **Country:** Serbia
- **Brewer:** Htes Zaiecar Pivara
- **Style.** Pilsner
- **Appearance:** Pale golden
- **Alcohol:** 4.7%
- **Serving temp:** 2–3°C

CHAPTER 3

Australasia

**Beer is the most popular
drink in both Australia and New
Zealand, which is surpising when
international attention has always
been focused on their successful
wine industries.**

Beer has been a feature of Australian life since the country was colonized by the British in the 18th century. Captain Cook brewed beer aboard his ship HMS *Endeavour* in order to make the stored water safe to drink through the process of fermentation. He had loaded the ship with four tonnes of beer when he left England, but a month later it had all gone! Cook also brewed beer from spruce needles when he first visited New Zealand in 1773, again with the purpose of purifying the water supply but with the added benefit of providing vitamin C to ward off scurvy.

Rum, known as 'grog', was being consumed in huge quantities in the new colony of Australia, by adults and children alike, but it caused unacceptable levels of public drunkenness, so early administrations decided to promote the drinking of beer. A government-owned brewery was set up in 1804 and soon other breweries joined it, kickstarting a boom in beer production. Australia's oldest brewery, Cascade, was set up in 1824, and is still operating today.

The first Australian beers were top-fermented, quick-maturing ales, based on English and Irish ales, but after a few years brewers began to experiment with local ingredients and create unique new beers. The first lager was brewed in 1885 in Melbourne at the Gambrinus brewery, and with the hot climate lager inevitably became popular for its refreshing qualities. Lager is still the most popular type of beer in Australia, accounting for around 95 per cent of all beers produced.

The sheer size of the country, combined with the cost of transporting bulk cargoes and, pre-Federation in 1901, different local laws, led to the emergence of strong regional brands, including Coopers in South Australia, Tooheys in New South Wales and Swan in Western Australia. Loyalty to these brands remains localized, even now transportation issues are a feature of the past.

A new generation of brewers has created a thriving industry that is producing a range of exciting new beers. There are now more than 100 craft breweries, which produce beers as varied as Southwark Old

Stout, Feral Brewing's Razorback Barley Wine and Little Creatures Pale Ale.

New Zealand has undergone a similar brewing revolution in the past 20 years. Lager remains the dominant style, as befits the home of scientist Morton Coutts, who developed the continuous fermentation process that makes large-scale production possible. However, a range of flavoursome beers is now emerging from a host of small breweries.

New Zealand's temperate climate makes it ideal for growing barley and hops. New hop varieties have been developed, particularly in the Nelson region, which was first identified as having the perfect conditions for hop-growing back in the 1840s. Varieties such as Nelson Sauvin, Motueka and Southern Cross have become popular with boutique brewers around the world, and drinkers can taste these hops in beers from Auckland's Epic and Liberty brewers, or Wellington's Tuatara, among others.

The capital city, Wellington, has branded itself New Zealand's Craft Beer Capital, and visitors can follow a

Beer has been a feature of Australian life since the country was colonized by the British

beer trail that takes in bars, off licences and breweries, whilst Nelson also aspires to the title with a diverse range of old pubs and breweries offering a huge variety of locally-crafted beers.

🇦🇺 GRAND RIDGE MOONSHINE

Named after the shady bathtub booze made famous in the 1920s in Prohibition America, Grand Ridge's Moonshine is classified by its brewers as a dessert beer owing to its high alcohol content and sweet, dark, fruity flavours. Almost like a sticky plum pudding in a bottle. Stylistically, it's known as a Scotch ale, a style that originated in Edinburgh in the 19th century.

TASTING NOTES: Fresh, crisp, with a mellow but floral hoppy aftertaste. Good with strong cheese or a fruity, boozy dessert like Christmas pudding.
- **Country:** Australia
- **Brewer:** Grand Ridge Brewery
- **Style:** Scotch ale
- **Appearance:** Dark brown
- **Alcohol:** 8.5%
- **Serving temp:** 10–14°C

🇦🇺 SIX STRING DARK RED IPA

With its deep red colour, Six String's Dark Red IPA is a testament to what can be done with caramel and chocolate malts combined in the right ratio. But don't be fooled by the dark appearance – this is a hoppy one with bags of aroma hops being added right at the end of the boil phase. Sweetness and bitterness in perfect balance.

TASTING NOTES: Toasted biscuit and citrus flavours with a strawberry cheesecake finish.
- **Country:** Australia
- **Brewer:** Six String Brewing Co.
- **Style:** Red ale
- **Appearance:** Red
- **ABV:** 6%
- **Serving temp:** 7–10°C

🇦🇺 CASTLEMAINE XXXX GOLD

Hugely popular in its home state of Queensland, 'fourex' was a well-known brand in the UK for many years in its canned form Castlemaine Export XXXX, until it became unavailable after InBev's licensing agreement expired. The XXXX refers to an age-old grading system for strong beers – although by today's standards, even the 4.8% export version is not particularly strong.

TASTING NOTES: Very light straw, corn notes and slightly sweet aftertaste.
- **Country:** Australia
- **Brewer:** Castlemaine Perkins
- **Style:** Pale lager
- **Appearance:** Pale yellow
- **Alcohol:** 3.5%
- **Serving temp:** 1–2°C

🇦🇺 REDOAK ORGANIC PALE ALE

A beer influenced by the British pale ales first brewed in Burton upon Trent in the 19th century. This beer is made using only organically-grown malts and hops, and a select strain of London ale yeast for a distinctively fruity taste. A superbly balanced homage to pale ales in their most traditional form.

TASTING NOTES: Soft stone fruits, sweet toffee malts and a nice bitterness in the finish. Great with roast chicken or British-style fish and chips.
- **Country:** Australia
- **Brewer:** Redoak Boutique Beer Cafe
- **Style:** Pale ale
- **Appearance:** Clear golden
- **Alcohol:** 4.5%
- **Serving temp:** 7–10°C

🇦🇺 LITTLE CREATURES PALE ALE

Often described as an American-style pale ale, Little Creatures in fact cleverly balances malt sweetness and hop bitterness in an easy-drinking beer more akin to the styles originally brewed in Burton upon Trent, England. Those first hoppy pale ales had to make the long voyage to India and their hoppiness diminished as they matured during the journey. This new Aussie classic is laced with locally-grown Galaxy and American Cascade hops and is bottle-conditioned.

TASTING NOTES: Fresh, crisp with a mellow but floral hoppy aftertaste.
- **Country:** Australia
- **Brewer:** Little Creatures Brewing
- **Style:** Pale ale
- **Appearance:** Clear orange
- **Alcohol:** 5.2%
- **Serving temp:** 4–7°C

DID YOU KNOW?

The very first pub in Australia was the Mason Arms. It opened in 1796 in Parramatta, New South Wales by James Larra, a freed convict.

🇦🇺 NEWSTEAD 3 QUARTER TIME

Newstead Brewing Company is renowned in its native city of Brisbane for providing a quality brewpub experience. Sometimes it's the excellent food that does the trick for people but more often than not it's this dangerously drinkable session ale. Named after the gentle and easy-going time signature in popular music, this is a central ingredient of any night on the town in Brisbane.

TASTING NOTES: Soft peach, juicy citrus and an easy-going moreish bitterness.
- **Country:** Australia
- **Brewer:** Newstead Brewing Co.
- **Style:** Session IPA
- **Appearance:** Hazy yellow
- **Alcohol:** 3.4%
- **Serving temp:** 3–5°C

🇦🇺 JAMES SQUIRE THE CHANCER GOLDEN ALE

Born in England in 1754, James Squire was transported to Australia where he was, according to local legend, the first person to cultivate hops. The Malt Shovel Brewery named a brand of beer in his honour and this British-style golden ale was one of the first beers off the line. Made with a combination of malted wheat, barley and Amarillo hops for a smooth, fruity flavour.

TASTING NOTES: Fresh, crisp with a mellow but floral hoppy aftertaste.
- **Country:** Australia
- **Brewer:** Malt Shovel Brewery
- **Style:** Golden ale
- **Appearance:** Pale yellow
- **Alcohol:** 4.5%
- **Serving temp:** 4–7°C

🇦🇺 COOPERS ORIGINAL PALE ALE

Thomas Cooper brewed his first batch of beer in 1862 as a remedy for his sick wife. Since then, five generations of his family have carried on the business. Currently, Dr Tim Cooper and electronics entrepreneur Glenn Cooper are at the helm. This is a bottle-fermented pale ale, brewed in the style of the old English pale ales from Burton upon Trent. The yeast left in the bottle can be added to the decanted beer to taste.

TASTING NOTES: Citrus fruits, sweet malts and smooth, soft carbonation. Great with a burger and very refreshing.
- **Country:** Australia
- **Brewer:** Coopers Brewery
- **Style:** Pale ale
- **Appearance:** Cloudy yellow
- **Alcohol:** 4.5%
- **Serving temp:** 6–10°C

🇦🇺 FOSTER'S LAGER

Ostensibly an Australian favourite, you'd be hard pressed to find any in Australia – the 'amber nectar' has not been advertised since the early 2000s. Foster's is brewed in the UK and is popular because of its low price and easy-drinking nature; it is the UK's second most popular lager.

TASTING NOTES: A very light flavour profile with just a small hint of malt and very little bitterness. Drink ice cold.
- **Country:** Australia
- **Brewer:** Heineken
- **Style:** Pale lager
- **Appearance:** Pale yellow
- **Alcohol:** 4%
- **Serving temp:** 1–2°C

PIRATE LIFE MOSAIC IPA

The initial recipe for this souped-up American IPA involved using Cascade hops and Simcoe in equal parts. However after one of the Pirate Life brewers spent a long night drinking a pale ale that used only the Mosaic hops, Pirate Life IPA became a single hop Mosaic beer as well. Originally brewed for the brewery's second birthday party this fast became a regular beer after demand proved so high!

TASTING NOTES: Candied fruit, juicy mandarins and light creamy element in the finish.
- **Country:** Australia
- **Brewer:** Pirate Life Brewing
- **Style:** IPA
- **Appearance:** Cloudy orange
- **Alcohol:** 7%
- **Serving temp:** 4–7°C

MURRAY'S WILD THING IMPERIAL STOUT

Stouts don't come much more exciting than this. Pouring a pitch black with a thick tan head, at 10% you'll detect some rum-like alcohol in the aroma as well as rich dark chocolate. Only 1,100 bottles of this were brewed, so if you find one, then save it for a rainy day: this beer ages as well as any fine wine.

TASTING NOTES: Chocolate, rum, coffee. Try it with vanilla ice cream or a warm chocolate brownie. Or both.
- **Country:** Australia
- **Brewer:** Murray's Craft Brewing Co.
- **Style:** Imperial stout
- **Appearance:** Black
- **Alcohol:** 10%
- **Serving temp:** 12–15°C

JAMES BOAG'S PREMIUM LAGER

Brewed in Tasmania, James Boag's is a premium lager made with a long maturation, as all lager should be. Crisp, slightly lemony and very refreshing, it has a lot more to offer in the taste department than many other pale lagers.

TASTING NOTES: Toasted bread, lemon peel and a very soft smooth finish. Very good to drink on a hot day.
- **Country:** Australia
- **Brewer:** J. Boag & Son
- **Style:** Pale lager
- **Appearance:** Pale yellow
- **Alcohol:** 5%
- **Serving temp:** 3–6°C

Former Australian Prime Minister Bob Hawke was previously the world record holder for the fastest drinking of a yard of beer (2.5 pints), when he downed a sconce pot in 11 seconds.

🇦🇺 FERAL HOP HOG

American-style India pale ale, heavily dosed with Yakima Valley hops and with a secondary dry hopping during fermentation, this beer has a resinous pine aroma and mouth-puckering bitterness. For hopheads only but, at only 5.8%, one they can drink all evening.

TASTING NOTES: Very strong acidic and pine notes on the palate, with a long, dry bitter finish.
- **Country:** Australia
- **Brewer:** Feral Brewing Co.
- **Style:** American IPA
- **Appearance:** Cloudy orange
- **Alcohol:** 5.8%
- **Serving temp:** 4–7°C

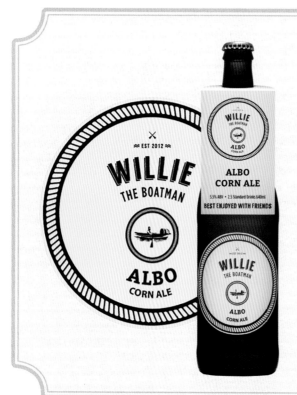

🇦🇺 WILLIE THE BOATMAN ALBO CORN ALE

Corn is often used as a cheaper substitute for barley in macro-brewed lagers and Pilsners. But corn also has a unique flavour of its own which the excellent Willie the Boatman brewery has tried to make the most of. This is the type of beer that American farmhands would brew to enjoy after a long day working their fields. Essential in the Australian heat!

TASTING NOTES: Light butter popcorn sweetness with the most delicate lemon finish.
- **Country:** Australia
- **Brewer:** Willie the Boatman
- **Style:** Pilsner
- **Appearance:** Pale straw
- **Alcohol:** 5.5%
- **Serving temp:** 3–5°C

TUATARA APA

This American-style pale ale has been through two incarnations, and since 2012 it uses homegrown hops due to a short supply of American produce. This is a smartly-made beer from a slickly marketed brewery – pronounced 'Too-Ah-Tah-Rah' – one that is fast becoming one of the most popular and trendy brands in the country.

TASTING NOTES: Biscuit malts, grapefruit aromas and big pine resin flavour. Classic with a hot dog or a burger.
- **Country:** New Zealand
- **Brewer:** Tuatara Brewing Co.
- **Style:** American pale ale
- **Appearance:** Cloudy yellow
- **Alcohol:** 5.8%
- **Serving temp:** 4–7°C

PANHEAD JOHNNY OCTANE RED IPA

Brewing out of an old tyre factory in Maidstone, Wellington, the Panhead brewers are the mad engineers of the Kiwi brewing scene. The Red IPA they brew (often called Canhead rather than Panhead) fuses a blend of well-roasted malts for those dark, brown bread flavours and employs American hops to lift the whole taste into IPA territory and add that satisfying bitter finish.

TASTING NOTES: Caramelized orange, biscuit cheesecake base and tangy fruit.
- **Country:** New Zealand
- **Brewer:** Panhead Custom Ales
- **Style:** Red IPA
- **Appearance:** Red
- **Alcohol:** 8%
- **Serving temp:** 4–7°C

PARROTDOG FALCON APA

Not all brewing goes according to plan and often brewers spend years refining recipes until they hit upon the right combination. It took ParrotDog a few attempts to get this APA right but now the Falcon is definitely in full flight having had its alcohol ramped up from 3.5% so that its wings are no longer clipped! Hoppy and clean, this makes a great middle ground session beer.

TASTING NOTES: Tropical fruit balanced with toffee and popcorn in the finish.
- **Country:** New Zealand
- **Brewer:** ParrotDog
- **Style:** APA
- **Appearance:** Light gold
- **ABV:** 5%
- **Serving temp:** 5°C

MOA BLANC

Moa Blanc is New Zealand's homage to the Belgian witbier style originally brought back to life by Pierre Celis in the late 1960s in the small village of Hoegaarden. But it has plenty in common with German wheat beer, too. Made with a blend of 50 per cent wheat and 50 per cent barley, a good dose of sediment remains in the bottom of the bottle to give its signature cloudy appearance. With banana, bubblegum and citrus in the nose, this is a refreshing summery beer.

TASTING NOTES: Banana, coriander and citrus followed by a smooth wheaty finish. Great with fish and Chinese dishes.
- **Country:** New Zealand
- **Brewer:** Moa Brewing Co.
- **Style:** Witbier
- **Appearance:** Hazy gold
- **Alcohol:** 5.5%
- **Serving temp:** 3–5°C

KERERU SWEET BIPPY

Brewing mostly British- and European-style beers, Kereru are well renowned for their knowledge of the Belgian style and their excellent Velvet Boot Belgian Dubbel has won awards for its faithful recreation of a classic style. Sweet Bippy takes this one step further with some extra clout, extra spice and some dark candy sugar sweetness to help amp up the flavour.

TASTING NOTES: Spicy fruit cake, boozy banana and hints of rum chocolate.
- **Country:** New Zealand
- **Brewer:** Kereru Brewing Co.
- **Style:** Quadrupel
- **Appearance:** Deep brown
- **Alcohol:** 9.3%
- **Serving temp:** 10–13°C

DID YOU KNOW?

'Ice brewed beers' are popular in New Zealand: the beer is chilled until the water freezes but the alcohol, with a lower freezing point, doesn't – so after removing the ice you get a more alcoholic beer.

🏴 MIKE'S IPA

Allegedly inspired by English pale ales of the past, this 9% alcohol double IPA has far more in common with the supercharged, highly hopped versions of IPA pioneered by American craft brewers. All the usual tropical fruit flavours you'd expect from very hoppy pale ale, with a fiery hop kick in the aftertaste.

TASTING NOTES: Passion fruit, lychee and pineapple balanced with a toffee malt base and a long, dry, eye-watering bitterness in the finish.
- **Country:** New Zealand
- **Brewer:** Mike's Drewery
- **Style:** Double IPA
- **Appearance:** Gold/amber
- **Alcohol:** 9%
- **Serving temp:** 8–13°C

🏴 EPIC ARMAGEDDON

A multi award-winning beer from a multi award-winning brewery! Epic's Armageddon IPA was voted best IPA in New Zealand in 2015. Not content with local domination though, it also scooped the same award in nearby Australia, and the not-so-nearby Sweden in the same year. Brewed to a devilish 6.66%, it's a perfect combination of New World hops and toffee caramel backbone.

TASTING NOTES: Florals, rose hips, grapefruit, peach, pine and toffee.
- **Country:** New Zealand
- **Brewer:** Epic
- **Style:** IPA
- **Appearance:** Clear orange
- **Alcohol:** 6.66%
- **Serving temp:** 4–7°C

🏴 BACH BREWING HOPSMACKER DOUBLE IPA

One of the many New World-style pale ales out there using hops from the hotter regions of the planet, Bach Brewing Hopsmacker pale ale uses a combination of locally-sourced Riwaka hops – a common theme for many New Zealand beers – and the more spicy, grapefruit-infused flavour of Cascade. The 2017 version is souped up to 8.2% for an extra smack of hops and bitterness.

TASTING NOTES: Spicy, pine resin in the nose and a nice amount of grapefruit, lychee and elderflower on the palate. Great with spicy dishes.
- **Country:** New Zealand
- **Brewer:** Bach Brewing
- **Style:** IPA
- **Appearance:** Clear amber
- **Alcohol:** 8.2%
- **Serving temp:** 4–7°C

🏴 LION RED

Produced by brewing giant Lion, this is a 4% alcohol session lager and a favourite among university students. In the mid-1980s, the brewery officially changed the name to Lion Red. Its amber colour, derived from the malts, relates it to the Vienna layers created in the 1840s.

TASTING NOTES: A very malt-forward lager, rich in caramel sweetness as well as a definite bitterness in the finish.

- **Country:** New Zealand
- **Brewer:** Lion Breweries
- **Style:** Vienna lager
- **Appearance:** Amber
- **Alcohol:** 4%
- **Serving temp:** 4–7°C

🏴 YEASTIE BOYS DIGITAL IPA

The Yeastie Boys have created this Digital IPA that is screaming with hoppy flavour from a blend of New Zealand's hop varieties and it's no surprise it won a gold medal from the Brewers Guild of New Zealand in 2012. The epitome of a modern, well-made and exciting hoppy pale ale.

TASTING NOTES: Passion fruit, lychee and caramel. Perfect with spicy barbecues and Indian curry.

- **Country:** New Zealand
- **Brewer:** Yeastie Boys
- **Style:** IPA
- **Appearance:** Medium orange
- **Alcohol:** 7%
- **Serving temp:** 4–7°C

DID YOU KNOW?

In 1770 Captain James Cook brewed the first beer in New Zealand as a cure for scurvy aboard his ship. He used the needles of an indigenous spruce tree 'with the addition of inspissated juice of wort' and molasses.

🏴 8 WIRED SAISON SAUVIN

First brewed in the farmhouses of France and Belgium, saisons were meant to be refreshing and safe to drink (water often wasn't) and were often well hopped. Saison beers can now be made with sackfuls of Nelson Sauvin hops. Earthy, pungent but very refreshing, this is definitely a beer worth savouring on a hot day.

TASTING NOTES: Cooked vegetables, earth, black pepper and citrus fruits. So versatile you can drink it with pretty much anything you like.

- **Country:** New Zealand
- **Brewer:** 8 Wired Brewing Co.
- **Style:** Saison
- **Appearance:** Hazy yellow
- **Alcohol:** 7%
- **Serving temp:** 4–7°C

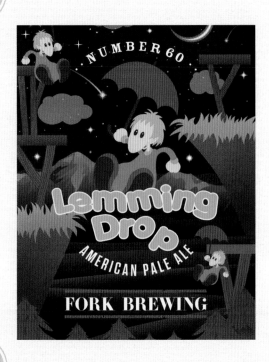

🇳🇿 FORK BREWING LEMMING DROP

Many brewers stick to tried and tested hops that are proven sellers but this can lead to many IPAs tasting similar. What Fork Brewing have done is create an APA with more interesting hops. The Lemon Drop hop exudes the flavour of its namesake fruit together with mint and green tea while the addition of Sorachi Ace adds an extra herbal note that's hard to place.

TASTING NOTES: Hints of dill, preserved lemon and lemon thyme.
- **Country:** New Zealand
- **Brewer:** Fork Brewing
- **Style:** APA
- **Appearance:** Dark gold
- **Alcohol:** 5.2%
- **Serving temp:** 4–7°C

🇳🇿 RENAISSANCE ELEMENTAL PORTER

Located in a region of Marlborough more famous for its sauvignon blanc grapes than for its craft brewing, Renaissance prides itself on making beer for the sophisticated palate. This is one of New Zealand's highest-rated beers, unusual for a porter, but no surprise when you taste the beautiful balance of chocolatey malts and crisp hops.

TASTING NOTES: Rich and full-bodied with a long roasty malt flavour and crisp hoppy finish. Drink with barbecue meats, coffee-based desserts and blue cheese.
- **Country:** New Zealand
- **Brewer:** Renaissance Brewing Co.
- **Style:** Porter
- **Appearance:** Dark brown
- **Alcohol:** 6%
- **Serving temp:** 8–12°C

🇳🇿 LIBERTY CITRA

Liberty's Citra is a lesson in how Citra hops are supposed to taste. This is a double IPA, meaning that almost twice the usual amount of malt is used, which releases extra sugars, and accounts for its 9% alcohol content. To balance this out a mountain of Citra hops are added, followed by a second dry hopping to complete this masterclass.

TASTING NOTES: Dusty lemon aroma, sweet caramel malt base followed by a tropical fruit hoppy flavour explosion.
- **Country:** New Zealand
- **Brewer:** Liberty Brewing Co
- **Style:** Double IPA
- **Appearance:** Clear gold
- **Alcohol:** 9%
- **Serving temp:** 8–13°C

CHAPTER 4

Rest of the World

Beer is enjoyed across the world and is now being produced in many different countries as innovative brewers look to meet the demands of new and growing markets.

China is the biggest market for beer in the world by volume, and is also the world's biggest brewer, producing more than 9.7 billion gallons (44 billion litres) of beer. Global brewery giants such as AB InBev and Heineken are therefore positioning themselves to collaborate with Asian brewers or buy up local brands in this fast-developing region.

Traditional 'beer' made with rice or millet was first brewed in India several thousand years ago. Beer as we know it today developed in the mid-19th century, when the colonial powers set up breweries to cater for European tastes. Prior to this, most beer had to be imported from Europe at great expense. The lengthy nature of the journey led to the development of the British India pale ale style. Today, pale lager is the predominant style throughout Asia, with some dark beers such as San Miguel Dark in the Philippines.

Until 1994 choice was fairly limited in Japan, because legislation prevented microbreweries being established unless they could produce 440,000 gallons (two million litres) a year. When this limit was dropped

to just 13,198 gallons (60,000 litres), the doors opened to a group of new brewers producing local beers, known as Ji Bīru.

Among the new names is Hitachino Nest, an exciting range of beers produced by Kiuchi Brewery, a traditional sake producer. Baird Brewing is another operator that is offering Japanese drinkers an alternative to bone-dry Pilsners.

Despite India's relatively low consumption of beer, brewpubs are springing up in some cities to cater for the new middle class. There are even microbreweries in China, sometimes using local ingredients such as Sichuan peppers, Chinese tea and date honey. With a population of more than 1.3 billion, turning even a fraction of China on to different beers presents a huge opportunity.

Africa is one of the smaller markets for beer in the world, accounting for only 6.6 per cent of production in 2012, however this figure is rising fast, and brewers see Africa as something of a new frontier.

Africa's thirst for beer is most commonly slaked by

resorting to local homebrew. This rough-and-ready beer is estimated to make up to four times the size of the bought beer market.

Multinational brewing companies such as SAB Miller are therefore producing more affordable beers, such as sorghum beer, a commercialized version of homebrew. SAB Miller has also launched an initiative to halve the price of beer by using ingredients cheaper than malt, such as cassava and sorghum. Brewers also hope that as more Africans achieve affluence they will choose more commercial options.

Brewing in South Africa dates back to 1658, when the first Dutch governor, Jan van Riebeeck, established a brewery at the Fort of Good Hope. Brewing gradually spread through the Cape, and South African Breweries (SAB) came into being in 1895 (as Castle Breweries), serving thirsty miners and prospectors. Although lager is the most popular drink in this hot continent, stouts, such as Guinness Export, have an enthusiastic customer base, and more Guinness is sold in Nigeria than anywhere else in the

Traditional 'beer' made with rice or millet was first brewed in India several thousand years ago

world, including Ireland.

Inevitably, Africa also has its own emerging craft beer scene, mostly focused on South Africa, with breweries like Jack Black's, Darling Brew and Boston Breweries bringing some much-needed variety.

● ASAHI SUPER DRY

A brewery that takes its environmental responsibilities very seriously, the Asahi brewery recycles everything it uses; the waste yeast product is sent to pharmaceutical companies and spent malt is used for cattle feed. This is the beer that kick-started a love of lager in Japan. The use of rice in the brewing mash is also something a little different and the beer's makers will tell you it results in less of a hangover the morning after. Whether that is true or not, Asahi commands more than 40 per cent of the Japanese brewing market for a good reason.

TASTING NOTES: As the name would suggest, incredibly dry at the end. Corn malts and bitter hops.
- **Country:** Japan
- **Brewer:** Asahi Breweries
- **Style:** Pale lager
- **Appearance:** Golden yellow
- **Alcohol:** 5%
- **Serving temp:** 3–5°C

● ECHIGO PILSNER

The Czech style of Pilsner lager appears all over the world. With the use of Saaz hops for their floral, slightly peppery quality and an increased malt presence, Echigo Pilsner is very much true to the old style. Brewed in the Niigata region on the north-west coast of Honshu, Japan's largest island, look out for this beer in its golden can.

TASTING NOTES: Bready malt flavours with a pronounced hop character from the Saaz hops. Pairs well with Monterey Jack cheese.
- **Country:** Japan
- **Brewer:** Echigo Beer Co.
- **Style:** Pilsner
- **Appearance:** Clear yellow
- **Alcohol:** 5%
- **Serving temp:** 3–5°C

● BAIRD DARK SKY IMPERIAL STOUT

Craft brewing has really taken off in Japan. Since its inception in 2000, Baird Brewing has been responsible for some of the country's best beer. Brewed in the tiny backroom brewery at their Numazu taproom, Dark Sky is about as serious as stout gets. Huge, hoppy flavours betray the brewery's American inspiration, while a blend of eight different malts balances the beer out.

TASTING NOTES: Floral and almost tropical hop aromas work well with the big chocolate and coffee flavours.
- **Country:** Japan
- **Brewer:** Baird Brewing Co.
- **Style:** Imperial stout
- **Appearance:** Dark brown
- **Alcohol:** 7.6%
- **Serving temp:** 8–13°C

● HITACHINO NEST BEER AMBER ALE

Brewed with a combination of two pale and two dark malts for a distinctive colour and toffee-like flavour, and two types of American hops for the fruity aroma essential in this type of beer, Hitachino Nest Beer Amber Ale is a perfect example of the American amber style. Pairs well with a wide variety of foods but especially chargrilled meats.

TASTING NOTES: Plenty of toffee, caramel and spicy bitter hops in the aroma with a very similar taste on the palate.
- **Country:** Japan
- **Brewer:** Kiuchi Brewery
- **Style:** Amber ale
- **Appearance:** Amber
- **Alcohol:** 5.5%
- **Serving temp:** 4–7°C

● YO-HO TOKYO BLACK

Up until 1994 it was illegal in Japan to brew beer unless you could produce more than 440,000 gallons (two million litres) per year. Once this law was relaxed, dozens of microbreweries were set up and the Yo-Ho Brewing was one of them. This beautifully silky black porter is one of their more popular brews, with a relatively low alcohol content and rich mahogany colour.

TASTING NOTES: Roasted malt, dried fruit and the hugely desirable chocolate-coffee combination typical of porter.
- **Country:** Japan
- **Brewer:** Yo-Ho Brewing Co.
- **Style:** Porter
- **Appearance:** Deep brown
- **Alcohol:** 5%
- **Serving temp:** 8–13°C

● YO-HO YONA YONA ALE

The phrase 'Yona Yona' translated from the Japanese means 'every night'. At 5.5%, this American-style pale ale is not a beer that will have you on the floor after two cans, yet it packs in masses of flavour. If the sign of a great brewer is the ability to make beer flavoursome without going overboard on strength, Yo-Ho Brewing is surely one of the greatest.

TASTING NOTES: Lots of melon, pineapple and other tropical fruits in the aroma. Great with a lightly spiced Thai curry.
- **Country:** Japan
- **Brewer:** Yo-Ho Brewing Co.
- **Style:** Pale ale
- **Appearance:** Clear amber
- **Alcohol:** 5.5%
- **Serving temp:** 4–7°C

● TIGER

Tiger was the first beer to be brewed in Singapore, in 1932. It soon became a much-decorated beer, winning awards for quality in London, Paris and Geneva. The recipe hasn't changed much since those days and it remains the flagship beer of the Asia Pacific Brewery. Tiger is widely available in more than 60 countries and is very popular in the United Kingdom.

TASTING NOTES: Light malt, light aroma and excellent for thirst-quenching.
- **Country:** Singapore
- **Brewer:** Asia Pacific Brewery
- **Style:** Pale lager
- **Appearance:** Pale gold
- **Alcohol:** 5%
- **Serving temp:** 3–5°C

🇨🇳 TSINGTAO

Tsingtao is bittered with domestically grown hops and uses water from the Laoshan mountain range – an area of China renowned for the purity of its water. When the brewery was founded in 1903, the beer was brewed in accordance with the German purity law of 1516; rice was introduced later, to cut costs.

TASTING NOTES: Light malt aroma with a very light malt flavour and a thin texture. Refreshing.
- **Country:** China
- **Brewer:** Tsingtao Brewery Co.
- **Style:** Pale lager
- **Appearance:** Golden
- **Alcohol:** 4.8%
- **Serving temp:** 1–2°C

🇨🇳 MASTER GAO BABY IPA

Returning to China from the US to run a pharmaceutical firm, Gao Yan is nonetheless the author of a homebrewing book that is held in high regard throughout China. Despite brewing beer that sells for eight times more than the majority of Chinese beer, Master Gao is doing rather well, producing around 2.4 million bottles of his Jasmine Tea Lager and this Baby IPA combined.

TASTING NOTES: Sweet with a note of mandarin and dried apricot.
Country: China
- **Brewer:** Master Gao
- **Style:** IPA
- **Appearance:** Copper
- **Alcohol:** 4.8%
- **Serving temp:** 4–7°C

香蕉小麥
BANANA WHEAT

类 型 小麦啤酒
STYLE HEFEWEIZEN
酒精度 5.5%
ABV

🇨🇳 GREAT LEAP BANANA WHEAT

The name of this Chinese-brewed Hefeweizen strongly suggests it was brewed with banana and indeed the taste appears to confirm this. The banana-like flavour however comes from that trademark of German brewing – Hefeweizen yeast. The first and biggest craft brewery in Beijing, Great Leap also operates the excellent brewery tap Brewpub #12.

TASTING NOTES: Banana and cloves with hints of bubblegum and spice.
- **Country:** China
- **Brewer:** Great Leap Brewing
- **Style:** Hefeweizen
- **Appearance:** Cloudy yellow
- **Alcohol:** 5.5%
- **Serving temp:** 4–7°C

≡ HAYWARDS 5000

India's population has historically preferred stronger types of alcohol, such as whisky or brandy, because they are cheaper and do the job of getting you drunk a bit faster! When they do drink beer, many Indians tend to go for the stronger stuff, such as Haywards 5000 – a very malty and strongly scented beer with 7% alcohol.

TASTING NOTES: Aromas of corn and grain with a hint of pungent hops in the background.
- **Country:** India
- **Brewer:** AB InBev
- **Style:** Malt liquor
- **Appearance:** Pale gold
- **Alcohol:** 7%
- **Serving temp:** 3–5°C

≡ ROYAL CHALLENGE PREMIUM LAGER

Since its launch in 1997 Royal Challenge has quickly become the second biggest-selling beer in India, thanks largely to its loyal customer base. Around 2.5 million cases are made every year and the beer is mostly sold for the domestic market rather than to export. A simple, easy-going pale lager that works well as an aperitif.

TASTING NOTES: A light beer with very low malt and hop profile.
- **Country:** India
- **Brewer:** Ab InBev
- **Style:** Pale lager
- **Appearance:** Clear golden
- **Alcohol:** 5%
- **Serving temp:** 2–3°C

DID YOU KNOW?

In 2011, Murali K. C. achieved the Guinness World Record for the most beer bottle caps removed with teeth in one minute. He removed 68 bottle caps!

KINGFISHER PREMIUM

The Kingfisher brand of premium lager takes a whopping 36 per cent of the beer market in India. It is also widely available in many countries all around the world and is possibly the most famous of India's beer exports. Very hoppy for its style, the hops not only impart a great aroma but also lead to a satisfying bitter finish.

TASTING NOTES: A very grassy hop aroma is followed by a light malt taste with a finish dominated by the hops.
- **Country:** India
- **Brewer:** United Breweries
- **Style:** Pale lager
- **Appearance:** Clear golden
- **Alcohol:** 5%
- **Serving temp:** 2–3°C

DID YOU KNOW?

Different Indian tribes have their own traditions of brewing rice beer which is an important role in their socio-cultural lives.

COBRA

Cobra was originally brewed in India for export to the United Kingdom. It's now contract-brewed in Great Britain. In 1989, Karan Bilimoria thought that Great Britain needed a less gassy lager and he founded the Cobra Brewery. The brand is now owned by Molson Coors and brewed in Burton upon Trent.

TASTING NOTES: Very light in colour, aroma and taste. Works well to put out the fire started by a spicy Indian curry.
- **Country:** India
- **Brewer:** Molson Coors
- **Style:** Pale lager
- **Appearance:** Pale gold
- **Alcohol:** 4.8%
- **Serving temp:** 1–2°C

☀ **MAGPIE BREWING COUNTRY FOLK**

Magpie Brewing is noted for its seasonal range and this naturally-fermented farmhouse-style pale ale was first created in 2017. The tangy, funky fruit flavours it gives off are from the Forbidden Fruit yeast strain but the finish is spicy and dry due to the use of rye in the malt mix. Thirst-quenching without being boring – this is the ideal spring beer.

TASTING NOTES: Creamy aromas with hints of red and slightly sour berries. Peppery in the finish.
- **Country:** South Korea
- **Brewer:** Magpie Brewing Co.
- **Style:** Farmhouse pale
- **Appearance:** Gold
- **Alcohol:** 5.6%
- **Serving temp:** 4–7°C

:◉: THE HAND AND MALT SLOW IPA

Not many brewers can boast their own farmland but the Hand and Malt brewery can do just that. The brewery grows its own hops in the nearby Chung Pyung area at what is the largest hop farm in South Korea. It also bakes bread with the yeast and feeds cows with the spent grains – drinking beer never felt so green!

TASTING NOTES: Floral hops with a light biscuit grain base, well balanced between bitter and sweet.
- **Country:** South Korea
- **Brewer:** The Hand and Malt Brewing Co.
- **Style:** IPA
- **Appearance:** Pale amber
- **Alcohol:** 4.6%
- **Serving temp:** 4–7°C

:◉: BUDNAMU HASLLA IPA

Serving handcrafted beers and homecooked food out of its brewery and bar, Budmanu is making waves on the South Korean brewery scene. This gorgeous IPA has garnered significant critical acclaim with its huge pine resin and malty backbone flavours making it the perfect match for those Korean barbecue dishes that have become so popular the world over.

TASTING NOTES: Sweet citrus fruit with hints of pine and grassy spice.
- **Country:** South Korea
- **Brewer:** Budnamu Brewery
- **Style:** IPA
- **Appearance:** Dark gold
- **Alcohol:** 6.1%
- **Serving temp:** 4–7°C

:◉: GALMEGI ESPRESSO VANILLA STOUT

Made with fresh local coffee beans and vanilla pods, this is one of the crown jewels of Galmegi Brewing's portfolio. The first microbrewer to emerge in the bustling port town of Busan in South Korea and also the operator of several taprooms in the region, Galmego is fast becoming one of South Korea's brightest brewing prospects.

TASTING NOTES: Rich coffee and sweet vanilla with dark chocolate finish.
- **Country:** South Korea
- **Brewer:** Galmegi Brewing Co.
- **Style:** Stout
- **Appearance:** Deep brown
- **Alcohol:** 5.5%
- **Serving temp:** 4–7°C

★ WINKING SEAL
BABY FATSO DRY STOUT

Bringing modern American BBQ classics to Ho Chi Minh City, Winking Seal is also taking influence from US craft brewing to bring new and exciting beer styles to Vietnam on a small scale. This exceptionally creamy and dry stout is given a smooth body by the addition of nitrogen during dispensing. The result is very quaffable and perfect with burnt ends or smoky ribs.

TASTING NOTES: Dry with hints of chocolate, coffee and roasty malts.
- **Country:** Vietnam
- **Brewer:** Winking Seal Beer Co.
- **Style:** Stout
- **Appearance:** Black
- **Alcohol:** 4%
- **Serving temp:** 10–13°C

▬ BINTANG

Bintang, or 'star beer', was made as a response to the popularity of pale lagers in other parts of the world. It is often compared to Heineken, not only because of its taste but also because the green bottle and the use of the red star as a logo are remarkably similar. Perfect refreshment in Indonesia's hot climates.

TASTING NOTES: Malty, toasted grain with hints of pepper and a citrus hoppy finish.
- **Country:** Indonesia
- **Brewer:** Multi Bintang
- **Style:** Pale lager
- **Appearance:** Clear yellow
- **Alcohol:** 4.8%
- **Serving temp:** 2–3°C

★ PASTEUR STREET CYCLO
IMPERIAL CHOCOLATE STOUT

One of the more luxurious beers produced in the country and indeed in the world. This gorgeous and rich chocolate stout is infused with cacao nibs which are specially selected and blended. The addition of local cinnamon and fresh vanilla beans adds a touch of class that helped this fantastic beer bring home the first gold medal for a Vietnamese beer at the World Beer Cup.

TASTING NOTES: Dark chocolate, creamy lactose and cinnamon.
- **Country:** Vietnam
- **Brewer:** Pasteur Street Brewing Co.
- **Style:** Imperial stout
- **Appearance:** Black
- **Alcohol:** 13%
- **Serving temp:** 10–13°C

STAR THREE HORSES BEER PILSENER

Bizarrely, the distribution of Coca Cola in Madagascar led to the creation of Three Horses Beer Pilsener after the French company responsible for the famous soft drink found a gap in the market for a locally-produced pale lager. After testing the water with 17 different recipes, they finally agreed the best one and in 1958 began production of the highest-selling beer in Madagascar.

TASTING NOTES: Ideal for a hot day when served freezing cold. Lightly herbal and lemony.
- **Country:** Madagascar
- **Brewer:** Brasseries STAR Madagascar
- **Style:** Pale lager
- **Appearance:** Light gold
- **Alcohol:** 5.4%
- **Serving temp:** 1–2°C

INLAND MICROBREWERY PILSNER

Clement Djameh trained in Germany, and now leads the charge in the microbrewing scene in Ghana. Using one of the many species of locally-grown sorghum instead of malted barley, Clement's brewing kit is not the most up to date having been bought mostly second-hand from Italy. He welded together his fermenter himself, and is even making his own fuel for boiling using palm kernel husks instead of expensive charcoal.

TASTING NOTES: Light honey, sweet lemon and extremely refreshing.
- **Country:** Ghana
- **Brewer:** Inland Brewery
- **Style:** Pale lager
- **Appearance:** Light gold
- **Alcohol:** Variable
- **Serving temp:** 1–2°C

DID YOU KNOW?

The Guinness World Record for driving over beer bottles was set by army driver Li Guiwen from Beijing when he took 8 minutes and 28 seconds to drive 60.19 metres (approx. 197 feet) along 1,798 bottles.

🏴 BOSTON BREWERIES BLACK RIVER COFFEE STOUT

The Boston Brewery is situated in the heart of Cape Town and is one of the craft beer landmarks of the city. Its tasting room at the Cape Quarter has become legendary, both as a place to drink beer from Boston Breweries and as one of the few places you'll find this Black River Coffee Stout on tap. Made with Ethiopian Yirgacheffe coffee extract.

TASTING NOTES: Big coffee, toffee and smaller hints of chocolate and brown sugar. A great way to wake up!
- **Country:** South Africa
- **Brewer:** Boston Breweries
- **Style:** Coffee stout
- **Appearance:** Pitch black
- **Alcohol:** 6%
- **Serving temp:** 8–13°C

🏴 DEVIL'S PEAK THE KING'S BLOCKHOUSE IPA

Here is a brewer that combines the best from modern American brewing with the traditional approach of Belgium to create beers with depth, character and flavour. Devil's Peak is looking to educate South Africa in how truly great beer can be and it is starting right here with this hop-charged American-style IPA. The King's Blockhouse is a perfect match for any spicy curries, thanks to its highly hopped bitterness and strong citrus flavours that cut through spice with ease.

TASTING NOTES: Lychee, passionfruit and general citrus fruits are balanced nicely with bitterness and biscuit malts.
- **Country:** South Africa
- **Brewer:** Devil's Peak Brewing Co.
- **Style:** IPA
- **Appearance:** Bronze
- **Alcohol:** 6%
- **Serving temp:** 4–7°C

DID YOU KNOW?

All of Devil's Peak Brewing Co.'s spent grain is donated to a farmer in Muizenberg who uses it to feed his livestock.

GLOSSARY OF TERMS

Abbey beers — generic term for beers produced by Trappist monks, beers brewed at other monasteries, or beers that are brewed in the style of these beers.

ABV — alcohol by volume; a measure of the alcoholic portion of the total volume of liquid, determined during brewing by the use of a hydrometer.

Ale — ale is produced by top-fermenting yeasts at warmer temperatures, namely around 4–13°C (40–55°F). Types include amber, pale, Belgian blonde, golden, brown, mild.

Alpha acids — the chemical component of hops that determine the bitterness of the beer.

Altbier — German traditional ale. 'Alt' means 'old', and an Altbier uses an old style of brewing, and is identified with the Rhineland, especially Düsseldorf.

Barley wine — a style dating from the 18th and 19th centuries, created for English patriots to drink in preference to French claret at a time when the two countries were often at war. A strong brew which is stored for many months.

Biere de garde — meaning 'beer for keeping', originates from the French/Belgian farmhouse ale brewing tradition of the late 19th century, centred in the Flanders region. Beers were brewed in the winter months for the summer farmworkers to be paid with.

Bitter — originally real ale, served fresh at cellar temperatures under no pressure. Now refers to a type of pale ale.

Bock — a type of German strong lager with a relatively high alcohol content (more than 6.25% ABV), malty with low hops bitterness, and often dark in colour. 'Bock' means goat in German. Types include helles bock, doppelbock and eisbock.

Bottom-fermented — the use at low temperatures of yeasts in the brew which sink to the bottom of the tank and thus have minimal contact with the air outside – produces lagers and pilsners.

Bottle conditioning — a secondary fermentation process where yeast is allowed to carbonate the beer naturally in the bottle.

Brewpub — a brewery that sells 25 per cent or more of its beer on site, often directly from its storage tanks, brewing it primarily for sale in the restaurant or bar.

Cask conditioned ales — ale which is fermented and carbonated naturally in the cask from which it is served, with no additional treatments. Often known as 'real ale'.

Champagne beer — a delicate, highly alcoholic and highly-carbonated style of beer, primarily brewed in Belgium with a lengthy maturation period. Some are cave-aged in the Champagne region of France and then undergo the remuage and disgorgement process whereby the yeast is removed from the bottle.

Continually hopped — the practice of adding hops at regular intervals throughout the boil process.

Craft brewery — small, independent breweries, using traditional ingredients (see microbrewery).

Doppel — German for 'double'.

Dry-hopping — the process where hops are added to the fermentation tank as the beer is maturing as well as during the boil process, where the oils may be lost.

Dubbel, tripel and quadrupel (single, double, triple and quadrupel) — the system of brewing strengths established by the Trappist monks.

Export — beers with a reputation for being superior since the expense of exportation requires a higher price tag. Stronger beers traditionally survived long sea journeys better, thus 'export' became a term for higher-strength brews.

Fermentation — the process whereby yeast consumes the sugars in the wort, producing alcohol and CO_2 as waste; the CO_2 is lost during this process.

Gateway beer — a beer which is drunk as an introduction to other types of craft beers.

Gravity — the relative density of wort at various stages during brewing. Usually expressed with the plato scale.

Hefeweizen — see *Wheat beer*.

Ice brewed beers — a process where beer is chilled until the water freezes but the alcohol, with a lower freezing point, doesn't – after removing the ice you get a more alcoholic beer.

IBU — International Bitterness Unit. The international standard for measuring the amount of bitterness in a beer. A highly-hopped beer such as an IPA will often have a higher IBU, while a stout or a light beer will usually have a low rating.

Imperial — style of pilsner or stout. Originally referred to a distinctive type of beer brewed in the 1800s in England for export to Imperial Russia. Now used to indicate a big and bold type of beer with double or even triple quantities of hops and malts, and a high alcohol content.

IPA — India pale ale. A style of beer originating in the UK and sold for export. A higher hop content in these beers helped preserve them for the long journey to India.

Keg — keg beers are served cold; they are brewery conditioned and undergo only the primary fermentation, they are then cold stabilized in the brewery and then pasteurized or sterile filtered; they therefore have no yeast and have gas added.

Kilning — the final stage of the malting process, where the malt is heated with hot air to stop its growth and give it stability. The time and temperature variation produces pale or darker malts.

Kölsch — a local speciality beer from Cologne, Germany, defined by an agreement of the Cologne Brewery Association known as the Kölsch Konvention. Kölsch is warm-fermented and then lagered, a style which links it to the Altbiers of western Germany.

Kriek — a style of Lambic beer from Belgium, using sour Morello cherries to ferment the beer. Traditionally the 'Schaarbeekse krieken' style of cherry is used, from where the beer gets its name.

Lager — a lager is produced by bottom-fermenting yeasts at cooler temperatures, namely around 0–7°C (32–45°F). Types include pale, helles, dark/dunkel, Vienna, Dortmund.

Lagering — storing at low temperatures, from the German word 'lager' meaning 'storeroom'.

Lambic — a dry, sour beer created through spontaneous fermentation. No yeast is added and the beer is exposed to natural ambient yeasts.

Malt liquor — a North American term for high alcohol beers (not less than 5% ABV) made with malted barley. In practice the term refers to beer made with inexpensive ingredients, eg corn, rice, dextrose, very little hops and a special enzyme to give greater alcohol content.

Märzen/Oktoberfestbier — before the days of refrigeration Marzen, or 'March' beer was brewed in the spring and kept in cold storage to be ready for consumption in the autumn. In October the brewers needed to empty their Märzen kegs before brewing again in the cooler months, hence the tradition of Oktoberfest began.

Mashing-in — the stage where the malt is cracked by being run through a malt mill. This eases the release of the sugars which are converted from starch in the malt as it is mixed with hot water.

Mash tun — the vessel used for mashing in.

Microbrewery — defined as a craft beer brewery producing less than 17,600 hectolitres of beer each year with 75 per cent or more of its beer sold off-site

Mild — see *Ale*.

Mouthfeel — a tasting term, used to describe beer in terms not covered by taste and smell, for example, body, texture and carbonation.

Pilsner — also known as Pilsener or pils. A type of pale lager taking its name from the Czech Republic city of Pilsen where it was first brewed in 1842, using the Bavarian techniques of brewing. Types include German, Czech and European.

Plato rating — a scale of measuring the specific gravity of beer in degrees (denoted as eg 10P, 15P), common in central and eastern Europe.

Porter — an 18th century London style, named for its popularity among London's street-market workers. A strong dark brown beer made from a blend of brown, pale and 'stale' or well-matured ales. The dark colour comes from the use of dark malts (unlike stouts which use roasted malted barley). A stronger version Baltic Porter was made for export across the North Sea to support Baltic trade.

Saison — a complex fruity Belgian farmhouse-style pale ale traditionally brewed in the winter for summer consumption; until recently this was described as an 'endangered' style although there has now been a revival, especially in the United States.

Schwarzbier — 'black beer' in German, usually means very dark lager.

Secondary fermentation — the process whereby the fermentation in the beer is restarted, usually in a different vessel from the initial fermentation.

Session beer — mild, easy-going beer with alcoholic content of usually less than 4% so that several can be consumed over an evening.

Sour ale — this phrase covers non-traditional sour ales which are typically brewed with an ale yeast and then inoculated with souring bacteria and yeasts to produce a tart and unusual taste.

Stout — traditionally the generic term for the strongest porters. See *Porter*. Types include dry, milk, oatmeal, oyster, coffee, imperial, Russian.

Top-fermented — ale yeasts are top-fermenting as they work at the top of the fermentation vessel at higher temperatures than lager yeast.

Wheat beer — beer with a large proportion of wheat as well as malted barley, usually top-fermented, creating a light, summery beer. Types include weissbier (including hefeweizen, dunkelweizen, weizenbock), witbier, and sour varieties such as Lambic, Berliner Weisse and gose.

Witbier — see *Wheat beer*.

Wort — unfermented beer, i.e. the liquid produced by mashing the grains, containing the sugars which will turn to alcohol during fermentation.

INDEX OF BEERS

10 Saints..75
1516 Black & Tan.....................................149
1936 Bière..163
3 Fountaine Oude Geuze 131
3 Monts...161
8 Wired Saison Sauvin...........................200

A

À la Fût La British a L'Erable 65
Aass Bock...178
Abbaye Des Rocs Brune 131
ABC Brewing Henrik Imperial Amber 178
Adnams Broadside....................................80
Affligem Tripel.......................................131
Against the Grain London Balling 38
Alaskan Amber...27
Ale-Mania Gose Mania 124
Alechemy Citra Burst 101
Alexander Keith's India Pale Ale 55
Alley Kat Olde Deuteronomy...................56
Alpine Beer Windows Up 45
Altenburger Schwarzes 123
Amager Wookie IPA................................172
Amstel Lager...165
Amsterdam Boneshaker IPA......................57
Anarchy Brew Co Anarchy Lager 81
Anchor Old Foghorn Barley Wine 46
Anderson Valley Boont Amber Ale 47
Arran Blonde...100
Arrogant Bastard Ale 37
Asahi Super Dry......................................206
Augustiner Helles....................................114
Ayinger Jarhundert 115

B

Bach Brewing Hopsmacker Double IPA......199
Bahamian Strong Back Stout 74
Baird Dark Sky Imperial Stout................206
Baltika No.4 186
Bamberg Thunderstruck 73
BapBap Toast..158
Barley Brewery Taccadibò........................156
Barley Station Bushwacker Brown Ale 66
Beamish Irish Stout................................107
Beau's Lug-Tread Lagered Ale 68
Beaver Brewing Bushes of Love..............149
Beavertown Smog Rocket 81
Beck's...121
Beer Hunters Mufloni Saison De Randonneur 181
Beer Valley Leafer Madness......................44
Bell's Amber Ale 54
Belle-Vue Kriek 135
Belzebuth Pur Malt 162
Berentsens Rogalands Pils 180

Berliner Pilsener 113
Bernard Celebration Lager 150
Bevog Kramah IPA 149
BFM √225 Saison 163
Big Sky Brewing Moose Drool Brown Ale 51
Bintang..214
Birra Tirana...187
Birrificio Del Ducato Sally Brown 154
Birrificio di Montegioco Runa 153
Birrificio Indipendente Elav Grunge IPA Alle Pesche 154
Birrificio Italiano Tipopils 155
Birro del Borgo Etrusca...........................157
Bissel Brewing Swish IPA 22
Black Isle Organic Blonde 99
Blackfoot River Single Malt IPA................29
Blanche de Bruxelles 134
Blue Jacket Rheinard De Vos 27
Bluestone Bedrock Blonde.......................109
Bohemian Regent Prezident 151
Boon Kriek...132
Boston Brewery Black River Coffee Stout......217
Boulevard Hibiscus Gose 28
Boundery Imbongo 106
Brains Bitter 109
Brasserie La Goutte d'Or Château Rouge 161
Brasserie Les 2 Frères Porter Baltique Hickson 70
Brasserie Saint James Daily Wages 35
Brassneck No Brainer 57
Brewdog Punk IPA 97
Brewfist 24k 156
Brewski Mangofeber DIPA........................174
Brick Brewery Red Brick Rye.....................80
Bridge Brew Works Dun Glen Dubbel.........29
Brimstone Enlightenment Blonde Ale 71
Bristol Beer Factory Southville Hop 82
BRLO Porter 114
Brooklyn Lager...54
Brooklyn Naranjito 30
Brugse Zot..133
Budnamu Haslla IPA................................213
Budweiser...27
Budweiser Budvar 152
Bura Brew Tornado 186
Burning Sky Plateau 82
Buxton Double Axe 90

C

Camba Black Shark 114
Camba Oak Aged Milk Stout Bourbon 123
Cantillon Kriek 138
Carib Lager...75
Carnegie Stark Porter..............................174
Castelain Ch'ti Ambree............................161
Castlemaine XXXX Gold...........................192

Celis White 139
Central City Red Racer IPA 62
Chimay Blue 143
Coal Harbour Woodland Sour Saison 56
Cobra 211
Cooper's Original Pale Ale................................... 194
Coors Light 23
Core Oatmeal Stout 23
Corona Extra.. 74
Corsendonk Pater 145
Council Beatitude Boysenberry Barrel Aged Imperial Tart Saison 22
CR/AK Brewing Perfect Circle 155
Crafty Devil Rock 'n' Roll Star.............................. 110
Crew Republic Foundation 11 127
Crouch Vale Brewers Gold 95
Cruzcampo 167

D

Dado Bier Original... 73
Dark Star Revelation.. 83
De Dolle Stille Nacht 132
De Koninck 146
De La Senne Taras Bolba 134
De Molen Hel & Verdoemenis 165
De Ryck Arend Tripel.. 147
Deck & Donahue Indigo IPA 160
Delirium Tremens 141
Denise Pale Ale 160
Devil's Peak The King's Blockhouse IPA 217
Dieu Du Ciel Péché Mortel 61
Dogfish Head 90 Minute Imperial IPA.................. 28
Dougalls 942 IPA 167
Driftwood Fat Tug IPA... 69
Duck-Rabbit Baltic Porter 35
Dugges Jasmne Dragon 176
Duvel 147

E

East London Brewery Quadrant 81
Echigo Pilsner.. 206
Eden Mill Rock Liquor 101
Einstök Icelandic Toasted Porter 180
Elbow Lane Angel Stout....................................... 102
Epic Armageddon 199
Erdinger Dunkel... 117
Evan Evans CWRW... 112
Evil Twin Even More Jesus 169

F

Fantôme 146
Farmageddon IPA 103
Fat Lizard Sweet Mary 390................................... 181
Felinfoel Double Dragon 111
Feral Hop Hog... 196
Firestone Walker Double Barrell Pale Ale 44
Five Points Railway Porter 80
Flack Manor Double Drop 84
Flensburger Pilsener 116
Flessa Bräu Mandarina Red Lager 116
Flying Dog Raging Bitch 40

Flying Monkey's Belle of the Barrel 69
Fork Brewery Lemming drop 201
Foster's Lager... 194
Founders All Day IPA 26
Four Winds Operis Brett Saison 70
Franziskaner Hefe-Weissbier................................ 117
Fremont Brewing Co Bourbon Barrel Aged Dark Star 22
Frog White Light 159
Früh Kölsch 117
Fuglsand Hvid Bock 169
Fuller's London Pride... 84
Fyne Ales Jarl 101

G

Galmegi Espresso Vanilla Stout 213
Galway Bay Buried at Sea.................................... 106
Gänstaller Bräu Affumicator................................ 121
Garage Beer Co W.A.R. 167
Goose Island IPA 41
Grand Ridge Moonshine 192
Grand Teton Bitch Creek ESB 51
Granite IPA 61
Granville Island Maple Cream Ale 66
Great Lakes Canuck Pale Ale 71
Great Lakes Harry Porter 62
Great Leap Banana Wheat 208
Greene King Abbot Ale 90
Grimbergen Blonde.. 133
Grolsch Premium Lager 166
Guinness... 104
Gulden Draak 148

H

HaandBryggeriet Haandbakk 177
Hacker-Pschorr Weisse 123
Hansa Borg Bayer.. 177
Harp Lager.. 104
Hartwall Lapin Kulta.. 183
Harviestoun Schiehallion 98
Haywards 5000... 210
Heineken 166
Het Anker Gouden Carolus Noel 134
Hiisi Pläkki 181
Himbergs BrauKunst Keller Bavarian Dry Hop Lager 113
Hitachino Nest Beer Amber Ale 207
Hoffbräu Münchner Weisse 121
Holsten Pilsener 128
Hornbeer The Fundamental Blackhorn 171
Howe Sound Pumpkineater Imperial Pumpkin Pie.................. 68
Hoyne Brewing Dark Matter 64

I

Ilkley Mary Jane IPA 94
Inland Microbrewery Pilsner 215
Innis & Gunn Original 90

J

Jackie O's Pub & Brewery Spirit Beast 2016................. 43
James Boag's Premium 195
James Squire Chancer Golden Ale........................ 194

Jämtlands Hell..176
Jever Pilsener..130
Jupiler..148

K

Kereru Sweet Bippy..198
Kingfisher Premium...211
Kinn Julefred..177
Kostritzer Schwartzbier.......................................129
Kronenbourg 1664..160
Kuhnhenn Raspeberry Eisbock...............................43

L

La Chouffe..144
La Trappe Quadrupel...166
Labatt Blue..55
Lagunitas IPA...34
Laitilan Kievari Imperiaali....................................183
Laugar Fibonatxi 0..168
Le Brewery Odo..162
Leffe Brune..145
Left Field Bang-Bang..65
Left Hand Brewing Milk Stout................................26
Lervig/Way Beer 3 Bean Stout..............................178
Liberty Citra...201
Liefmans Goudenband...147
Lindemans Pecheresse...142
Lion Red..200
Little Creatures Pale Ale......................................193
Live Oak Hefeweizen...24
Locher Appenzeller Hanfblüte...............................164
Löwenbräu Original...122
Lübzer Pils...124

M

Magic Hat #9...32
Magic Rock Cannonball..95
Magpie Brewing Country Folk................................212
Maisel's Weisse Original.......................................125
Malheur Bière Brut..139
Malmgård Barley Wine...183
Marble Dobber IPA..96
Marble Imperial Red..31
Marston's Pedigree...87
Master Gao Baby IPA..208
Matuška Hellcat Imperial IPA................................152
Maui Coconut Hiwa Porter.....................................38
McAuslan St-Ambroise Oatmeal Stout.....................66
Meantime Yakima Red..91
Menabrea 1846...157
Mendocino Black Hawk Stout..................................31
Mendocino Eye of the Hawk...................................32
Metalman Pale Ale...104
Meteor Pils...159
Michelob Original Lager...53
Mike's IPA..199
Mikkeller Beer Geek Breakfast..............................170
Mill Street Tank House Ale.....................................57
Moa Blanc..198
Molson Canadian Lager..59

Molson Coors Blue Moon..34
Mt Begbie Brave Liver Scotch Ale...........................64
Murphy's Irish Stout...106
Murray's Wild Thing Imperial Stout.......................195
Muskoka Kirbys Kölsch...59

N

Narragansett Autocrat Coffee Milk Stout.................32
Nastro Azzurro Peroni..157
Nebraska Brewing Mélange a Trois..........................40
Newstead 3 Quarter Time......................................193
Nickel Brook Raspberry Uber..................................61
Nils Oscar God Lager..175
Nøgne Ø India Pale Ale...180
Nômada Tu Jardín..168
Nørrebro Bryghus Ravnsborg Rod..........................171
Norrlands Guld Export...175
Nynäshamns Bötet Barley Wine Jamaican Rum Cask.....176

O

Oakham JHB...91
Odell Cutthroat Porter...26
Oedipus Thai Thai..165
Oettinger Hefeweissbier.......................................130
Off Color Apex Predator..25
Okult No.1 Blanche..164
Omnipollo Noa Pecan Mud Cake Bourbon................174
Ørbæk Fynsk Forår..172
Orkney Dark Island Reserve..................................100
Orkney Raven Ale..97
Orval...146
Oskar Blues Bourbon Java Ten Fidy.........................34
Other Half All Citra Everything...............................41
Otley Motley Brew...109
Otromundo Strong Red Ale.....................................73

P

Pabst Blue Ribbon...37
Paname L'oeil de Biche...159
Panhead Johnny Octane Red IPA............................197
Parish Ghost in the Machine....................................35
ParrotDog Falcon APA...197
Pasteur Street Cyclo Imperial Chocolate Stout.........214
Paulaner Salvator..127
Pauwel Kwak..141
Pelican Umbrella New-World IPA.............................39
Pilsner Urquell..150
Pipes Smoked Lager...112
Pirate Life Mosaic IPA..195
Plank Dunkler Weizenbock....................................120
Porterhouse Oyster Stout......................................107
Powell Street Old Jalopy Pale Ale............................58
Pressure Drop Pale Fire..85
Primátor Double 24..150
Propeller London Style Porter.................................59
Pulpit Rock Saftig..37
Purple Moose Madog's Ale....................................112

Q

Quilmes...73

R

Radeberger Pilsner 124
Redemption Trinity.. 85
RedOak Organic Pale Ale 193
Reina Oro 168
Renaissance Elemental Porter 201
Revelation Cat Black Knight 153
Ribstone Creek Old Man Winter 63
Riedenburger Dolden Sud IPA 113
Riegele Noctus 100 127
River North Brewery Mr. Sandman 28
Rochefort 8.. 133
Rockmill Juicy Melody 185
Rodenbach Grand Cru 141
Rogue Dead Guy Ale... 53
Royal Challenge 210

S

Sambrook's Russian Imperial Stout 86
Sambrook's Wandle.. 80
Samuel Adams Boston Lager.................................... 50
Samuel Smith's Oatmeal Stout 94
Schlenkerla Rauchbier Marzen 129
Schneider Aventinus 128
Sharp's Doom Bar 95
Side Launch Mountain Lager 68
Sierra Nevada Pale Ale 51
Sinebrychoff Koff Porter 184
Siren Liquid Mistress 84
Six String Dark Red IPA 192
Ska Modus Hoperandi 38
Skovyst BøgeBryg Brown Ale 169
Sleeman Honey Brown Lager 58
Sly Fox 113 24
Smuttynose Really Old Brown Dog 41
Spaten Oktoberfest 130
St Austell Korev 96
St Bernardus Abt 12 142
St Feuillien Blonde.. 142
Staropramen Premium Lager................................... 151
Stigbergets Amazing Haze 175
Stonehammer Continuity Baltic Porter 62
Straight to Ale Laika Imperial Stout 45
Svaty Norbert IPA... 152

T

Teerenpeli Julmajuho 184
Tempest Brave New World 97
Terrapin Wake-n-Bake Coffee Oatmeal Imperial Stout ... 46
The Bruery Mischief 23
The Flying Dutchman Nomad More Complicated Than Your Girlfriend
Stout 184
The Hand and Malt Slow IPA 213
The Kernel Table Beer 96
Theakston Old Peculier.. 88
Thornbridge Jaipur.. 90
Three Horses Pilsner 215
Tiger 207
Tiny Rebel Haduken 110

To Øl Liquid Confidence 171
Toccalmatto Russian Imperial Stout Wild Bretta....... 156
Tomislav Tamno.. 186
Tomos Watkin OSB 110
Tooth and Nail Truce 70
Toppling Goliath King Sue 54
Tree House Julius 45
Trillium Mettle 40
Tripel Karmeliet 145
Tripel Van De Garre 143
Trois Dames Saison Houblon 163
Trouble Brewing Dark Arts Porter 103
Tsingtao... 208
Tuatara American Pale Ale 197
Twickeham Fine Ales Naked Lady 82
Two Roads Ol' Factory Pils...................................... 43
Tyskie Gronie 185

U

Unibroue La Fin du Monde...................................... 65
Untapped Ember 111

V

Vagabund Szechuan Saison 120
Vedett Extra Blond... 138
Victory Golden Monkey 30

W

Warpigs Kicked to Sleep 172
Weihenstephaner Hefeweissbier 128
Weihenstephaner Pilsner 122
Weird Beard Black Perle 85
West Sixth Pay it Forward 44
West St Mungo Lager 98
Westmalle Trappist Dubbel 139
Westvleteren 12 135
Wild Beer Co Wild Goose Chase 88
Wild Rose Cherry Porter.. 64
Williams Brothers Fraoch Heather Ale...................... 100
Willie the Boatman Albo Corn Ale 196
Windsor & Eton Knight of the Garter 91
Winking Seal Baby Fatso 214
Worthington's White Shield 87
Wylam Jakehead IPA... 87

X

Xyauyù 155

Y

Yards General Washington Tavern Porter 30
Yeastie Boys Digital IPA... 200
Yo-ho Tokyo Black 207
Yo-ho Yona Yona Ale 207
Yuengling Dark Brewed Porter 36

Z

Zajecarsko Svetlo 187

PICTURE CREDITS

Parragon would like to thank all the contributing breweries for sending great images and to the following brewers in particular:

Page 22, Bissell Brewing Swish IPA: Bissell Brothers; 26, Founders All Day IPA: Founders Brewing Co.; 26, Left Hand Brewing Milk Stout: Left Hand Brewing Co.; 44, Firestone Walker Double Barrel Pale Ale: Firestone Walker Brewing Company; 46, Terrapin Wake-N-Bake Coffee Oatmeal Imperial Stout: Terrapin Beer Co.; 47, Anderson Valley Boont Amber Ale: Anderson Valley Brewing Company; 68, Beau's Lug-Tread Lagered Ale: Beau's; 85, Weird Beard Black Perle: Weird Beard brew Co; 96, St Austell Korev: St Austell Brewery; 138, Cantillon Kriek: ©Brasserie Cantillon;

Photographer credits: 25, Off Color Apex Predator: photo ©M. Kiser/Good Beer Hunting; 27, Bluejacket Rheinard de Vos: photo ©Rose Collins/Neighborhood Restaurant Group; 29, Bridge Brew Works Dun Glen Dubbel: photo ©Matt Sanchez – Digital Relativity; 34, Oskar Blues Bourbon Java Ten Fidy: photo ©Jeremy Farmer; 35, Brasserie Saint James Daily Wages: photo ©Fielding Cathcart; 37, Pulpit Rock Saftig: photo ©Erik Dutcher; 64, Hoyne Brewing Dark Matter: photo ©Kelly and Phil Jones; 65, Left Field Bang-Bang: photo ©Justin Spencer; 70, Four Winds Operis Brett Saison: photo ©Alison Page; 71, Brimstone Enlightenment Blonde Ale: photo ©Mike Sansano; 80, Brick Brewery Red Brick Rye: photo ©Slawek Tomas; 94, Ilkley Mary Jane: photo ©John Hope Photography; 102, Elbow Lane Angel Stout: photo ©Naomi Kamat; 116, Flessa Brau Mandarina: photo ©Anne Winkler; 149, 1516 Black & Tan: photo ©Aleksandar Bubalo; 160, Deck & Donohue Indigo IPA: photo ©Jean Marie Heidinger; 169, Evil Twin Even More Jesus: Label design by: Martin Justesen | New York Cantillon; 172, Amager Wookiee IPA: photo ©Morten Tietze; 183, Malmgard Barley Wine: photo ©Anna Autio is the photographer; 196, Willie the Boatman Albo Corn Ale: photo ©Per Ericson, retouching by Sarah Barker at Pocket Rocket Productions; 217, Devil's Peak The King's Blockhouse IPA: photo ©Ewald Sadie

iStock images: 5, 6, 8, 9, 10, 11, 12, 13, 14, 15, 16, 17, 18, 20, 21, 48, 49, 76, 79, 92, 93, 105, 108, 118, 119, 136, 137, 188, 190, 191, 195, 202, 204, 205.

Shutterstock images: 33, 216